'ARTHURS', 'NELSONS' & 'SCHOOLS' AT WORK

'ARTHURS' 'NELSONS'
& 'SCHOOLS' AT WORK

S. C. Townroe

IAN ALLAN LTD
LONDON

First published 1973
Revised edition 1983

ISBN 0 7110 1292 X

Published by Ian Allan Ltd, Shepperton, Surrey;
and printed by Ian Allan Printing Ltd at their works
at Coombelands in Runnymede, England

Contents

Cover: 'Schools' class 4-4-0 No 902 *Wellington*.
Painting by George F. Heiron

**Front endpaper: 'Schools' No 920 *Rugby* approaches
Chislehurst Junction with a Charing Cross-Dover train,
16 September 1948.**   *E. R. Wethersett/Real Photographs Co*

**Back endpaper: 'LN' No 30858 *Lord Duncan* waits to leave
Bournemouth West with the 5.05pm to Waterloo in the
mid-1950s.**   *T. G. Hepburn/Rail Archive Stephenson*

**Title page: 'King Arthur' No 30781 *Sir Aglovale* roars past
Weald Intermediate signalbox with an up boat train in 1949.**
F. R. Hebron/Rail Archive Stephenson

**Left: 'Schools' No 30919 *Harrow* passes Purley on a Victoria-
Newhaven relief boat train, 17 April 1954.**   *C. Hogg*

Preface

The Southern Railway's 'King Arthur' class of 74 4-6-0 express passenger locomotives became one of the most popular types in the country during the years of the grouped railways. They were to be seen everywhere, from Ramsgate to Exeter, from Oxford to Brighton. Whether you took your summer holiday on the Continent or in Devonshire it was almost certain that the journey by rail would be behind a 'King Arthur' at some stage, an engine with a workmanlike appearance and a legendary name. To locomotive enthusiasts, for whom this book is written, they were more than just a class, for there were to be four precise groups or batches of engines varying in detail one from the other and representing the growth of a design over a period of years.

The 'King Arthur' class had not long been named when another more powerful 4-6-0, the 'Lord Nelson', appeared on the scene. Sixteen engines of the 'Nelson' class were not, however, likely to do more than take a little of the cream of the express traffic away from the 74 'Arthurs', and, in fact, they only succeeded in taking away a few star turns, mainly in the way of Pullman expresses. Even then, 'Arthurs' were often to be seen working in place of 'Nelsons', and the whisper went round amateur railway circles that the 'Nelsons' were just white elephants. The lack of really definite evidence to that effect merely stimulated such rumours. 'Con-

fidentially, old man,' one amateur might say to another, ' "X" told me that they are always under repair'; or 'It was a rotten run — the driver told me at Victoria that the "Nelsons" won't steam'. Partisans of the 'Arthurs' were not slow to add first to the fire of contention, naturally. 'The "Nelsons" had to hand it to the "Arthurs" west of Salisbury, you know.' 'Nelson' supporters replied by quoting a comment which a leading locomotive engineer was alleged to have made after a footplate trip on an 'Arthur', to the effect that it was a 'crude engine'.

The most powerful 4-4-0 in Europe! That distinction was claimed for a new design of 4-4-0 introduced by the Southern Railway in 1930, and wide interest was aroused in railway circles at the revival of the four-coupled type for main line work, in view of the general preference for six-coupled types.

There were certain loading gauge restrictions over the London-Hastings route to be met by the design. It was hardly anticipated that the new engines would prove to have such a wide usefulness over all the Southern main lines, or that they would, in the course of their career, run the six-coupled engines so close in performance.

Superlatives were often used in describing new locomotives, and descriptions of that kind could be as meaningless as the grandiloquent claims made by US film companies for each new production of their studios. It has been wisely said that the true worth of any design must be judged by long-term results. The long view must be taken because, amongst other things, the repair and maintenance expenses and the fuel consumption could only be truly assessed after a period of years in traffic. If the design is to be considered for

Below: No E453 *King Arthur,* **c1926.** *Lens of Sutton*

a place amongst the élite, the performance and reliability of the engines must have been maintained when they were no longer new, when they were matched against other and possibly newer designs, and when, under changing traffic conditions, they were given loads to handle in excess of those for which they were intended. On this basis, a just assessment of the 'Schools' class engines and their work must be that their designer produced an outstanding class of locomotive.

The fact that amongst the enginemen in particular the popularity of these engines never waned was a tribute in itself. Whatever the odds, they displayed on the road a response to handling and a degree of stamina which found favour with the practical man on the footplate.

Like all engines, the 'Schools' bore an official classification, namely 'V' class. Some types became known merely by letters, as Bs or Xs, while others acquired nicknames, not always complimentary; the 'Schools' were always spoken of as such. 'Give me a "School" any day, with a fair load' was a remark often heard from experienced drivers.

The theme of this volume was originally written by the author in two booklets published by Ian Allan, entitled *The Book of the Schools Class* (1947) and *King Arthurs and Lord Nelsons of the SR* (1949). Subsequently, the publishers asked me to rewrite them in a combined, and less potted, version which included some recollections of the Southern Railway and Region when the author was one of the locomotive engineers.

This book appeared as *Arthurs, Nelsons and Schools of the Southern*, published in 1973. The present volume is produced as a result of the popularity of the 1973 title and, apart from being generally enlarged, includes additional material gathered by impartial observers on locomotive running and performances, an additional chapter on the preserved loco-

Above: The last 'Arthur' to work over the South Eastern section. No 30782 Sir Brian at Ramsgate with LCGB 'Kentish Venturer' rail tour, 25 February 1962. Brian Stephenson

motives, contributed by Michael Harris, new tabular matter and a vastly increased selection of photographs.

In compiling the original booklets the author was indebted to the late H. Holcroft, who was responsible for much of the design work on Maunsell's locomotives, and who later published his own memoirs, material from one volume of which has been incorporated in this book. Acknowledgement is due to former members of the Southern Railway, including L. Lynes (Maunsell's Carriage & Wagon Assistant), M. S. Hatchell (Works Manager), the late A. Earle Edwards (Traffic Superintendent), the late J. P. Maitland (Shed Superintendent, Nine Elms), S. A. Downs (District Locomotive Superintendent). Train running details have been collated from articles published in railway journals such as *Trains Illustrated* and *Railway World* by the late Cecil J. Allen and the late Norman Harvey. Thanks are due to the photographers and to the donor of prints from pre-Group official negatives which are privately preserved.

A bibliography is included of publications found useful in writing this book.

Finally, this book must be dedicated to the memory of men whose lives were bound up with the steam locomotive, and whose cheerful good humour may perhaps be faintly detected in these pages.

S. C. Townroe
Upham, Hampshire
October 1982

1
The Southern and its First Chief Mechanical Engineer

At the time of the amalgamation of the railways in Britain into four group companies in 1923, the railways south of the Thames which were to form the new Southern Railway did not enjoy much of a reputation for speed, comfort and punctuality. In the public esteem they were not in the same street as the Great Western — which could probably have claimed the largest band of devotees — or the London & North Western or Great Northern. By 1939, the Southern had become known as 'Britain's brightest and best-run line', an image of which the foremost ingredients were the regularity and frequency of its electrified services, the geniality of its staff as portrayed by that poster character, 'Sunny South Sam', and by the comfort and punctuality of its main line steam trains. The latter were to be associated with its three principal types of express locomotives, the 'King Arthurs', the 'Schools' and the 'Lord Nelsons', which are the theme of this book.

Of those 140 locomotives, five have survived for preservation. 'King Arthur' class No 777 *Sir Lamiel*, 'Schools' class No 925 *Cheltenham* and No 850 *Lord Nelson* were withheld from scrapping by the British Railways Board for the National Collection. All have now been restored to working order, as described in Chapter 14. 'Schools' class No 926 *Repton* was sold to a purchaser in Vermont, USA and No 928 *Stowe* was acquired by Lord Montagu for his museum at Beaulieu. *Stowe* is now on the Bluebell Railway and in regular use.

Four years elapsed between the Armistice of 1918 and the creation of the Southern Railway, and of the GWR, LNER and LMS, in 1923; four years of uncertainty for railway management, years in which forward planning for the rehabilitation of the war-worn railways in the South was inhibited. The Government, indeed, retained the control of the railways, which had begun at the outbreak of war, until 1921: meantime those railway politicians who had from time to time argued in favour of nationalisation aired their views more vehemently. The Ministry of Transport, in 1920, proposed in a White Paper the fusion of the private companies into six groups to be known as the Western, North-Western, Eastern, North-Eastern, Scottish and London groups. In due course a counter-proposal came from the Railway Companies Asociation for five groups; four were the ones eventually adopted in 1923, the fifth was to have been a 'London group' to co-ordinate the special transport problems of the Metropolis, an idea that has been revived more than once.

From the point of view of development the period of Government control was not completely sterile; various committees were set up to examine matters of common interest to the railways. The design of standard locomotives for British

railways was one, to which a major contribution was made by R. E. L. Maunsell, Chief Mechanical Engineer of the South Eastern and Chatham Railway (SECR) who had become CME of the government-sponsored Railway Executive Committee during World War 1. Another committee examined the possibility of converting the home railway system to the Continental loading gauge, to facilitate the circulation of European rolling stock via the cross-Channel train ferries developed during the war. However, when the committee had calculated the enormous cost of converting the SECR alone, the idea was promptly dropped! The shortcomings of that company's system, with its loading gauge restrictions and the limited axle loads which its bridges and track would bear, were to become one of the many problems which confronted the new Southern management.

In 1923, the Southern began the task of combining the three separate organisations of the London & South Western, the London, Brighton & South Coast and the South Eastern & Chatham Railways, plus some minor companies into one body. The task involved the kind of upheaval with which railway staff have more recently become familiar. For the first year there were three General Managers, an arrangement which enabled the three eminent title-holders of the constituent companies jointly to oversee the amalgamation and conveniently allowed two of them to carry on until due for retirement, leaving Mr H. A., later Sir Herbert, Walker of the LSWR to reign supreme from 1924 onwards. Geographically, the Southern divided itself into three sections, Eastern, Central and Western, corresponding approximately to the former company territories, and into five administrative divisions, London (East), London (Central), London (West), Southern (Southampton) and Western (Exeter). As the smallest of the four Groups, the Southern retained much of the atmosphere of a pre-1923 company. Any part of the system, except west of Exeter, could be visited on business without involving a night away from home, and all the officers could regularly meet one another. Headquarters meetings were held in the committee rooms in the Charing Cross Hotel, where month by month the General Manager was to hold his Traffic Officers Conference, attended by all divisional (later, district) officers to keep them in the picture.

The Southern was singular in having a one-word title to adorn its locomotives and rolling stock, and its letter headings!

The selection of a Chief Mechanical Engineer was not difficult to resolve. R. W. Urie of the LSWR was 68 years of age and on the verge of retirement. He had been CME at Eastleigh since Dugald Drummond's death in 1912 and was to leave some excellent locomotives for the Southern including the 20 4-6-0s which were to become the basis of the 'King

Arthur' class. He favoured the simple six-coupled locomotive with two large outside cylinders; no fewer than 12 designs of 4-6-0 were prepared in outline, with variations on wheel and cylinder sizes, as well as three possible 2-6-0s in appearance like foreshortened 'H15' 4-4-0s. A fine 4-8-0 with 5ft 1in coupled wheels and a tractive effort of 30,555lb had been proposed as far back as 1914 (see below). L. B. Billinton of the LBSC was 39 years of age; he had served overseas with the rank of Lieutenant-Colonel during World War 1 and his absence from the railway scene, and his experience, which was limited to his own company, could not have been to his ultimate advantage. R. E. L. Maunsell, on the other hand, was a mature 54 years of age, having been CME of the SECR since 1913 and, more importantly of the Railway Executive. With his prominence in the profession and his experience on other railways before going to the SECR, his appointment caused no surprise. L. B. Billinton accepted compensation terms, and a 'handsome piece of presentation plate' from his staff, and retired to live the rest of his life in the country, in Sussex.

Thus, the locomotive engineer who was in due course responsible for the 'Arthurs', 'Schools' and 'Nelsons' was Richard Edward Lloyd Maunsell, the son of a Dublin lawyer and a graduate of Trinity College, Dublin, two influences which were to make him a first-class administrator. His training as an engineer took place on the Great Southern & Western Railway (GS&WR) of Ireland, a company which perforce maintained its locomotive and rolling stock on a limited budget and where Maunsell no doubt learned the importance of careful costing, and of a policy of make-do-and-mend. After a spell of locomotive running experience on the Lancashire & Yorkshire Railway as Shedmaster at Fleetwood, Maunsell followed the custom of many young engineers in those days and took a post on one of the railways in the Commonwealth, in his case on the East Indian Railway. He became the District Locomotive Superintendent at Asansol, the author's grandfather then being the DLS at Allahabad, and in India the difficult conditions under which locomotives operated, climatic and otherwise, imprinted upon his mind the assets of simplicity and utter reliability in design. Rudyard Kipling's story of 'The Bold 'Prentice'* well portrays the Indian railway scene.

Maunsell returned home to be Locomotive, Carriage &

*Land and Sea Tales, Rudyard Kipling, Macmillan & Co.

Below: Proposed Urie 4-8-0 freight locomotive.

Wagon Superintendent of the GS&WR, and thence to Ashford as CME of the SECR.

Maunsell was a thoroughly practical locomotive man; humble in his unpretentiousness and ready to delegate to his assistants. With these qualities, and with an Irish twinkle in his eye, he made an excellent leader and the men he picked to work under him stayed loyally with him throughout his time on the Southern.

The burden which fell on his shoulders during the formative years of the Southern Railway was a heavy one became of continual pressure from the General Manager and the Board toward fulfilment of great schemes. The need to produce electric multiple-units in ever-increasing numbers brought unprecedented design and production problems, and some ingenious conversions of steam stock. By 1938 there were over 3,000 coaches of electric stock, a tenfold increase over 1923; during the 1930s much of it was newly-built corridor stock for the main line extensions to Brighton, Worthing, Eastbourne and Portsmouth. The decisions about stock requirements were not always reached with a generous time allowance for construction before the publicly announced opening dates; in fact it became a standing joke among the workshop staff that almost impossible target dates were set in order to keep everybody's noses to the grindstone. Maunsell made it a point of honour that his rolling stock must be ready in good time to start the new services, and it always was, though there would be a last-minute scramble to find missing bits and pieces. At any rate, when changes in detail design were proposed by other interested departments including the General Manager's, after building had started, Maunsell was a man to put his foot down firmly and say 'no' to such interference.

The steam locomotive stock was in poor shape in 1923. Before he could concentrate on new locomotives of his own design, Maunsell had to draw up a programme for giving all the existing ones a thorough overhaul and to that end to use his available workshop facilities to the best advantage. As events turned out, Maunsell's contribution in new designs was on a small scale compared with the opportunities afforded to his colleagues on the other group companies to replace the old with the new. Electrification, and everything to do with it by way of new stations and signalling, received priority in capital expenditure, and the steam locomotive side of the organisation on the Southern soon became the Cinderella, so far as money was concerned. Much ingenuity was expended in modifying and rebuilding older locomotives

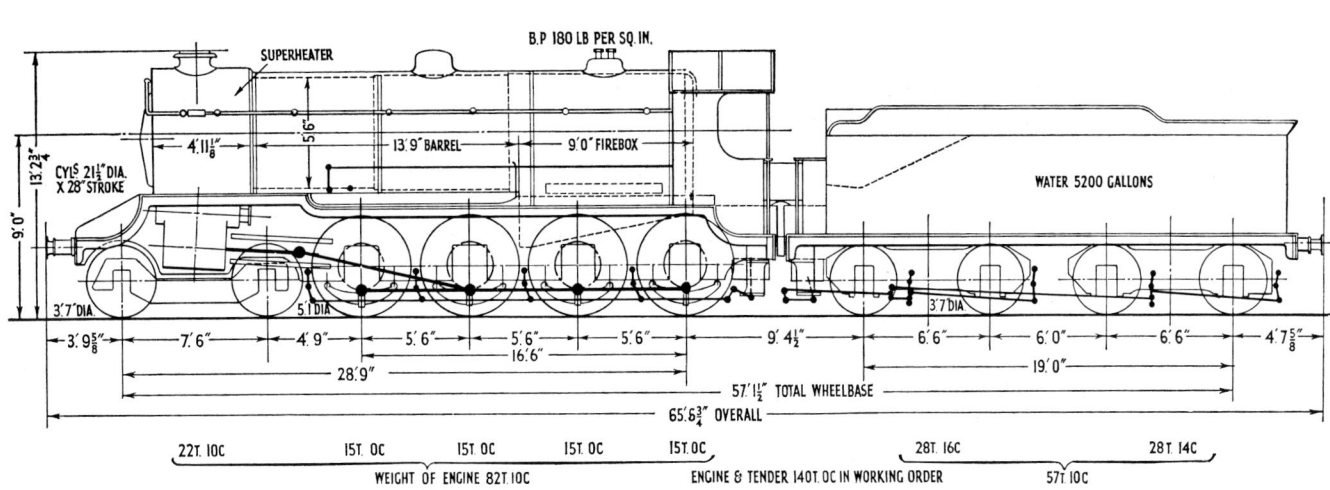

which, in retrospect, would have been better written off.

The strain upon Maunsell eventually told on his health and after two long illnesses he retired in 1937. When approached on the eve of his retirement, regarding the choice of a parting gift from his staff, he demurred: he wanted no expensive presentation, no silver plate or the traditional mantel clock. It would please him, however, to be given albums of photographs of his assistants, managers and foremen.

In the year of his retirement the direct line to Portsmouth was electrified. For it, he was responsible for the first main line electric units incorporating the innovation of nose-end gangways. Thirty-four years afterwards the 4-COR units were replaced by more modern stock on the Portsmouth line, but were still running with the original and wholly satisfactory design of gangway. It would have pleased him, almost as much as the survival of his steam locomotives, as an example of value for money, and of faithful service. These were the keynotes of his own conduct. When appointing his principal assistants in the early years, he said to one of them, Lionel Lynes, 'I expect you will either stay with me for a month, or 30 years!'. All his officers stayed with him.

Above: R. E. L. Maunsell.

Left: Portsmouth electrification: 4-COR unit No 3058 on the train formally inaugurating electric services to Portsmouth, at Waterloo, 1 July 1937. City of Portsmouth coat of arms carried on the gangway. *Ian Allan Library*

Below: Maunsell rebuild: 'E1' 4-4-0 No 163 on a down train at Sydenham Hill in pre-Grouping days. *Ian Allan Library*

2
The Southern's Inheritance of Locomotives

When William Stroudley became the Locomotive Superintendent of the London, Brighton & South Coast Railway in 1870, it possessed 233 locomotives made up of no fewer than 72 different types. During his 20 years in office he succeeded in enlarging the total stock but, by a process of standardisation, confined it to a mere seven classes.

In 1923, the Southern Railway inherited from its constituent companies a total of 2,281 locomotives made up of 125 different classes, with an average age of 28 years. A picture of the types of locomotive in service at the amalgamation may be gained by categorising them by wheel arrangement (omitting a few odd ones) thus:

Tender locomotives

4-6-0	73	4-4-0	606
2-6-0	30	0-4-2	116
0-6-0	340	4-2-2-0	6
4-4-2	11		

Tank locomotives

4-8-0T	4	0-6-0T	188
4-6-4T	7	0-6-4T	5
4-6-2T	7	4-4-2T	120
2-6-4T	1	0-4-4T	464
0-6-2T	134	0-4-2T	112

Maunsell hoped, at one stage, to replace a large proportion of the older locomotives by nine standard types of his own, which between them would employ only five patterns of boiler; these were to be:

Tender locomotives

Wheel arrangement	Class	Traffic type
4-8-0		Mineral (not built)
4-6-0	Lord Nelson	Passenger
4-6-0	King Arthur	Passenger
4-4-0	Schools	Passenger
4-6-0	H15	Mixed
2-6-0	U	Mixed
4-6-0	S15	Goods
2-6-0	N	Goods

Tank locomotive

0-8-0T	Z	Shunting

The opportunity to fulfil this plan was denied to Maunsell and when he departed, in 1937, the Southern stock of 1,814 locomotives still included over 70 classes. Although he contributed 340 new locomotives, the average age had risen to 32 years!

Between 1923 and 1938, the average age of the tender locomotives rose from 25 to 28 years, and that of the tank locomotives from 30 to $38\frac{1}{2}$ years.

The main reason for the survival of the veterans has already been mentioned; another reason was the trade slump of the early 1930s which caused proposals for new designs to be held in abeyance. Among the victims were Maunsell's Pacific, an enlarged 'Lord Nelson' later re-drafted as a three-cylinder 2-6-2, and a 4-8-0 freight locomotive. Other victims of the slump were the managerial staff who had to accept a $2\frac{1}{2}$% reduction in their salaries!

Between 1932 and 1937 only 100 new locomotives were built. Twenty 'Q' class 0-6-0 tender locomotives were built in 1938 to Maunsell's design, after his retirement. The medium-sized 0-6-0s, such as the Wainwright 'C' class and the Drummond '700' class, played a useful role on the freight workings and the 'Qs' were intended to cover withdrawals of the older 0-6-0s as they reached a condition otherwise involving expensive repairs. But the threat of war made scrapping inadvisable, and brought a further reprieve for the veterans.

The preponderance of 4-4-0 tender locomotives at the amalgamation reflected the general standard of loads and speeds on the Southern lines and the extent to which passenger trains were made up of timber-built non-corridor bogie coaches and even six-wheelers. It is true that another main line company, the Midland, had remained a '4-4-0' line but it had an ample number of locomotives with which to double head the heavier trains. Other companies were well provided with 4-6-0s whereas of the 73 4-6-0s in the new Southern stock, all ex-LSWR, only 20 were suitable for express work. Twenty-five were Drummond four-cylinder machines built for passenger work but down graded to secondary passenger or freight work because of poor design features.

Eight-coupled freight locomotives, again plentiful elsewhere, did not exist on the Southern. There was indeed no heavy mineral traffic to justify them and the few Robinson ex-ROD 2-8-0s which were on trial on the LSWR in 1920, with a view to the purchase of more, were not acquired because of their limited usefulness. Not until 1943, with the arrival of the wartime Austerity 2-8-0s, could Southern enginemen enjoy handling eight-coupleds with excellent adhesion and brake power.

More numerous than the 4-4-0s were the passenger tank engines, indicating the amount of local, and short-distance, passenger services, and branch lines. For that kind of work there was little advantage in fitting them with later developments such as superheaters and piston valves. Almost without exception they were reliable and easy to maintain, and they continued at work unmolested, long after the Southern Railway era.

In the early years of the LMS and the LNER, the transfer

of locomotive types from one section to another produced some interesting results by way of comparative trials, and incidentally the claim that certain types were best suited to the territory of their origin was exposed as a fallacy. The pooling of resources also enabled the available locomotive stock to be utilised to the best advantage. So far as the Southern was concerned there were many difficulties in the way of so doing. The loading gauge on the Eastern section was less generous than on the Central and the Western sections. More serious still, in constructing the South Eastern and the London, Chatham & Dover Railways the depth allowed between the track and the formation level, for ballasting, was in time to prove entirely inadequate for the increasing train speeds and weights of locomotives. The shortcomings of the permanent way in Kent were destined to be demonstrated dramatically by a number of derailments of the 'River' class 2-6-4 tanks, culminating in 1927 with the disaster at Riverhead, near Sevenoaks, and considerable expenditure on the track, and on the underbridges, had to be incurred on the three main routes to Dover, via Chatham, via Maidstone and via Tonbridge.

The composite loading gauge, to which nearly all new Southern locomotives and rolling stock were built, was dictated by that of the Eastern section. Ex-LBSCR and ex-LSWR locomotives required for use on that section which did not conform to the composite gauge had first to have their cab roofs and footsteps cut back, denoted by a yellow triangle on the buffer beam. Even tighter restrictions applied to, and still remain on, the Tonbridge-Hastings line.

Companies like the LBSCR which used the Westinghouse air brake were in the minority, and the vacuum brake became the standard throughout the country, although the LSWR and LBSCR electric stock fitted with the air brake retained it. Fifty years later, the air brake was to be used on all Southern Region stock. The ex-LBSCR air-braked locomotives represented a considerable proportion of the locomotive stock and it was essential that most of them, at any rate, should be able to work vacuum braked trains. It was not possible simply to strip them of the air brake and replace it by vacuum, as all the brake rigging was designed for operation by air cylinders, which occupied less space than vacuum cylinders anyway. The solution, which of course took time, lay in the fitting of ex-LBSCR locomotives with vacuum ejectors and with dual brake controls. The locomotive brakes remained air operated, and by means of a proportional valve the activation of the driver's air brake control also applied to the same degree as the vacuum brakes on the train. The necessary proportional valve was devised and patented by a Brighton Works foreman, E. M. Jackson.

Other differences were not always welcomed when engines were transferred to other areas. A left-hand driving position was standardised on the LSWR and LBSCR, but the SECR locomotives were right-hand drive. In keeping with the locomotive controls, the signals of each company had been sited in positions where they would be best seen from the driver's side. Drivers eventually got used to the existence of both left-hand and right-hand drive types, which persisted to the end of steam, although the opposites were occasionally the cause of minor collisions when two locomotives moving in the same direction in a marshalling or locomotive yard met at points, neither driver having seen the other! The arrangement was much more disliked by the firemen, not all of whom could readily become ambidextrous in wielding a shovel accurately. When, for instance, ex-LSWR 4-4-0s of Classes 'T9', 'L11'

and 'L12' were drafted on to the Eastern section to ease a shortage of power, fireman and driver would be found occupying the same side of the footplate, with obvious friction.

Differences in the direction of rotation, clockwise or anticlockwise, of control handles proved to be something of a menace. Regulators, hand brake wheels and blower valves could be hurriedly, and so incorrectly, operated, hence the kind of incident which occurred at Nine Elms when an ex-Brighton tank went through the boundary wall into 'The Brooklands Arms'. When the 0-8-0 tank engine *Hecate* was acquired from the Kent & East Sussex Railway, it had a reversing lever which one pulled back for forward travel and vice versa: immediate modifications were made before any walls were demolished. Blower valves had to be standardised to open clockwise, and the handles clearly marked, since any mistake in the use of the blower could result in a 'blow-back' with possibly fatal burns.

The Brighton tank engines of the 'E' classes were popular shunting engines because of the air brakes, hence their longevity and their eventual appearance on all divisions. By contrast, some of the LSWR 'G6' shunting engines relied upon the hand brake alone until the Southern got around to providing them all with vacuum brakes. Just as primitive were the Brighton 'A1' and 'D1' tanks, 'C3' 0-6-0 goods engines, and others, which possessed only crosshead-driven feed pumps, and not until 1930-32 were they all equipped with injectors: meantime only ex-Brighton enginemen could manage them and they were definitely not types to be sent elsewhere than to Central section depots! Even though most engines were straightforward enough to drive, there were niceties of handling, and of all the types those which took longest to become accustomed to were Drummond's engines. The Drummond steam reverser was of somewhat small dimensions so that it could be fitted neatly out of sight between the frames and close to the reversing shaft and valve gear. In contrast, the Ashford engines used the massive Stirling steam reverser, mounted outside, as large as, and often mistaken for, a Westinghouse air pump. It was a most dependable device, whereas Drummond's was finicky and temperamental and if its various cocks, glands and leather washers were not serviced by skilled fitters, it would alter the cut-off or change from foregear to back gear on its own.

Incidentally, the standard of workmanship of running shed fitters, and the educational standard required to pass as a driver, were highest on the LSWR, largely the legacy of Drummond's interest in the Mutual Improvement Classes by which the staff gained their technical knowledge — in their off-duty hours, moreover.

The injector controls on Drummond's 'T9' and other classes of 4-4-0 were, unusually, on the floor of the cab, where they could be set by a tap of the heel. The fireman could simultaneously adjust the injector steam supply and have a hand free to steady himself. It worked well, and enabled the fireman to set an injector working without excessive back-rushes of steam and water from the injector overflow. But the heel-tapping required practice. Drummond himself could not have ridden on his own locomotives or he would surely have improved the weather protection of his cabs. As it was, the 'T9' cab roof only partially covered the space between engine and tender, and the cab side cutaways were unnecessarily large. There were no doors: only a chain between engine and tender to prevent the crew from falling overboard. When the Stewarts Lane (Eastern section) men saw their first 'King Arthurs', they promptly dubbed the 'T9s', the 'Queen Annes'.

Another difference between the pre-grouping Southern companies, which affected locomotive design and handling techniques, lay in the varying types and sources of coal. In order to minimise the cost of coal insofar as haulage charges were involved, the choice of certain collieries as sources of supply was affected by geography. The LSWR used mainly Welsh coal, which was distributed over its system via the Severn Tunnel and Salisbury, whereas for the LBSCR and SECR coal from the Midlands and Yorkshire would travel via the West London or Widened Lines. Regular travellers used to claim that they could tell which railway they were riding on, simply by the smell of the coal! The Midlands and Yorkshire coals tended to be gassy, quick-burning coals, with a high residue of ash. This type of fuel required a grate with ample spacing between the firebars to allow the ash to fall into an ashpan of ample proportions. Conversely, Welsh coal made very little ash, and LSWR fireboxes were shallow and the firebars closely spaced to minimise loss of unburnt fuel into the ashpan. Here again were differences in design which brought complications, not only in fuel supplies to locomotive depots but also in the quantity of ashpan and smokebox refuse which could limit the time a locomotive could spend in traffic between visits to the ashpits.

After amalgamation, the Southern continued to use the same sources of coal supplies, except that the Kent coalfields were by then producing good quality coal from Chislet and Snowdown, which was sent to Eastern section depots, for main line work. Betteshanger, a cheap, low-grade Kent coal, was sent all over the system for the exclusive use by shunting locomotives. The tall, hopper-type coaling plants installed at Stewarts Lane, Feltham and Nine Elms were for preference supplied with hard Yorkshire coal as it did not readily pulverise when tipped into a 400ton capacity hopper.

The price paid per ton of locomotive coal was higher in the south than elsewhere. Figures for 1908 published by the railway companies show that the LSWR was paying 17s 9d, the LSBCR 17s 11d and the SECR 15s 9d per ton, whereas the other companies were paying an average of 10s to 12s per ton. The price paid by the Southern companies was partly due to the longer haulage from the collieries — the Kent Coalfield was a later development — and partly because passenger train working required better grades of coal than freight train working. In the South the proportion of passenger train miles to freight train miles was of the order of 75% to 25%, whereas in the Midlands and the North the proportion was the other way round.

The cost of fuel was the largest item in the annual expense account of a locomotive department, a matter which the management endeavoured by various means to keep in the minds of enginemen. Prior to 1914 many companies operated a system whereby the drivers received a bonus when the locomotive allocated to them achieved a better-than-average coal consumption. The system encouraged a certain amount of fiddling, whereby the men who loaded the coal on the engines would be bribed to falsify their bookings, or coal would be taken off another engine or from the stacks which were held in reserve at the locomotive depots. Attempts were made to discourage malpractices; for example by whitewashing coal on tenders and in stack so that any interference could be noticed, and in the end the bonus system fell into such disrepute that it was dropped; moreover it became inoperable with the growing practice of common-user locomotives. On the Southern, there continued to be published at the locomotive depots, until 1939, a monthly statement of the coal consumption the individual locomotives used on main line passenger work, but the figures as between one locomotive and another could vary for so many reasons outside the enginemen's control that their publication was merely a general reminder for economy.

With the train loads and speeds which prevailed at about the time of the amalgamation, a figure of 30-35lb per mile could be expected from locomotives working passenger trains; on freight trains the consumption would range from 60-90lb per mile, according to conditions. The lowest averages prevailed in the South, with little heavy freight traffic.

On the SECR and the LBSCR, few locomotives had boilers with a grate area of 20sq ft and over. An increase on this figure had been a feature of post-1918 rebuilds such as the Ashford 'D1s' and 'E1s' and the Brighton 'B4X'. Notable exceptions were the LBSCR Atlantics with 31sq ft and the 'I3' with $23\frac{3}{4}$sq ft, both very successful. Coal economy was not improved by the need to thrash smaller locomotives: Holcroft recalls that the spark-throwing by Stirling 'B1s' and 'F1s' rivalled that associated with Crewe locomotives!

On the LSWR, Drummond had, as early as 1899, provided his passenger 4-4-0s of Class 'T9', 'S11' and 'L12', with 24sq ft of grate, increased to 27sq ft on the 'D15s' and 31sq ft on his 4-6-0s. The LBSCR 'Remembrance' class Baltics were limited by other design considerations to 26.7sq ft, so that when rebuilt as tender engines in 1934 for use on the Western section, they did not rank much above the Drummond 'T14s' in performance.

Along with generous grate areas Drummond, with an eye to economy, like the true Scot he was, equipped his locomotives with various coal-saving devices; steam driers in the smokebox; cross water tubes in the firebox; and water heaters in the tender. He also enforced a rigid surveillance over the enginemen to make sure they handled the controls in the most economical way, with wide-open regulators and short cut-offs for maximum expansion; hence it is not surprising that the overall coal consumption per train mile was lowest on the LSWR, as the following figures, again for the year 1908, show:

LSWR	46.9lb per mile
LBSCR	51.4lb per mile
SECR	59.9lb per mile

On the other hand, Drummond's devices were expensive to fit and maintain, so what was gained on the swings was lost on the roundabouts. The same conclusion was ultimately reached, in the closing years of steam in Britain, that complicated equipment, which theoretically saved money by lower fuel consumption, cost in one way or another more than it saved.

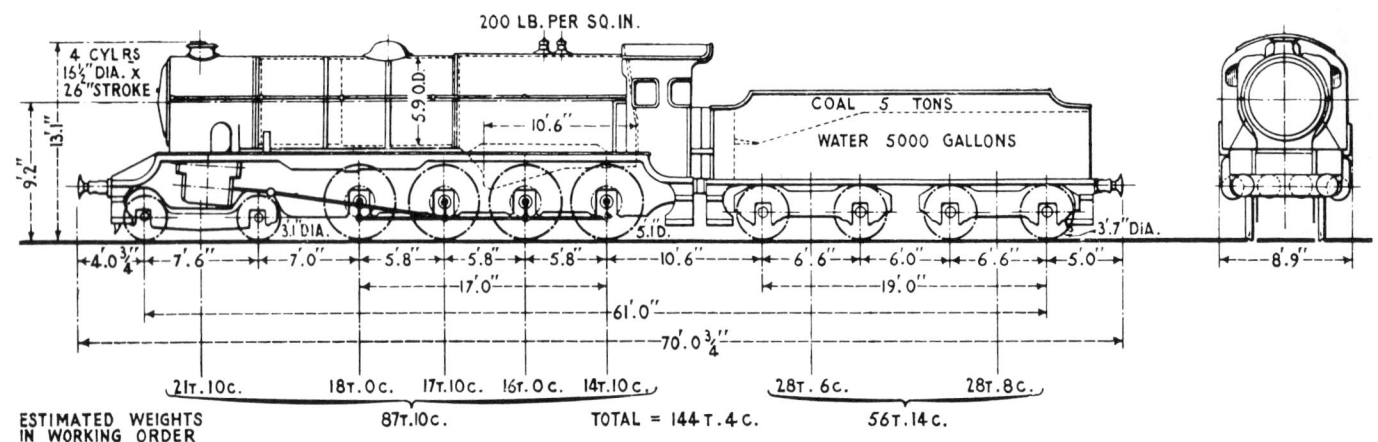

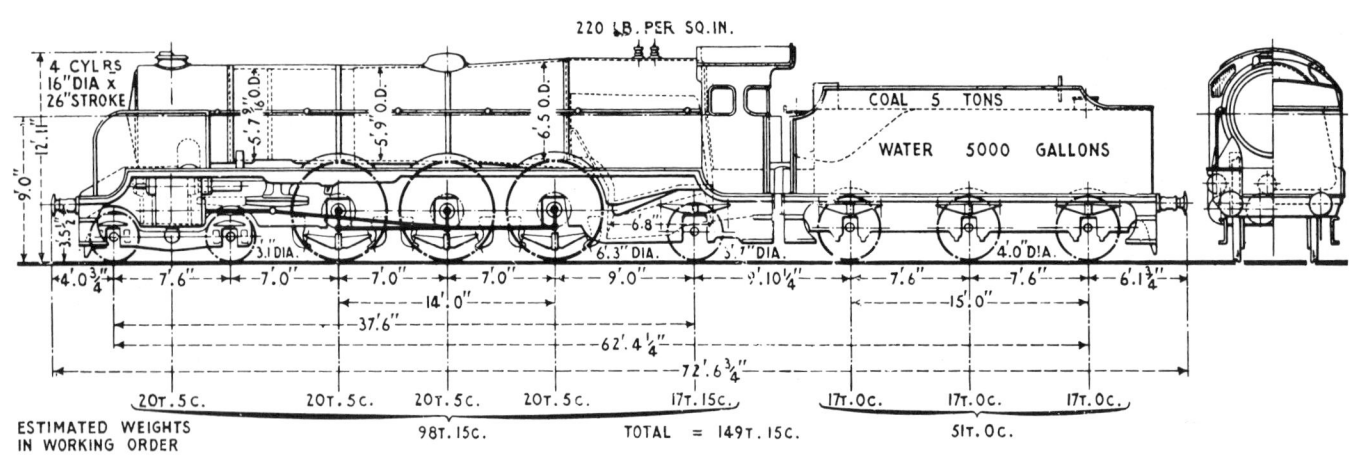

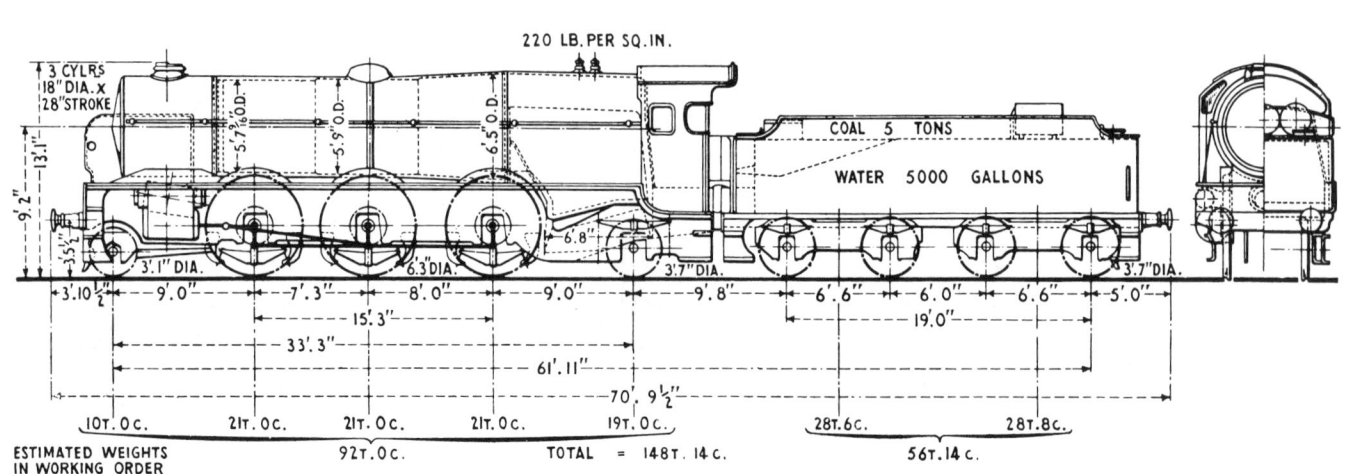

Left: Three proposed Maunsell designs that were not built: (Top) Four-cylinder 4-8-0 for mineral traffic. (Centre) The 1933 Pacific for boat trains. (Bottom) The 4-6-2, redrafted as a three-cylinder 2-6-2.

Southern pre-Grouping designs at work in the late 1930s. (Above) Ex-LBSC 'D1' 0-4-2T No 2357, New Cross, March 1937. (Right) Ex-SECR 'R1' 0-4-4T No 1704, on a Sevenoaks-Tonbridge push-pull, Hildenborough, July 1939. (Below right) Ex-LSWR 'L11' 4-4-0 No 155 near Angmering in April 1937, with a Portsmouth-Brighton train.

All: E. R. Wethersett/Real Photographs Co (24910/23156/23384)

Above: Ex-LBSC 'C3' 0-6-0 No 2303 at Hackbridge, on a pick-up goods, June 1938.

Below: Ex-SECR 'C' 0-6-0 No 1719, Hither Green, May 1934.
Both: E. R. Wethersett/Real Photographs Co (23177/24922)

Above: 'Z' 0-8-0T No 953,
Hither Green, June 1935.
*E. R. Wethersett/Real
Photographs Co (24937)*

Left: 'River' 2-6-4T No A807
River Axe. Ian Allan Library

Below left: Ex-LBSCR 'K'
2-6-0 No 2337.
*E. R. Wethersett/Real
Photographs Co (24905)*

Brighton legacy:

Top: Baltic tank No B333 *Remembrance*
O. J. Morris

Above: 'B4X' 4-4-0 No B56. *Ian Allan Library*

Right: Rebuilt 4-6-4T — 'N15X' 4-6-0 No 2329
Stephenson. *BR*

**Above: Last Maunsell design:
'Q' 0-6-0 No 540, Oxted,
September 1948.**
*E. R. Wethersett/Real
Photographs Co (23280)*

**Drummond designs
compared:**

Left: 'E10' 4-2-2-0 No 371
Ian Allan Library

**Below left: On the Central
section, 'T9' 4-4-0 No 304
with the down 'Eastbourne
Limited', at Patcham.**
H. Gordon Tidey

3
A Crisis: Locomotives in Travail

A young engine cleaner had often to undergo some form of initiation ceremony, such as being daubed with soot, after which he would be held under the outlet of a water column while somebody turned the valve. The young Southern Railway was likewise destined to suffer a cold douche, in the form of criticism and ridicule by the popular press.

During its first year, all seemed set for a prosperous future. Passenger traffic was buoyant, with 59 million passenger journeys in 1923, representing a 26% increase over the total for the constituent companies in 1913. Competition from private cars and from air transport to the Continent was negligible. Although few people enjoyed holidays with pay, the South Coast was a popular venue for day trips and good business was done with excursion trains. The staff of the three companies carried on much as before with their own methods of working whilst the new management, seemingly in no great haste, reshaped its organisation and centralised its headquarters at Waterloo station. But the postwar public was not inclined to be as tolerant as it had been of delays and discomforts.

Postwar reductions in the length of the working day of offices and workshops had the effect of concentrating commuter traffic in the morning and evening and over-taxing the steam hauled suburban services.

On the Eastern (SECR) section, as yet untouched by electrification, the suburban train consisted of six-wheelers drawn by an 0-4-4T. On the main line there was no corridor stock apart from a few boat train sets built at Ashford in 1922, and some LSWR stock had to be hastily transferred, to form trains with the occasional Pullman car in the rake. Some Drummond engines were also sent on loan. South Western officials, already put out by the appointment of ex-SECR men to top jobs, including the Chief Mechanical and Chief Civil Engineers, regarded such loans as the penalty of an enforced marriage with an inferior Kentish railway system. On the busiest day of the Easter rush in 1924, of the 36 down boat trains from Charing Cross and Cannon Street, the majority were formed of non-corridor, non-lavatory coaches, some with nothing better to haul them than elderly 'M3' 4-4-0s or Stirling 'O' class goods engines with 5ft 2in driving wheels and 140lb pressure. The annual exodus of South Londoners to the hop-fields of Kent drew forth the roughest specimens of South Eastern stock; the customers did not complain, since there was ample room under the hard seats for the concealment of ticketless families. Regular passengers were convinced that hop-pickers' trains could be found in general circulation!

Conditions were less Dickensian on the Brighton line, although at holiday times a trip to the seaside was likely to be made in suburban stock behind a Billinton 'E4' 0-6-2T with

stops for the locomotive to take water and for the passengers to relieve themselves. The LBSCR had only 11 Atlantics, seven Baltics and the two 4-6-2 tanks *Abergavenny* and *Bessborough* in its front rank: Newhaven boat trains and the 'Sunny South Express' to and from the North via Willesden might have nothing better than a Gladstone 'B1' class 0-4-2. At any rate the Brighton management had ambitious plans for further electrification on the 6,600V overhead system. When the Southern decided to standardise 600V third-rail traction, these plans were, naturally, held up. But such was the urgency to cope with commuter traffic that extensions of the overhead electrification were made to outer suburbia and it was not until 1929 that conversion to third-rail had been completed on the Central (Brighton) section.

On the Western section the LSWR at the time of the grouping had, to quote M. P. White, 'firmly laid the foundations of a service which was frequent, regular and punctual. Everywhere the average was excellent, and there was nothing spectacular either in speed or waywardness. These were the foundations upon which the Southern built up its own distinctive tradition'. Before World War 1 ended, the LSWR started to rehabilitate itself with new locomotives and rolling stock. By 1923 there was the latest thing in hump marshalling yards at Feltham, and in the reconstructed Waterloo station the LSWR had the largest station in Britain, handling the largest number of trains, 1,034 daily. South Western men would have much preferred to join forces with the Great Western. East of Waterloo there was that 'Hornby' railway — the name under which the Meccano firm had just put its new O gauge train sets on the market. 'How far is it to Brighton?' asked an LSWR man of an LBSCR man who boasted of Baltics and Pullmans, 'only 51 miles!' 'Why, we fly-shunt further than that!'.

At Victoria, a dividing wall separating the SECR and the LBSCR portions of the station, demolished during 1924, was somehow symbolic of the many obstacles to be overcome before the Southern could operate as one railway, and one team. The staff continued to wear the uniforms and badges of the old companies. Many of them had not long been demobilised from the Forces. Others were recent recruits in place of the railwaymen who had lost their lives. Following the war, the railway companies and the railway unions had come together and drawn up conditions of service and 'who-does-what' agreements which were to apply nationally; they also produced an admirable and workable constitution for negotiations between management and staff at local and regional levels. Nevertheless, unification of the conditions could not be achieved overnight. The introduction of an eight-hour, instead of a ten-hour, day for railwaymen also involved additional recruits.

The constituent companies had competing services to towns served by more than one of them, and to eliminate the duplication of the longer and slower routes the Southern recast its timetable.

There is, time has proved, no quicker way to upset the travelling public then by altering the pattern of train service to which they have become accustomed, however good a case may be made for changes. In 1924, such changes were construed as lack of consideration for the public by a new railway monopoly. The railway companies were largely to blame for their traditional aloofness toward public criticism; they made little attempt to foster relations with press and public. It was, anyway, impossible to please everybody all the time.

The Southern soon came to realise the value of public goodwill, and to create a new department to take care of advertising and publicity. Its first task was to combat the press attacks which increased in volume and virulence towards the end of 1924, seizing upon every minor delay or incident out of which to make headlines. The Southern was an easy target; it had been a bad summer: trains crawling behind time or standing motionless in mid-section, trains ending up at the wrong station or not starting through lack of engines. A shortage of seating had not been helped by the withdrawal of coaching stock for conversion into electric trains. Above all, it was trouble with the locomotives that really upset the applecart. Taking each locomotive failure as the loss of more than five minutes on a passenger train or replacement of the locomotive before completing the journey, there were 267 failures in the month of August 1924; moreover one may guess that, things being what they were, not every case was reported. Eight locomotive failures a day were bound to play havoc with the timetable, and the figures did not include 'non-mechanical casualties' attributed to mis-management by enginemen, shortage of water in boiler or tender, shortage of coal, boiler priming (overdue for washout, perhaps), slipping and over-loading. There were late starts due to 'Awaiting locomotive' or 'Late arrival off previous service', which might be the reaction from a failure, or was, quite likely, the impounding of locomotives by traffic disruption at terminal stations, thus delaying coaling and watering for the next trip. No wonder the Southern operators welcomed the electric multiple-unit! The worst culprits amongst a host of causes of mechanical failure were the over-heated big-ends, slide bars and eccentrics. The use of white-metal of inferior quality, a legacy of wartime, had something to do with bearing troubles but even at that comparatively late stage in the art of design the reliability of big-ends was far from perfect. Drummond's inside big-ends were notorious and only by fitting additional felt oiling pads into recesses in the bearing surface could a reasonable mileage be obtained without overheating. Next on the list were leaking or broken boiler tubes: again, many boilers were overdue for complete re-tubing. In the six years between the armistice and 1924 it had not been possible to give every locomotive a general overhaul in works. Other causes high on the list were over-heated axleboxes, injector and feed pump defects, leaking pipes and joints, followed closely by failures due to loose fittings. The steel wheel pounding on the steel rail produces vibrations guaranteed to shake loose nuts and bolts not firmly secured by locking washers and split pins. A fresh hazard had appeared, in that bits that fell off were liable to cause fireworks in contact with the conductor rail. A vigorous campaign against preventable failures and the introduction of new locomotives gradually brought about an improvement. In August 1927, the total failures for the busiest month of the year had fallen to 93 compared with the 267 cases in 1924. Whatever action could be taken to improve the condition of existing locomotives for 1925 it was obvious that new express passenger locomotives must be procured at once, hence the directors urged Maunsell to finalise a design which could be produced quickly in some numbers, and to find a locomotive building firm which could execute a contract at short notice. The locomotive drawing offices were at once put on overtime to prepare specifications for tendering by outside industry. The 'King Arthurs' were on the way.

A promise of better things to come was made by Sir Herbert Walker at a meeting at the Savoy Hotel in January 1925, to which representatives of local authorities on the Southern system had been invited. Sir Herbert admitted, with some candour, that there had been serious shortcomings, and his announcement that £10 million was to be spent on modernisation was sufficient to silence the opposition.

On the operating methods of the railway Sir Herbert Walker was to impose strict disciplines. All trains, loaded or empty, and all regular light engine movements had to be worked to timings as published to the staff in the working timetables. No recovery allowances were incorporated in train schedules, as they were regarded as conducive to an easy-going attitude on the part of drivers; to minimise inter-ference from permanent way works the civil engineer had first to seek approval for any temporary speed restrictions and their number was limited on any given route. All additional trains, whether revenue-earning or for some railway purpose, such as ballast carrying or coaches going to a works for repairs, had to be shown either in a weekly printed notice or else on a stencilled notice to be circulated 24 hours beforehand. The notices were delivered to all stations, signalboxes, locomotive depots and to anyone else likely to be concerned, eg inspectors of every rank and interest.

The running of an extra train at a few hours' notice, by telephonic arrangement, was countenanced only in certain circumstances. Sir Herbert's dictum was 'Plan Your Traffic'; a shaft which was aimed particularly at those station and yard masters who would, by lack of foresight, want to have their own yards cleared of surplus stock immediately by an extra train which might merely move the congestion from A to B and interfere with passenger traffic in doing so. Any extra trains likely to be required on odd days — for example, Ocean Liner trains — were allotted Q or ghost pathways in the working timetables which kept clear of any other trains.

Sir Herbert did not hold with the use of Traffic Control Offices, believing that thereby initiative was taken away from outdoor staff in immediate contact with the running of trains and transferred to clerks in offices. When war came in 1939, it became essential to have some form of control in order to arrange trains at a moment's notice, though out of respect for Sir Herbert, they were not termed Controls but Train Super-vision Offices.

This apparent prejudice against the telephone, as an adjunct to laziness, or as a potential cause of misunder-standings, certainly resulted in the survival of an antiquated telephone system. A limited number of direct telephone lines radiated from Waterloo to manual exchanges at some of the principal stations, but otherwise there existed a network of omnibus circuits, notorious for the number of inquisitive ears likely to overhear conversions, and for the poor quality of audibility. By official circulars staff were from time to time urged never to use the telephone as a substitute, time permitting, for written communications!

In one respect the omnibus telephone system was unrivalled, before the era of the transistor radio, and that was in the transmission of news; the winner of the Derby was circulated within minutes of the race! It was also used to warn of the presence of officialdom in the area. The late A. Earle Edwards used to recount how, as an assistant district officer, he had reproved a signalman for being on duty in an unshaven condition, thereby incurring himself a nickname derived from a much-advertised brand of shaving cream, as he was soon to discover. He arrived at a country signalbox by car and, the signalman being engaged, he answered a call on the telephone circuit to hear a voice say 'Look out, Jack, old "Shavex" is around!'.

West of Salisbury there was, until 1939, no trunk telephone line. Business was still transacted by the single-needle telegraph, using the Railway Clearing House Code. Coded telegrams were the principal means of communicating with the other railway companies. The code-word BOYNE was known to locomotive men, as a warning that no water was available at a particular station — eg 'Boyne Basingstoke'. 'Clyde Basingstoke' meant that water had been restored. On the occasion of an annual office outing, it was customary to send a 'Boyne' telegram to the place at which the party was due to take lunchtime refreshment! Other locomotive code words included CHENG for changing engines, NORUN for a failure and, with less obvious derivation, COLORADO to order a pilot engine and HEBREW for a train with an assisting engine.

To keep station, signalbox and office clocks correct, before the days of the BBC, a time-signal used to be transmitted over the telephone and telegraph system from headquarters at 10am each morning: the further the station from London, the less accurately the clocks were liable to read. Some drivers used to try and time their trains by reading station clocks en route, for not every driver possessed a watch. By a curious anomaly, guards were supplied with watches to enable them to compile their train journals, but drivers were not, and the custom remains the same on BR today. The majority of drivers, anyway, preferred to have their own watches, and at every locomotive depot there was always somebody who made a lucrative hobby out of watch and clock repairing. The Southern gingered up its timekeeping by Lost Time Tickets requiring drivers to answer for as little as one minute lost. A driver would do almost anything rather than put pen to paper.

Southern trains after Grouping:

Below: Ex-SECR 'J' 0-6-4T No 207 passes Sydenham on a down train, c1923/24. *Lens of Sutton*

Bottom: Ex-LBSC 'K' 2-6-0 No 340 at Honor Oak with a down train, c1923/24. *Lens of Sutton*

Above: Ex-SECR 'B1' 4-4-0 No 454 comes round the curve from Shortlands, on the line to Beckenham Jn, with an up train. Note the dc third rail already in position. *Lens of Sutton*

Below: Ex-LSWR 'M7' 0-4-4T No E669 near Walton-on-Thames with a Woking-Waterloo train, 1927. *F. R. Hebron/Rail Archive Stephenson*

**Right: Ex-LSWR motive
power on the Central section:
'L12' No 421, near Redhill,
May 1930.**
*E. R. Wethersett/Real
Photographs Co*

**Below: LSWR electrification:
an up electric train leaves
Hounslow for Waterloo.**
Lens of Sutton

4
New Design

In attempting to discern the predigree of the 'Arthurs', 'Schools' and 'Nelsons', we find ourselves tracing through the threads of a tangled web. These threads lead us back to earlier engines from which experience had been gained and to designers whose ideas had influenced the parent CME. Interwoven with these threads are others which represent the economic circumstances ruling at the time, the developments of the traffic, the strength of the civil engineering works, and the mechanical equipment possesed by the railway concerned.

In the prosperous days of railways and steam locomotives, engineering journals were able to publish details of a new locomotive in almost every issue. There would be a photograph with the impressive caption 'Designed by Mr C. Y. Lindercock, Locomotive Superintendent, Great Smashem & Cheatham Rly'. In the following month would appear an article on the 'fine 4-4-0 express locomotive designed by Mr C. O. Upling of the Long, Slow & Winding Rly.' Careful comparison of their principal dimensions might reveal that there were only slight differences in the sizes of the working parts, albeit each locomotive conformed outwardly to the parent designer's, or company's, distinctive styling which prevented anyone from thinking that one was a copy of the other. Both were almost certainly a modified or slightly enlarged version of an earlier design. There was nothing wrong in that. The steam locomotive grew up by a gradual process and few designers could afford to risk any dramatic experiments. But there was a curious isolationism about the railway design offices. They could have learned so many useful lessons from one another. Books of locomotive diagrams supplied to senior officers would carry stern warnings, such as the one in our Eastleigh diagram book: 'This book is issued to Mr . . . . . on the understanding that it is for his personal use only and must not be lent to anyone else on any pretext whatever. The information it contains is confidential and must not be passed on'.

Swindon had the reputation of being the most secretive place. Yet there was little that could not be discovered about GWR locomotives by some mild espionage, and one hardly need go so far as that when GWR locomotives could be observed in action in half the counties of England. A knowledgeable observer could spot the long travel of the valve spindle as one of Churchward's engines moved off, and hear the sharpness of the exhaust. Passing at speed, the barely audible beats and the wide sweep of the connecting rods gave clear indication of the high expansion ratio. The higher than average boiler pressure of 225lb was a published figure. On each side of the smokebox, large steam pipes took a direct route to the outside steam chests. No patents covered these features. Swindon locomotives passed daily beneath the windows of Eastleigh drawing office where new locomotives, such as the 'H15' and 'N15' 4-6-0s, were being designed with short travel valves, 180lb boiler pressure and indirect steam pipes. The drawing office staff were ruled in schoolmasterly fashion by a chief draughtsman, who did not expect his staff to venture as far as riding on footplates and was never known to do so himself. Any suggestions from the shop floor or from the running department for alterations to drawings, by improvements, were strongly resented. If the case was a good one, the design would be changed but not in the form originally suggested!

Before the amalgamation five companies possessed dynamometer cars for locomotive road testing. These were not in everyday use and it is difficult to believe that, had they wanted to do so, other CMEs could not have come to some arrangement to hire one.

The advances in design achieved at Swindon stemmed from Churchward's interest in what other locomotive engineers were doing: the use of higher boiler pressures and long piston strokes in the United States, and in France the fine workmanship put into locomotives working on the compound principle. A generation later, Gresley's 4-6-2s for the Great Northern main line were inspired by the success of a prototype Pacific built by an American locomotive manufacturer which had distinguished itself on the Pennsylvania Railroad and on the stationary testing plant at Altoona.

Maunsell, too, believed, in his own words, in 'looking around for the best practice'. He mixed as often as possible with fellow engineers, at international railway conferences and at meetings in London of the Civil, Mechanical and Locomotive Engineers Institutions. In his first design, for the SECR, the 'N' class 2-6-0, he acknowledged that the cylinders and long valve travel had followed the practice of Swindon, on which he went one better by adding a Horwich development, higher superheat temperatures. The new coaches built at Ashford for the Continental boat trains, in 1922, must, he told Lionel Lynes, his carriage and wagon officer, 'ride as well as the London & North Western coaches' — a tall order when the latter were running on the 'finest permanent way in the world', as the LNWR claimed, and the SECR probably had the worst!

Impetus toward collaboration between the railway CMEs had been given when, while the railways were still under government control after World War 1, a committee, which included such eminent men as Gresley (GNR), Churchward (GWR), Fowler (MR) and Hughes (L&YR), was charged with the task of drawing up specifications for standard locomotives. The committee was dissolved after amalgamation, ultimately to come to life again under nationalisation in the form of a design team drawn from all the Regions of British Railways. With a few arguable exceptions, the BR standard locomotives incorporated the best features of the locomotives designed during the previous 25 years. The leader of the BR design team, E. S. Cox, later wrote '... there finally emerged an end product which exploited nearly all the practical, as distinct from the theoretical, possibilities of steam traction. To such men as Gresley, Maunsell, Stanier, George Ivatt and Riddles the historian must rightly accord the credit for original thought and application which assured its success'. (E. S. Cox; *Locomotive Panorama* Vol 2; Ian Allan, 1966.)

Before his installation as Southern CME, Maunsell had cast a critical eye over the products of Brighton and Eastleigh. The Brighton school of design was evidently out of touch with the best developments elsewhere; the latest design, the Baltic 'Remembrance' class, was a handsome heavyweight. As a tank locomotive it was pointless because it was never used to work fast trains with bunker leading, it was always turned. The Brighton 'K' class 2-6-0 did good work but the Ashford 'N' 2-6-0 did better. Maunsell saw in the Eastleigh 'N15' 4-6-0s many of the good points which long experience had taught him to adopt in his own design policy. Here were some locomotives built for strength and durability, everything about them was accessible and a pit was only needed for ashpan emptying. Both smokeboxes and ashpans were of such a size so that neither needed to be emptied too often of ash and char. There were no gadgets or fancy fittings. The bearings throughout were of generous dimensions. Lubrication of cylinders, valves and axleboxes was provided from the footplate, where the enginemen could control it. Many of the components were standard with other Urie types.

The LSWR had steadily invested in new locomotives throughout most of its history. Between 1918 and 1923, in spite of postwar difficulties, 49 new locomotives had been built, which was more than the combined output of Ashford and Brighton. Eastleigh Works was the most modern in the country. Its running sheds were generally the best laid out and the best equipped on the Southern. In many ways, the LSWR had more in common with the larger companies north of the Thames; it was financially stable, the civil engineering works had from the beginning been constructed soundly with sufficient capital, and the traffic had shown a steady growth. The originating freight traffic exceeded that of both the LBSCR and SECR put together. It had substantial investments in property and in docks. It was the only Southern company on which through locomotive workings were long enough to involve the provision of dormitories and lodgings for enginemen, and the only company with a four-track main line for 50 miles out of London. These were some of the threads mentioned at the beginning of this chapter which had influenced locomotive development.

The first 4-6-0s on the LSWR had been built by Drummond in 1905, the 'F13' class, with four cylinders. Two inside cylinders beneath the smokebox drove the leading pair of driving wheels, and two outside cylinders were positioned adjacent to the leading coupled wheels to drive the middle pair. The divided drive arrangement of a four-cylinder engine followed that adapted with the 4-2-2-0 type No 720 produced in 1897. That locomotive had in turn been based, it is held on good authority, upon Webb's LNWR 2-2-2-0 type divided drive locomotives which had evidently taken Drummond's fancy, not on account of the compound expansion so much as of the free running of uncoupled pairs of driving wheels. Engine No 720 performed less well than the ordinary two-cylinder 4-4-0s but, nothing daunted, Drummond built five more 4-2-2-0s in 1901 with smaller boilers. In all his 4-2-2-0s, as with Webb's, the inside and outside cylinders were separated by a length of frame. The stresses set up by the thrusts of separate cylinders caused fatigue cracks in a portion of the frame which could not be made deeper without fouling the bogie wheels. In action, they were temperamental machines. The inside and outside sets of cylinders would operate alternately in and out of phase with one another, which upset the balancing and the even draught on the fire. The engines, Nos 720 and 369-373, became known to the staff as 'Butterflies' because they appeared at work on fine days at the peak of summer traffic, but seldom at other times. Drummond would have been sensible to have rebuilt them as straight two-cylinder 4-4-0s, and one suspects that it was the loss of face which prevented him. George Whale was at the time reverting to two-cylinder 4-4-0s after he succeeded Webb as CME at Crewe.

Drummond was an obstinate Scot and in due time his obstinacy cost the company more money because the five 'F13' 4-6-0s cracked their frames in just the same places. Transmitting the drive in that way certainly avoided the concentration of weight and stress on one driving axle and the principle was employed by other engineers. It was the location of the cylinders which caused trouble. A better arrangement was to have the cylinder blocks in line and to divide the drive by differences in the length either of the piston rods or the connecting rods, or both.

Picking holes in the work of past designers, of course, can sound supercilious, so let us hasten to imagine the difficulties that they had to contend with, on the LSWR in particular. The only instrumentation that was available for test purposes was the steam engine indicator which drew a diagram of the compression and expansion within the cylinder. Alloy steels, case hardening processes, crack detectors, strain gauges, and so on, were non-existent, or in their infancy. Ultrasonic testing and industrial X-ray photography lay in the future. When parts of a locomotive broke or developed cracks the cause was often a matter of guesswork, the cure to increase the thickness of metal. Engines were allowed to run with cracked spokes, frames, hornblocks and cylinder castings, provided that the cracks were marked and regularly inspected by running shed fitters for any sign of worsening.

Drummond's attempts to produce a successful four-cylinder 4-6-0 were examples of trial and error. In chronological order they were:

Nos	*Date*	*Cylinders*	*Boiler tubes*	*Firebox Water tubes*	*Scrapped or rebuilt*
330-334	1906	16in×24in	340×1¾in	112×2¾in	1924-25
335	1907	16½in×26in	340×1¾in	112×2¾in	1914
453-457	1908	15in×26in	247×1¾in	84×2¾in	1925
448-452	1910	15in×26in	247×1¾in	84×2¾in	1925-27
443-447	1911/12	15in×26in	247×1¾in	84×2¾in	1915-18
458-462					(mods)

Full details are available in reference books. The above changes show that the cylinder sizes were reduced, an indication that the cylinders were at first too large for the boiler's steaming capacity. Although the boilers were reduced in size and in the number of tubes when the cylinders were bored at 15in, the gas flow and the steaming could well have been better in spite of the reduction in heating surfaces A grate area of 31.5sq ft — larger than on the 'King Arthur' class —

was provided on all the engines, and 6ft 0in diameter coupled wheels, and 175lb boiler pressure, until the final batch, 443-47 and 458-62, which had 6ft 7in wheels and 200lb pressure. The latter engines had outside sets of valve gear to operate the four valves, with rocking shafts to the inside valves, and Eastleigh never found a way of setting the valve gear which would give equal port openings on all four valves. By their appearance they looked capable of timing the 'Atlantic Coast Express'; instead they were more suitable to work stopping trains to Basingstoke.

No one from amongst the ex-LSWR technical staff who was around in Southern days could quite explain the logic behind Drummond's experiments with his 4-6-0s. All agreed, anyway, that the first 16 belonged to the 'Couldn't-pull-pussy' class. In the last year of his life, in 1912, Drummond reverted to a 4-4-0 type with the excellent 'D15' class which became for a time the mainstay of the Bournemouth express services. On this same route in 1937 another 4-4-0, the 'Schools' class, was destined to rival the performance of the 4-6-0s.

Below: Eastleigh product: 'H15' 4–6–0 No 485 on a down Basingstoke train, Hersham, June 1938.
E. R. Wethersett/Real Photographs Co (23300)

Bottom: Maunsell 'N' 2-6-0: No 810 *Ian Allan Library*

Drummond locomotive designs:

Left: 'T7' 4–2–2–0 No 720, as fitted with large boiler, and with indicating gear, at Nine Elms *Ian Allan Library*

Right: 'D15' 4–4–0 No 469. *Ian Allan Library*

Below right: 'F13' 4–6–0 No 334, leaving Salisbury with a freight for Eastleigh. *Ian Allan Library*

28

Above: In original condition, 'P14' 4–6–0 No 448.

Left: Rebuilt, 'T14' 4–6–0 No 443. *Both: Ian Allan Library*

Below left: In final condition, 'T14' 4–6–0 No 460. *S. C. Townroe*

Urie 4-6-0s:

Top: 'N15' No 736.
Locomotive Publishing Co

Above: 'H15' No 482.
Ian Allan Library

Right: 'H15' No 486.
Ian Allan Library

5
The Development of the 'Arthurs'

Nobody dared criticise Drummond's engines while he was alive — at least not openly. He held that there were no bad engines of his, only bad enginemen. It did not reach his ears that the initials LSWR on the water cart tenders of his four-cylinder locomotives stood for 'Lazy Swines Won't Run'. After his death, R. W. Urie rebuilt No 335 to his own 'H15' design, and was dealing similarly with Nos 330-334 at the the time of his retirement. He had financial authority to rebuild Nos 448-457 but had not made up his mind about the details of the conversion. The last 10 'Paddleboats' were destined to survive, with Maunsell modifications, until after World War 2 except for No 458, blitzed in 1940.

Urie's 'N15' class 4-6-0s could run, and had plenty of power with 22in×28in cylinders, and a well-tried type of boiler; their weakness was that steam pressure could not be reliably maintained. The Running Dept tried all the remedies; the chimney and blast pipe alignment was checked with a plumb-line, smokebox joints made airtight, tubes swept daily, and superheaters regularly water tested for steam leakage. When Maunsell heard of the steaming difficulty, he had No 742 fitted with the cylinder indicating gear, and readings were taken on a run from Waterloo to Salisbury in February 1924. In spite of expert handling the steam pressure gradually fell back until it was only 100lb at Hook: the highest indicated horsepower figure obtained was 950, with the pressure standing at 150lb, and at Hook it was as low at 650ihp. A month later, No 742 took the road again after having the steam ports enlarged, and the exhaust release point set a little earlier to sharpen up the blast. These alterations proved ineffective, so the next step was to alter the design of the chimney and petticoat pipe. Urie's distinctive, slightly Gallic stovepipe chimney on the 'N15s' was made of small diameter, in the belief that the exhaust would escape with considerable velocity and carry smoke and steam above the level of the cab windows, a problem that was to become serious, as will be related.

The stovepipe chimney on No 742 was replaced by the larger diameter pattern as used on the 'H15' class. It was a nicely proportioned chimney which, with minor alterations and the addition of a capuchon, was to look well on the 'Arthurs', 'Schools' and 'Nelsons'. The larger petticoat pipe used with the 'H15' chimney enabled the blastpipe cap to be enlarged from 5in to $5\frac{1}{8}$in, and on the next trial run with No 742 the steaming was much more consistent and the horsepower was up, to 1,250ihp.

Maunsell had by then decided to rebuild Nos 448-457 into his own version of the 'N15' with 200lb boiler pressure, $20\frac{1}{2}$in diameter cylinders, long lap $6\frac{9}{16}$in travel valves and with his design of superheater with 337sq ft of heating surface instead of 308sq ft with Urie's superheater. The main steam pipes to the valve chests took a direct path, out of the smokebox sides. The air passages through the ashpan dampers to the grate were more generous that on the Urie 'N15'. On test, No 451 proved capable of sustaining 1,500 indicated horsepower at 190lb pressure, a 20% improvement over No 742.

In the course of general repairs during 1927-29, the Urie 'N15s' were given replacement Maunsell superheaters, and the worn 22in diameter cylinders were linered down to $20\frac{1}{2}$in, except for No 755 which continued to run with the larger diameter without any appreciable advantage. As Nos 736-755 were to survive for 40 odd years, it was a pity that apart from the foregoing alterations they were left alone when they could have been placed on a par with the Maunsell version.

Below: Original Urie design for a 'King Arthur', as built from 1918. The coupled axle weights were later corrected to 58t 7cwt.

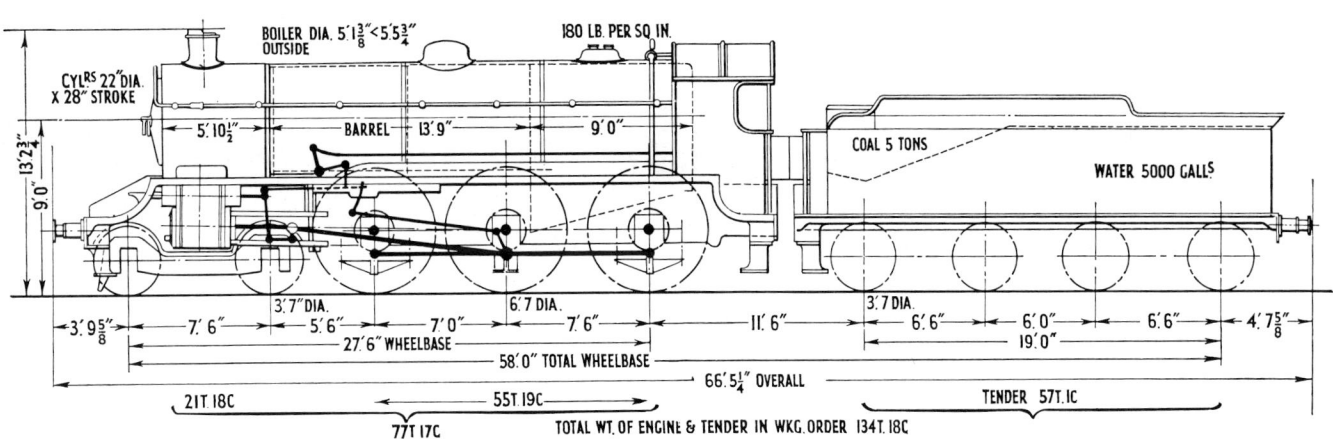

The reason was that they satisfactorily filled a niche in the pattern of traffic requirements, coping with Southampton boat traffic, van trains and semi-fast passenger trains; it was thus difficult for the Running Dept to prove that further expenditure on them could be justified. In the mid-1930s, when new design work was practically at a standstill, the technical staff applied their minds to various ways of gingering up the Urie 'N15s'. One simple method would have been to increase the boiler pressure from 180 to 200lb, but the works people were able to prove that the boiler repair costs of the 'Arthurs' with 200lb pressure were appreciably greater than the 180lb boilers. It had been found necessary to have a number of spare 200lb boilers on hand, without which the target overhaul time for an 'Arthur' could not be maintained.

An improvement in the valve events offered possibilities, and Nos 740/3/5/6/8/52 were equipped with double ported valves which should have afforded better steam admission and a freer exhaust. Their effect on performance was very small. Better results followed the fitting of Nos 736/7/41/52/55 with Bulleid's arrangement of the multiple-jet blastpipe and wide chimney.

Reverting to our story; when the storm broke in 1924 and it became imperative to supply some new passenger locomotives at once, without waiting for Maunsell's four-cylinder 4-6-0 design, the obvious course lay in taking the improved 'N15' design prepared for rebuilding Nos 448-457 to the Western section loading gauge, and altering details, such as the cab, to suit the composite loading gauge. This was to provide an 'N15' type 4-6-0 which could run on the Central section and on the Eastern section once the main line to Dover via Tonbridge had been improved by the Civil Engineer to carry locomotives with axleloads of 20 tons. The 30 additional locomotives which were decided upon, could not be built immediately at Eastleigh Works, and an urgent contract was undertaken by the North British Locomotive Company of Glasgow. Known in the trade as The Combine, the NB Co was the largest locomotive building firm in Europe, formed by the amalgamation of three former Glasgow firms, Sharp, Stewart & Co, Neilson, Reid & Co, and Dubs & Co, and the three workshops, Queens Park, Hyde Park and Atlas Works had a potential output of 700 locomotives annually. Delivery of the series No 763-792 began in May 1925, barely six months after the placing of the Southern's order.

The locomotives, fully erected except for coupling and connecting rods, were towed from Glasgow to Eastleigh. Some ran hot on the journey, with overheated coupled axlebox bearings, which the contractors had made too neat a fit and with insufficient working clearance. By July, enough of them were serviceable to take over the Dover boat trains, loaded to 425 tons instead of 300 tons.

It was at this time that the 'N15s' began to appear with names. The circumstances in which the names came to be bestowed on them have been related by Sir John Elliot who was later to become Chairman of British Railways, and of London Transport. As Mr Elliot he wrote: 'I was at the time, 1925, Public Relations Assistant to Sir Herbert Walker. One day he sent for me and told me that a large number of new express engines were to be built at Eastleigh and Glasgow, and that he would like some special publicity given to them, suggesting that if I could find an appropriate name for them, he would recommend it to the Board of Directors. After a few days I submitted a list of the names of Arthur's Knights of the Round Table, pointing out the connection between them and places on the Southern Railway.'

Certainly, the romantic and dignified names were most suitable for locomotives, the most human of machines; more suitable, one might suggest, than the names of places. Many a parent, dragged to the end of the platform before starting time by a youngster eager to see the engine, 'Dad', must have been taxed with questions about *King Arthur* or, more difficult still, about such Norman-French names as *Sir Meliot de Logres*.

It is fairly well-established that Arthur did exist, though he was a duke rather than a king, and that about 500AD he was the leader of the Britons against the Anglo-Saxons who invaded the country during the years following the departure of the Romans. He succeeded for a time in holding back the barbarian invaders, to preserve the orderly and peaceful existence which Britons had enjoyed under Roman rule, and his exploits were handed down by myths and legends. William of Malmesbury, in the 12th century, referring to the fables about Arthur, described him as 'a man worthy to be celebrated not by idle fictions but by authentic history. He long upheld the sinking state and roused the broken spirit of his countrymen to war'. Nennius, writing in the 9th century, mentioned twelve battles in which Arthur was victorious but the British place names cannot be identified. Geoffrey of

Below: An NB Loco Co 'King Arthur' as new.

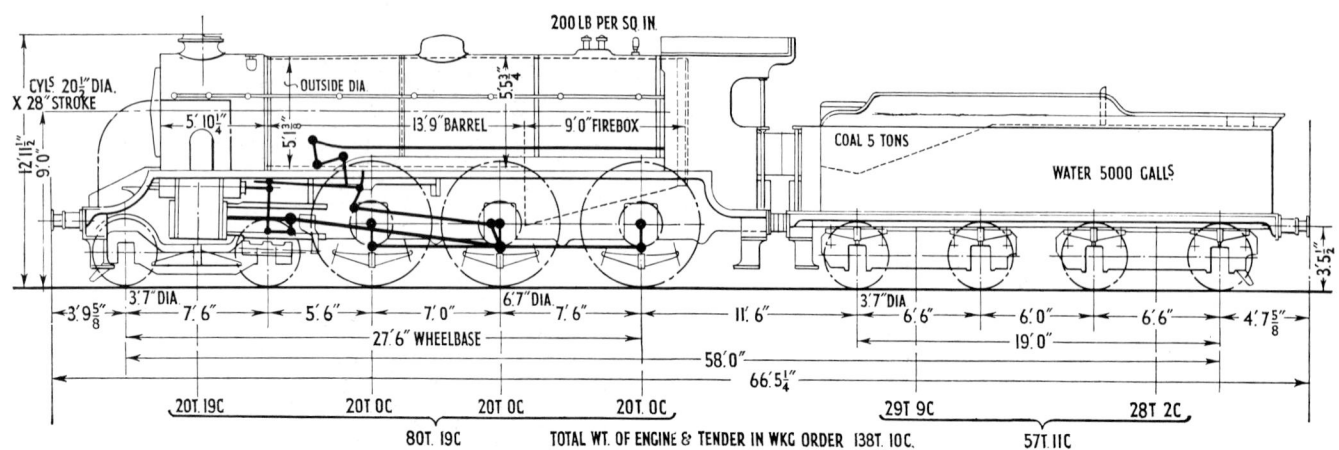

Monmouth, another 12th century writer, produced an historical romance. *The History of the Kings of Britain*, containing stories of Arthur; the book in due course inspired Sir Thomas Malory in the 15th century to write the dreamland tales in his *Morte d'Arthur*. More recently, Alfred, Lord Tennyson's 19th-century peom, *The Idylls of the King*, presented King Arthur as an ideal hero of English chivalry.

The connection between King Arthur and places in Southern Railway territory, such as Canterbury, Winchester, Old Sarum (Salisbury), Glastonbury, Camelford and Tintagel was, therefore, based on mediaeval legends. That these places were associated with the stirring events of the 5th and 6th centuries AD, historians accept as not entirely fanciful.

Fourteen more 'Arthurs', Nos 793-806, were built at Eastleigh between March 1926 and January 1927 to work on the Central section. The Baltics could handle the 'Brighton Belle' and other primary services to the coast, but with only seven of them in total and seldom all serviceable, they were being helped out by the 'River' class 2-6-4 tanks, those much-lamented engines, well-liked by drivers in spite of a tendency to roll. Their riding was, in fact, much steadier on the Central than on the Eastern section. Experiments to improve it were cut short by the Sevenoaks accident. Some Drummond 'L12' 4-4-0s, 'Bulldogs', were also at work on such trains as the 'Eastbourne Sunday Pullman'.

The last batch of 'Arthurs' was provided with six-wheel tenders because the Civil Engineer considered the bogie tender, weighing $57\frac{1}{2}$ tons — with more than 22 tons of water! — to be too heavy for the Central, and certainly the mileages involved did not warrant the provision of so much water. A stock Ashford pattern of six-wheel tender was used, to suit which the drag-box of the 'Arthur' had to be specially adapted, so that the 793-806 batch could not easily be changed to bogie tenders. The dc electrification to Brighton was not expected to displace them as early as 1933 but they were quite suitable for the Kent Coast trains.

The SR Board had authorised the construction of 15 'Arthurs' to follow No 792, but No 807 was not built and the number remained blank; instead the 15th became No 850 *Lord Nelson*, described in the next chapter.

The 'Arthurs' were the first locomotives in Great Britain to be fitted with smokebox 'wings', or deflector plates, and their introduction to British practice came about in the following way. In 1902 the LSWR began the installation of pneumatically-operated points and signals on the main line, first at Grateley and later over the 24 miles between Woking and Basingstoke. On the latter, four-track section, the signals, carried on gantries, were placed immediately over each track with the object of indicating clearly to which line they applied. With the signals so placed, there was one snag: the driver's line of sight could be interrupted by the steam and smoke from the chimney. A much better arrangement, adopted when the Southern Railway installed colour-light signalling between Waterloo and Hampton Court Junction, was to place each signal slightly to the left of the track to

which it applied. With left-hand drive engines — the majority — if a driver wanted to make certain of his correct signal he had, to quote Col Hall, the SR Signal Engineer of the time, 'only to cock his head over the side of the cab to see the right one'.

As locomotive boilers grew in size and chimneys got shorter, so the difficulties of sighting signals increased, and with more efficient valve gears the exhaust steam left the chimney at less velocity, with a tendency to drift down over the cab windows. Such a tendency was more pronounced with head or following winds than with cross winds. On the Woking-Basingstoke stretch the prevailing winds, south-westerly in Britain, blew in the same direction as the track. Another main line likely to be similarly affected was the GWR West of England route, but that company placed its signals away from the centre of the track, and its locomotives had taper boilers and a width of cab which took advantage of a generous loading gauge.

By 1925, the improvements incorporated in the Maunsell 'Arthurs', which have previously been described, made signal sighting from these engines even more tricky, and drivers on the Western section petitioned Maunsell for a remedy. He, as was his wont, cast around to see whether other railway administrations were seriously troubled, and found that the German Railways obtained good results by fitting large rectangular plates vertically each side of the smokebox. Plates of this pattern were fitted to No 772 *Sir Percivale* working on the Western section in 1926. Though effective, they seemed a somewhat clumsy solution, so experiments were made to see whether small wings around the chimney would give the same results. They did not. A further alternative was tried, with a circular plate extending around the upper half of the smokebox, but this too, failed. Maunsell then reverted to the German pattern but reduced in size: satisfactory results were achieved with plates as high as the handrails, well radiused on the top front corners. With these compromises the 'Arthurs' and 'Nelsons' were permanently fitted. Thus far, a solution had been reached by trial and error; in 1931, scale models of a 'Schools' class and a 'U' class with taper boiler were submitted for wind-tunnel tests at the National Physical Laboratory, and various patterns of deflector plate were tested in miniature. One pattern extended the whole length of the engine from smokebox to cab. It was established that the projection of the plates forward of the smokebox provided the necessary up-draught to carry smoke clear of the boiler top. Without them, the air disturbance caused by the front of the smokebox gave rise to areas of low pressure around the boiler. Deflector plates were also adopted for certain LMS and LNER locomotives, but the GWR found no need of them.

The SR enginemen were pleased with the improved visibility, and soon discovered another advantage of deflector plates: pheasants and partridges that flew into the path of the engine were neatly trapped and ready for collection at the next stopping place!

Urie 'Arthurs':
Above: No 739. *Lens of Sutton*

Below: No 747 passes Esher with a down train, c1923.
O. J. Morris/Lens of Sutton

Above: No E748 with a down train, passing Clapham Jn, c1924/25. *A. W. Croughton/Lens of Sutton*

Below: No 752 Linette arrives at Bournemouth West with an express from Waterloo, c1924/25. *Lens of Sutton*

Urie 'Arthurs' in SR days.

Above: With Lemaître exhaust, No 752 *Linette* passes Earlsfield, with a Waterloo-Bournemouth train, July 1947.
John P. Wilson

Below: No E755 *The Red Knight,* fitted with a louvred chimney.
Lens of Sutton

Above right: No E737 *King Uther* passes Raynes Park with an up West of England train, c1930. The engine is fitted with a Maunsell NBL Co boiler.
F. R. Hebron/Rail Archive Stephenson

Right: No 737, c1937, waiting to leave Waterloo with a Bournemouth train. By then, fitted with Maunsell smokebox door and snifting valves. *C. R. L. Coles*

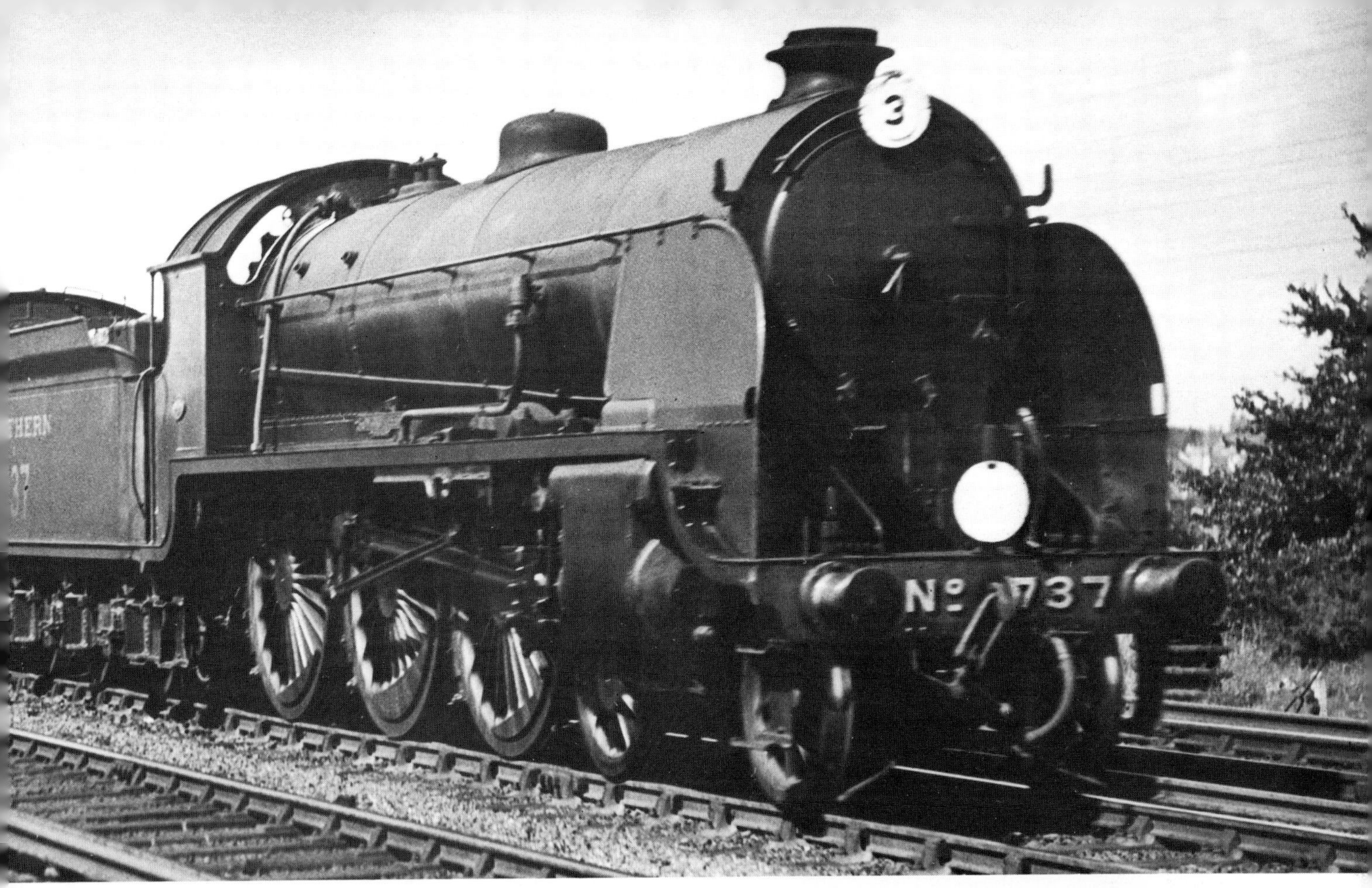

SOUTHERN
737
No 737

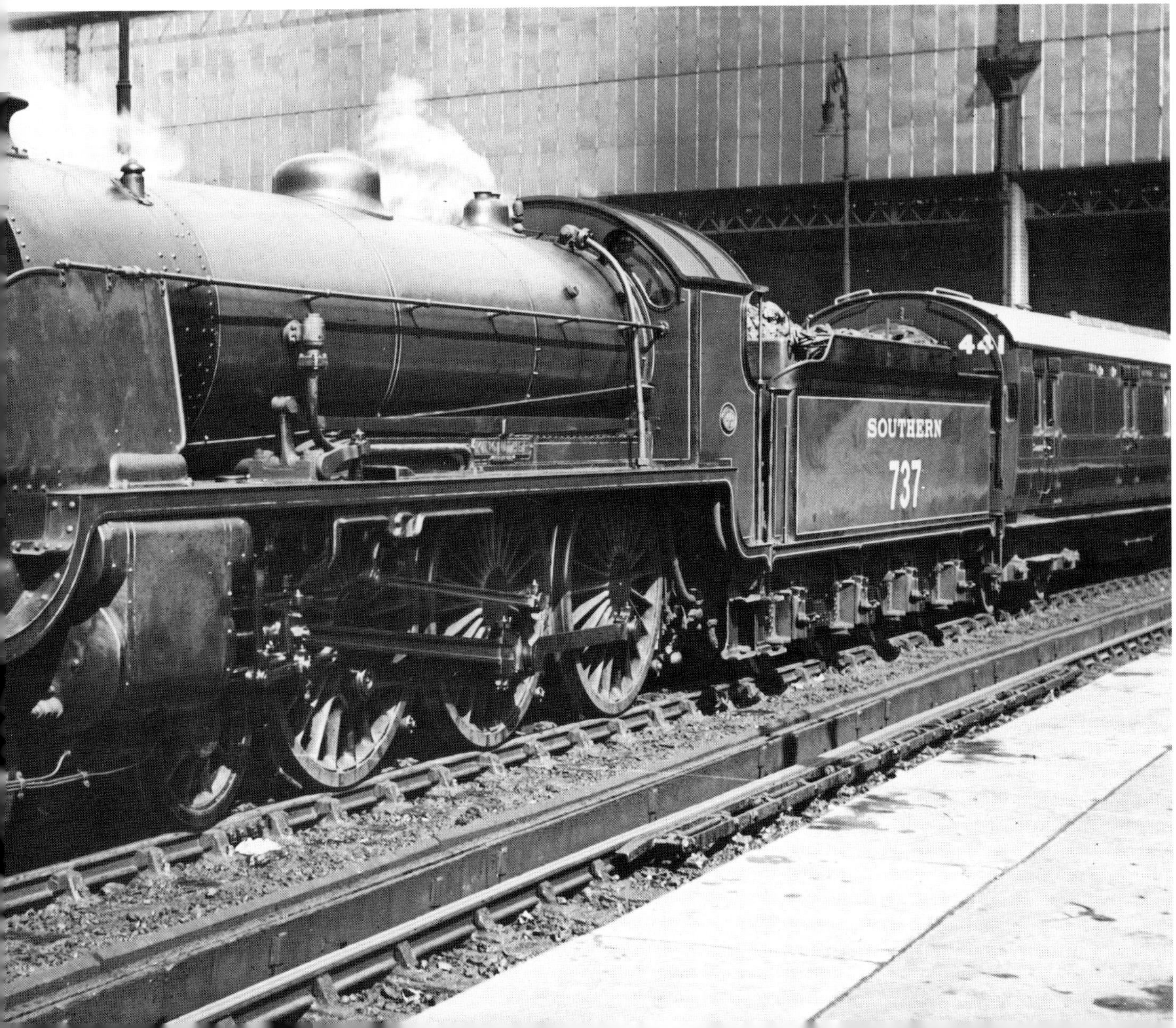

441
SOUTHERN
737

SOUTHERN
453

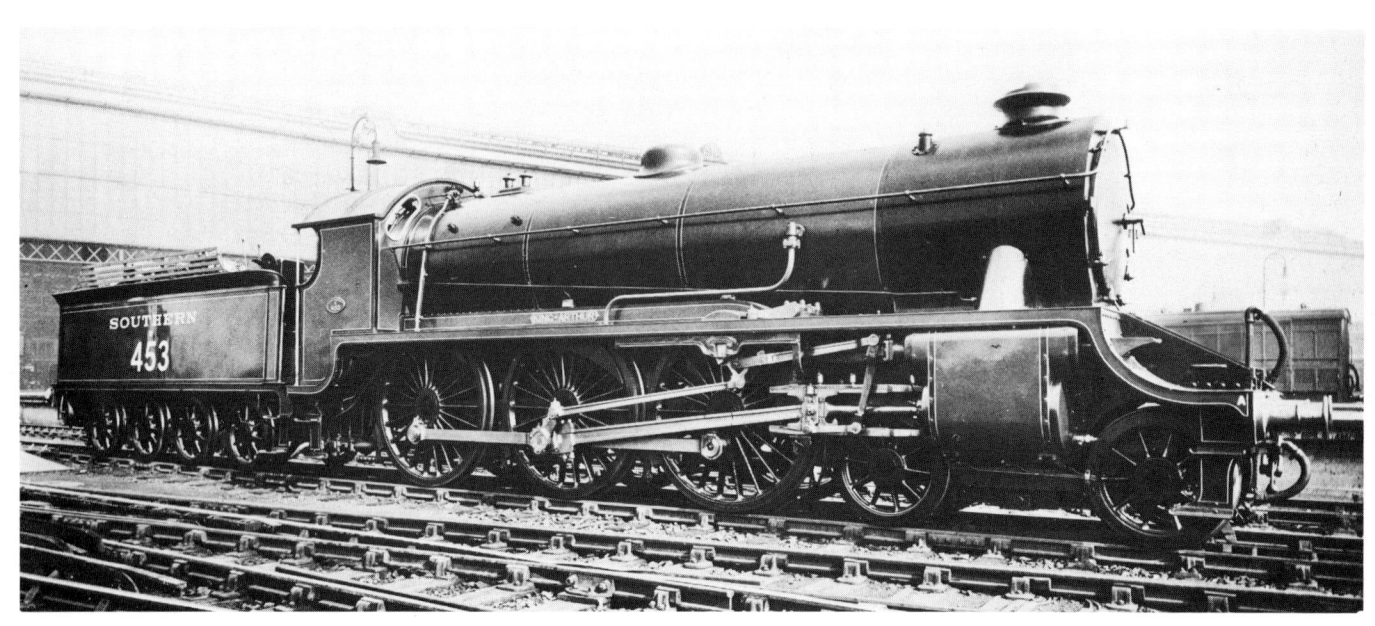

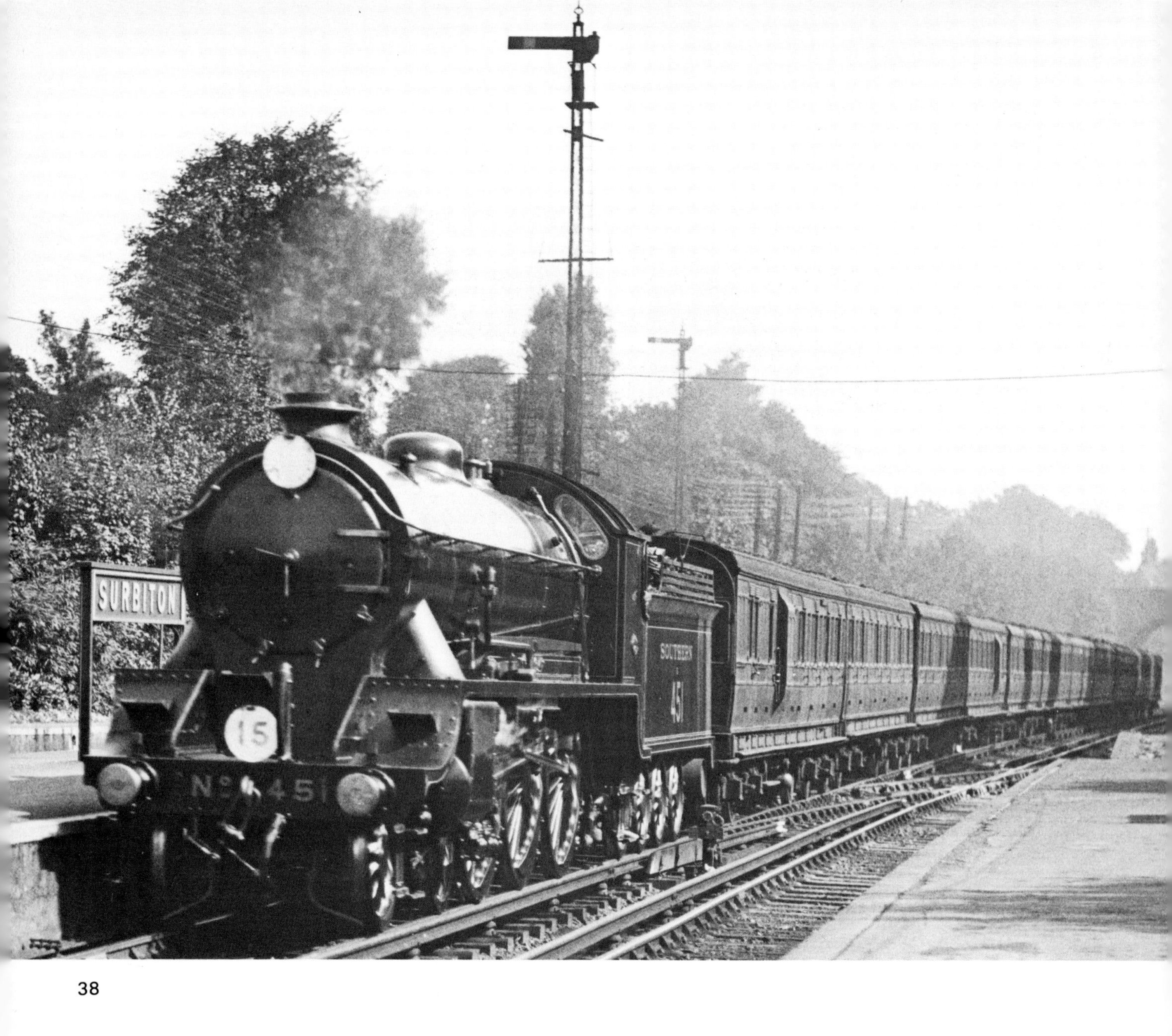
SURBITON
SOUTHERN
451
15

Eastleigh 'Arthurs'.

Above left: SR publicity photograph of No E453 *King Arthur,* as built. *BR*

Left: No E451 *Sir Lamorak* passes Surbiton with a down West of England train, 10 September 1930. *F. R. Hebron/Rail Archive Stephenson*

Above: No E452 *Sir Melliagrance* at Raynes Park with a Bournemouth-Waterloo express, 10 September 1926. *F. R. Hebron/Rail Archive Stephenson*

Right: No E453 *King Arthur,* as fitted with small experimental smoke deflectors, c1926/27. *Lens of Sutton*

Below right: An NBL Co-built 'Arthur' in transit, seen at Gorgie Junction in 1925 behind a North British 'S' 0-6-0. The train, which includes two 'Arthurs', the leading one No 769, has stopped for examination. *P. Ransome Wallis*

'Scotch Arthurs' on boat train work:

Above: No E764 *Sir Gawaine* approaches Dover Marine on a down working, c1927.   *Lens of Sutton*

Below: No E765 *Sir Gareth* marshals its train at Dover Marine, c1927.
Lens of Sutton

Right: No E769 *Sir Balan* breasts the summit between Beckenham Jn and Shortlands with the 11.10am Victoria-Dover Marine, 1928. Smoke deflectors fitted, and LSWR-style numerals on buffer beam.
F. R. Hebron/Rail Archive Stephenson

Below: No E771 *Sir Sagramore* comes round the connecting spur from Bickley to Petts Wood with the 11.00am Victoria–Dover Marine Pullman boat train, autumn 1925. *Lens of Sutton*

Bottom: No E783 *Sir Gillemere* between Woking and Brookwood with a down express, early 1930s. *F. R. Hebron/Rail Archive Stephenson*

Above: No E784 *Sir Nerovens* at Southampton West station (later Central) with an up express, c1926. *Lens of Sutton*

Below: No E786 *Sir Lionel* speeds through Esher with a special train for Bournemouth, September 1925.
F. R. Hebron/Rail Archive Stephenson

Left: No E772 *Sir Percivale* waits to depart from Waterloo with the 2.30pm to Bournemouth on 23 October 1926. As fitted with German pattern experimental smoke deflectors.
F. R. Hebron/Rail Archive Stephenson

'Arthurs' on the Central section:

Above: No E794 *Sir Ector de Maris* near Merstham on the Quarry Line with the 3.05pm Victoria-Brighton 'Southern Belle', May 1928. *F. R. Hebron/Rail Archive Stephenson*

Below: No E805 *Sir Constantine* under ac electric overhead electrification, passing Clapham Junction with a Victoria-Brighton train, c1928/29. *James R. Clarke/Lens of Sutton*

Above right: No 806 *Sir Galleron* stands at Charing Cross with a Dover train in the late 1930s. *Lens of Sutton*

Right: On the Eastern section, *Sir Percivale*, with experimental deflectors, passes Herne Hill with a Dover-bound boat train, c1927. *Lens of Sutton*

Below: Illustrating an alternative experiment in smoke deflection, No E783 *Sir Gillemere* near Walton-on-Thames with the 12.30pm Waterloo-Bournemouth, 1927.
F. R. Hebron/Rail Archive Stephenson

6
The Design of the 'Nelsons'

In 1915 the story went round railway engineers' offices that some 4-6-0 locomotives had been built by Hawthorn, Leslie & Co of Newcastle for the Highland Railway, only to be debarred by the company's Civil Engineer; in consequence the Locomotive Superintendent who designed and ordered them had either been dismissed or compelled to resign. The locomotives had subsequently been bought by the Caledonian Railway. The full circumstances were not made public but for some reason there had been a lack of liaison between the officers concerned about the maximum axleload that the Highland's track and bridges could safely bear.

The affair served as a reminder, where such was necessary, that locomotives were necessarily growing in size and weight, and that the margin of safety incorporated in the design of bridges built many years previously was gradually being reduced. The time was approaching when some bridges would be seriously overstressed, with the possible repetition of earlier disasters. Cast iron components were prone to fail without any warning; bridges of riveted, wrought iron had the advantage that signs of distress, such as buckled plates and broken rivets, could afford some warning of trouble. Stresses increased with train speeds, but the extent of the stressing which was taking place was unknown, until the arrival of the electrical strain gauge made accurate measurement possible. It had been a broken cast iron bridge girder that caused a serious derailment on the LBSCR at Norwood in May 1891; the locomotive involved was an 0-4-2 of the 'B1' class, No 175 *Hayling*.

In 1923 a Bridge Stress Committee, consisting of 10 eminent civil engineers, was formed to investigate the problem. Five years later its report was published, and one of its points was that three- and four-cylinder locomotives, by virtue of better balancing than two-cylinder types, were much to be preferred.

It was during the same period that Maunsell was developing his design for a locomotive capable of running over all the Southern main lines with trains of 500 tons at 55mph average speed. The SR limit of axleloading was 21 tons, and the weight on the 'King Arthur' driving axle was already within 16cwt of the limit at 20 tons 4cwt. No easement of the limit was likely; the Southern Chief Civil Engineer, George Ellson, was a member of the Bridge Stress Committee and, as a former engineer on the SECR, he knew that some bridge reconstruction work was necessary, before even the 'Arthurs' could pass over the Eastern section routes.

The 'Lord Nelson' design deserves a special place in the history of British locomotive development, as an exercise in ingenuity to secure a significant increase in the power of a 4-6-0 type with a minimal increase in weight. As it turned out, the empty weight of a 'Nelson' engine at 77 tons 2cwt was only 1ton 1cwt greater than an 'Arthur' of the final 793-806 series, and yet the tractive effort was raised to 33,510lb against the 25,321lb of the 'Arthur'. The weight, in working order, on each coupled axle of the original 'Nelson' was 20 tons 13cwt compared with 20 tons 4cwt on the driving axle of the 'Arthur' and after the 'Nelsons' had been given new cylinders and a redesigned front-end by Mr Bulleid, the axle weights were still within the 21ton limit.

In view of the findings of the Bridge Stress Committee, it was to be expected that thereafter Maunsell's proposals for express locomotives were multi-cylinder types: the three-cylinder 'Schools' class 4-4-0 which followed the 'Nelsons', and the three-cylinder 2-6-2 and four-cylinder 4-6-2, neither of which got beyond the drawing board. Some reduction in the hammer-blow of the two-cylinder 'Arthurs' was achieved meanwhile, recalculating the proportion of balancing weights for the reciprocating parts. Subsequently the correct balance of driving wheels was checked by spinning them in the special machine at Eastleigh.

In working out the 'Nelson' design, considerable time was spent on a complete investigation into the problems of balancing reciprocating masses, and the arrangement of setting the cranks at 135 degrees to give eight beats or 'impulses' per revolution of the coupled wheels offered advantages in the reduction of stress on axleboxes and motion parts. Holcroft had pointed this out in a paper read in 1920. The motion parts were made out of the latest high-tensile steel and the working parts of the 'Lord Nelson' were a model of neatness combined with strength. In order to test the eight-beat principle beforehand, a Drummond four-cylinder, No 449, was altered to that crank arrangement in 1924. It created a more even draught on the fire and there was less tendency for the blast to pull the fire to pieces when the engine was working heavily at slow speed. On the other hand, it was argued that the blast would be too soft to be fully effective, and that four impulses instead of eight would be better for starting heavy trains. The trial proved that the strength was quite adequate. Some years later the last of the class, No 865 *Sir John Hawkins*, had the crank settings altered to four beats, to enable direct comparisons to be made between it and the others. After a long period it was clear that there was no difference. Some drivers declared in favour of No 865, others considered that the 'bark' had improved, but not the 'bite'. The alteration to the engine was one of several experiments with others of the class, of which more anon.

The only British locomotive on which the eight-beat crank setting had been tried was a four-cylinder 0-6-0 tank engine produced in 1922 by the North Staffordshire Railway. The intention there was to improve the acceleration of suburban trains, but the engine was unsuccessful. After *Lord Nelson* had appeared, five LMS 'Claughtons' were fitted with Caprotti valve gear and eight-beat cranks, and the Crown Agents utilised the same setting in some Pacifics built by Vulcan Foundry for the then North Western Railway, India (later Pakistan Railways).

The 'Nelson' boiler was based on that of the Maunsell 'N' class 2-6-0 boiler, enlarged to the limit of the composite loading gauge. The grate area of 33sq ft was the largest of any British 4-6-0, except the GWR 'King' class of 1927; to achieve it the firebox was 10ft 6in long and although it was only 18in longer than the 'King Arthur' firebox the extra distance of the front firebars from the firehole required a lot more skill in the use of the shovel. If the fireman was unable to shoot shovelfuls of coal to the far front of the box two things happened: the unfed areas of grate would burn thin and large volumes of cold air would be drawn in, and coal which fell short of its intended place would form a high ridge across the middle of the grate, to add further to the difficulty of hitting the front. The result was a rapid fall in steam pressure; meanwhile the fireman endeavoured, with the aid of a long fire-iron not easily manipulated when travelling at speed, to spread the fuel more evenly over the grate. Stirring the fire was, on any locomotive, liable to lead to the condition described as 'having 100lb of smoke and no steam'. The 'Nelson' boiler steamed freely in the hands of a fireman who had mastered it, but disappointing runs were to be expected otherwise. For this reason the 'Nelsons' were allocated during their lifetime to only four depots — Nine Elms and Stewarts Lane up to 1939, and later to Eastleigh and Bournemouth, and so far as possible kept out of the hands of enginemen who did not get regular practice with them.

The copper firebox tubeplate and the steel throat plate, at the junction of firebox and boiler barrel, were elaborate pressings with pronounced ogee curves, and the tube holes in the firebox plate came close to the radii at the root of the flanges. Evidence of stress in these portions of the boiler took the form of cracks, and leakages from the tube seatings, stresses which were aggravated by allowing an engine to stand with the blower on, dampers and firedoor open and the grate not fully covered. Attention from running shed boilersmiths accounted for rather frequent days out of steam and out of service, but the position improved after minor improvements and when the three-roller tube expander was replaced by the five-roller, less likely to distort the tube holes.

With competent firing, and careful boiler maintenance, the 'Nelson' was a first-class locomotive, capable of keeping the faster schedules with ease. The four separate sets of Walschaerts valve gear gave accurate beats; the good balancing obviated any feeling of riding on a reciprocating engine, and the regular drivers and firemen became very attached to them. But as it turned out, the 500ton trains for which they were intended were few; the regular ones were those made up of Wagons-Lits stock for the 'Night Ferry', and 'Golden Arrow' and 'Bournemouth Belle' which loaded to 12 Pullmans in the summer. A 500ton train of ordinary SR stock involved 14 coaches and a dining car, and only one platform at Waterloo could accommodate a train of that length. For the regular interval expresses 12 coaches were normally sufficient and within the capacity of the 'Arthurs'. Hence it came about that much of the mileage run by 'Nelsons' could have been performed by a less powerful type, and at less cost per mile, as a 'Nelson' consumed more coal with its larger grate, and more oil with four cylinders, and was more expensive to overhaul than the two-cylinder

'Arthur'. History does not relate the basis on which the operating department calculated the need for 16 'Nelsons', in 1928, but traffic forecasts had reason to be optimistic, and having passed through a period of acute shortage, the management was anxious to have more reserves of motive power.

With a boiler pressure of 220lb, cylinder $16\frac{1}{2}$in diam and 6ft 7in diameter coupled wheels, the tractive effort of *Lord Nelson* exceeded that of the GWR 'Castle' class. The publicity people at Paddington had made much of the claim that the 'Castle' was the most powerful express passenger engine in the country and when *Lord Nelson* ousted it from that position, the publicity from Waterloo was not slow in pointing this out, though it was hardly likely to produce a rush of passengers eager to travel to the West of England by the SR route instead of the GWR! It was much to Maunsell's distaste, since the CME staff at Swindon had been most co-operative in supplying information (about design problems of four-cylinder locomotives) while the 'Nelson' was in embryo stage. Collaboration was much to be preferred to pointless rivalry.

No 850 *Lord Nelson* left Eastleigh Works in August 1926, with the flourish of press trumpets that befitted 'the premier express locomotive in the British Isles'. In those days a new locomotive aroused interest everywhere it went. Maunsell was pleased and honoured when King George VI and Queen Elizabeth the Queen Mother (then Duke and Duchess of York) took a short footplate trip on No 850 in the course of a visit to Ashford Works on 21 October 1926 — appropriately, Trafalgar Day.

Two years elapsed before any more 'Nelsons' were built. No 850 underwent a series of coal consumption trials on booked services; no special runs were made and no dynamometer car was used. Maunsell was determined to discover, and to put right, any faults in the first engine, rather than build a number and be faced with the expense of alterations to the batch. During the initial trial period, No 850 worked all the principal trains on the Eastern and Western sections without difficulty. On the trip customarily given for the benefit of the press, a 12-coach train was taken easily at the 55mph average from Waterloo to Salisbury. On 27 July 1927, the 10.45am Victoria-Dover boat train, carrying the King of Egypt and his suite, was the heaviest single-engined train to have been worked out of Victoria, extra Pullmans for the royal party having made the load up to 480 tons full.

Thus assured that the engine was reliable, that the boiler steamed freely and that the coal, oil and water consumption figures were reasonable, Maunsell could confidently proceed with the building of a further 15 engines, Nos 851-865, in 1928. Meantime, *Lord Nelson* had bowed to *King George V* for the top place in the power rating of British locomotives. The GWR 'King' class was, however, heavier. A review of the bridges on the GWR brought to light the fact that, on the routes where a heavier and more powerul locomotive than the 'Castle' class could be employed with advantage, an axleload of $22\frac{1}{2}$ tons was permissible; also that bridges built by the GWR since 1900 had been designed for axleloads up to that figure — a far-sighted precaution.

With Chatham, Portsmouth and Plymouth dockyards and other Naval bases on its system, the Southern was prompted to use the names of famous admirals and the gunmetal plates which bore them were applied in style; no mere surnames on oblong plates but with massive, curved plates. The longer ones took two men to lift them: no weight saving there!

The 'Nelsons', as new, were hand-painted by the traditional methods, being taken to a warmed paint shop and given numerous coats of flat, undercoat and gloss, well rubbed down. The Southern, after deliberating as to which of the passenger locomotive liveries used by constituent companies looked the most presentable after two or three years of weathering, came down in favour of the green used on the LSWR and introduced by Urie in 1913. This was described as sage green, and known in the paint shop as Parsons Green — not a reference to a London suburb nor to the colour of the vicar's lawn, but to the name of the manufacturer. The colour was subject to slight changes in shade as years went on. Lining was in chrome yellow. Brass number plates were fitted to the cab sides. The appearance of the finished locomotive — without the ugly deflector plates — could appropriately be termed 'ship-shape' meaning, according to the *Universal English Dictionary*, 'arranged as a good seaman would approve of'. In 1927 the 'Royal Scot' 4-6-0s of the LMS appeared, with a distinct likeness to the 'Lord Nelson', the result of friendly collaboration between Derby and Waterloo. The three-cylinder 'Royal Scot' proved to be the better of the two. The boiler was almost a copy of the 'Nelson' boiler but had a slope and depth of grate that was easier to fire and the chimney and blastpipe dimensions turned out to be correct for good draughting and steaming, more by fortunate choice than from any testing data available.

Their shorter engine wheelbase gave the 'Scots' a steadiness of ride inferior to the 'Nelsons'. In December 1929 the leading coupled wheels of a 'Nelson' working an up boat train became derailed at Kent House, and after damaging a short length of track the wheels rerailed themselves and the train arrived at Victoria with the driver blissfully unaware of what had happened. That kind of off-and-on again derailment was not unknown with freight wagons but very rare with locomotives. By an odd coincidence, a 'Royal Scot' did the same thing at Weaver Junction a few weeks afterwards. The occurrences naturally raised the question as to the extent to which the bogie and the leading coupled wheels 'steered' a locomotive on curves, and led to a review of the design of bogie side-control springs.

The 'Scots' also suffered from drifting steam, and Derby tried at least four versions of mini-deflectors, just as the Southern had done before adopting the large deflectors already applied to 'Arthurs' and 'Nelsons'. Incidentally, Doncaster also spent much time with devices of its own before deciding that, after all, Maunsell had been right.

Above: No E850 *Lord Nelson*, **on shed at Nine Elms in 1927.** *Lens of Sutton*

Left: *Lord Nelson* **takes the 11.00am boat train from Victoria through Herne Hill, c1928.** *F. R. Hebron/Rail Archive Stephenson*

Above: No E855 *Robert Blake* has just passed Chelsfield with the up 'Golden Arrow' in 1929. *F. R. Hebron/Rail Archive Stephenson*

Below: No 857 *Lord Howe* on shed at Stewarts Lane, November 1931. *O. J. Morris/Lens of Sutton*

Right: No E853 *Sir Richard Grenville* (with six-wheeled tender) heads the second part of the 2.00pm Victoria-Dover Marine boat train through Orpington, in the winter of 1928/29. Note the staff accommodation in the coach body hut! *F. R. Hebron/Rail Archive Stephenson*

Above: No 865 *Sir John Hawkins* stands at Waterloo in the early 1930s. *Lens of Sutton*

Left: No E853 *Sir Richard Grenville* (with Urie eight-wheeled tender) nears Chelsfield with the 4.00pm Victoria-Dover boat train, 1930. *F. R. Hebron/Rail Archive Stephenson*

Below left: No E856 *Lord St. Vincent* near Dunton Green with the up 'Golden Arrow', 1930.
F. R. Hebron/Rail Archive Stephenson

Above right: Alias No E861, *Lord Nelson* on display in Liverpool for the Liverpool & Manchester Railway centenary exhibition, September 1930. Recast nameplates were fitted.
T. G. Hepburn/Rail Archive Stephenson

Right: No E858 *Lord Duncan* with the down 'Golden Arrow' near Chelsfield, July 1931. Urie tender.
H. Gordon Tidey/Real Photographs Co

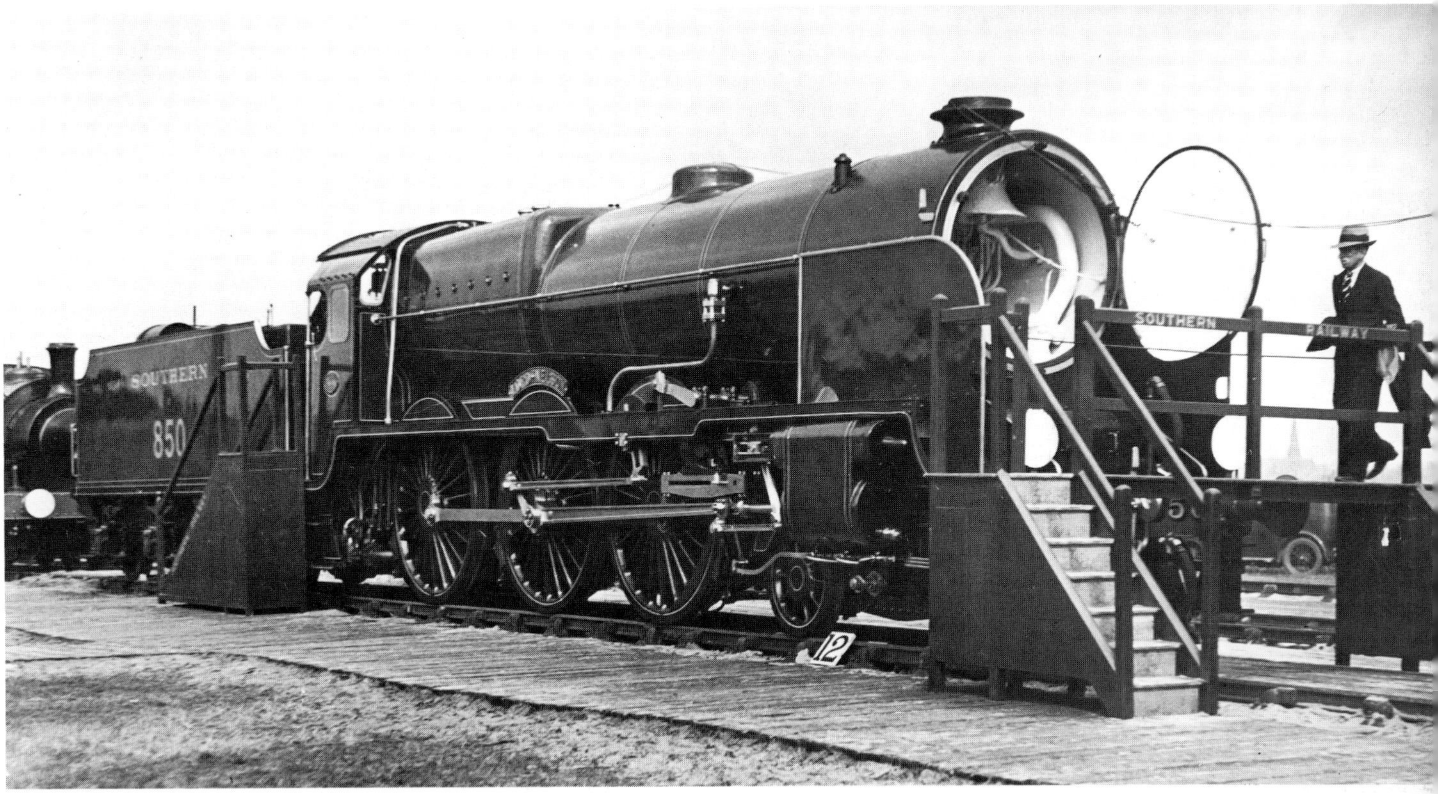
SOUTHERN
850
SOUTHERN
RAILWAY
12

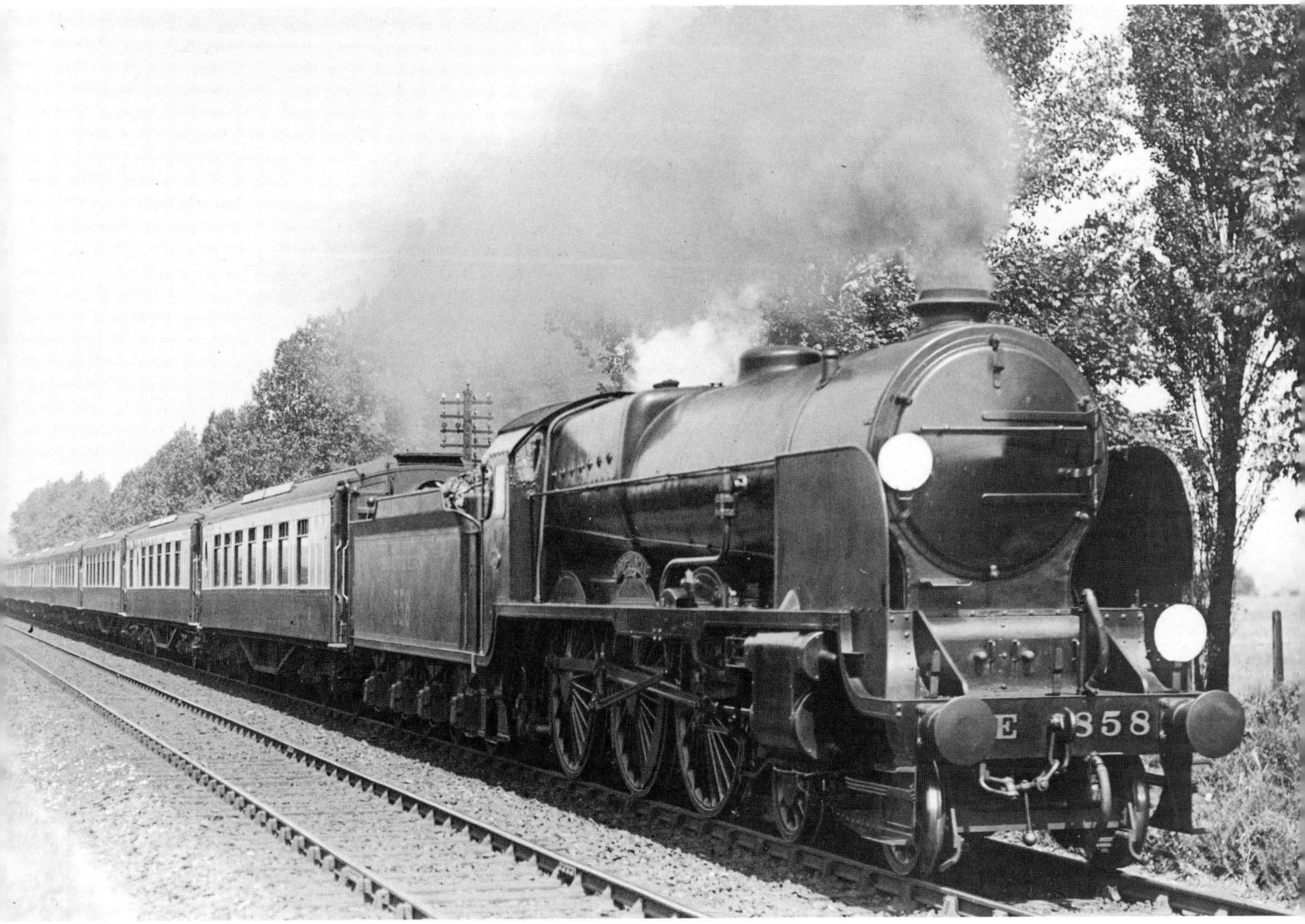
E 858

7
'Arthurs' and 'Nelsons' from the Footplate

The ban on footplate riding, imposed for safety reasons, was lifted for members of the railway press and for persons in associated supply industries such as steel, brake and signalling equipment and so on. A few put their experiences into print. Cecil J. Allen made copious notes and his ride on No 850 *Lord Nelson* is quoted in Chapter 12. O. S. Nock has written of his trips on 'Schools' and 'Nelsons' in *Southern Steam* (David & Charles, 1972). Little else, unfortunately, has been written about 'Arthurs', 'Nelsons' and 'Schools', but we have an authority in H. Holcroft and his *Locomotive Adventure* Volume II.

Holcroft was one of three designer-draughtsmen who occupied a room next to Maunsell's private office. Being the youngest and fittest, he was sent out to ride on the footplate and to give Maunsell — who was a stickler for the truth — unbiased feedback, He kept a diary of his working days which gave him material for writing in his retirement. His footplate work was mainly concerned with proving the competence of the new engines.

Holcroft was immediately involved with the SR 'Arthurs' on the appearance of No 453 *King Arthur* early in 1925. He records that it was tried on the Eastern section between Charing Cross to Dover and back in April 1925, and then he was concerned in a series of trials to compare the results of using South Wales or Yorkshire coal, and incidentally to observe the new locomotive. Holcroft concluded that more Yorkshire coal was burnt by No 453 than Welsh, but less was used in lighting up. The steaming of No 453 was noted as 'very good throughout the trials, irrespective of the coal used . . . less damper opening was needed with the Yorkshire coal to maintain full pressure in the boiler, but more supplementary air admitted at the firedoor was needed to consume the gases (from combustion)'. Typical engine working between Waterloo and Salisbury and return was characterised by Holcroft as full regulator and cut-offs of 18-23% on the down journey and 18% cut-off, accompanied by most running on the small valve, returning to London. The coal consumption during the 15 trials in April and June 1925 emerges as 34-41lb/train mile down to Salisbury and 29-47lb/train mile up to Waterloo; the absence of steam heating in the later trials obviously affected results. In November 1925, Holcroft notes that 'Arthur' No 451, then E451, fitted with indicator shelter and gear, following a series of trials, was worked 'a bit heavy' and reached Salisbury from Waterloo in 76min with 281 tons tare against a 92min schedule.

One interesting exercise involved a comparison of the different approaches to locomotive handling by enginemen. Holcroft found that the shorter cut-offs used by some crews made the 'Arthurs' freer steamers, the more expansive

working being a feature of Western section drivers. Accordingly, Maunsell decided to carry out coal trials with two 'Arthurs' in the hands of Nine Elms and Battersea drivers, each working on both sections. The locomotives selected were Nos 778 (Nine Elms) and 768 (Battersea). Holcroft rode on No 778 and a Test Engineer on the Eastern section engine. Yorkshire coal was used for both locomotives and each made six out and back trials on each section. Working under test conditions was carefully controlled: the boilers were washed out before each set of trials and the coal carefully weighed. Each engine performed the same duties, with the same turns of duty and the same enginemen. As a result of the 24 trial runs it was clear that the Nine Elms driver, H. W. Gray, was more economical to some degree. The average daily results showed that the total amount of coal consumed by No 778 was appreciably less than used with the driving techniques adopted for No 768. On the Eastern section trials, No 778 used 7,588lb coal (daily average) in running; No 768, 9,237lb, and on the Western section, No 778 8,084lb and No 768, 8,905lb. Holcroft also noted that the Battersea men tended to run with boiler pressure just below blowing off point; with Ramsbottom safety valves this may have been acceptable, but as applied to the 'Arthurs' the result was that the action of the pop safety valve wasted steam. Whether the results of the trials were entirely conclusive must be open to question, Holcroft noting that 'weather conditions also favoured No 778'.

To conclude, Holcroft was to say in Vol 2 of *Locomotive Adventure* that the 'Arthurs': 'did the job they were designed for in a completely competent manner; they were economical in running, rode well and were easy to maintain . . . one could always anticipate how they would measure up to a job'. Perhaps significantly, he did not ride on the footplate of an 'Arthur' later than November 1926; there was nothing more to be said.

As to the 'Nelsons', Holcroft rode on No 850 in the autumn of 1926. His first trip with No 850 on a boat train to Dover, on 22 October, was inconclusive, three permanent way checks caused delays that were not recovered.

However, the choice of driver may have had some effect as he was full of praise for a second run when No 850 was handled by Driver Stuckey, a name which occurs in C. J. Allen's footplate ride with this engine. By December 1926, No 850 had returned to the Western section working between Waterloo, Salisbury and Exeter. Holcroft's experience was that No 850 steamed well and was worked on full regulator and with frequent changes of cut-off. This was on trains of 330 tons tare at the heaviest. He was also present on indicating trials with No 850 which were carried out between

Waterloo and Exeter and return with a 16-coach, 521ton train. The maximum horsepower recorded on the trials was 1,467 at 55mph and at 24% cut-off.

It was 1936 before Holcroft had another close look at the working of a 'Nelson'. This time, his remit was to investigate why No 853 on the Eastern section was not 'up to the mark'. On 400ton boat trains from Victoria-Folkestone Junction and back, the locomotive was worked hard, particularly on the outward journey, with late cut-offs, and the water level was not maintained despite the use of two injectors at times. The train was checked in each direction which partly explained the failure to keep time. However, Holcroft considered that the locomotive was not superheating properly. In August 1937, he travelled on No 862 fitted with the Kylchap blastpipe and double chimney. He was impressed, 'it was very lively and free running . . . and time lost . . . was quickly recovered'. Notably, full boiler pressure and water level were achieved without trouble.

Unfortunately, Holcroft had few chances to ride on 'Schools' class engines and has little of interest to say regard-ing their performance. However, he noted that the advantage of more adhesive weight on a 4-6-0 is offset by greater internal friction as compared with a 4-4-0; if the 'Arthurs' and 'Schools' were found to be capable of developing the same indicated horsepower — as had been the results of indicator tests between London Bridge and Eastbourne with 'Schools' No 909 in 1931 — it was not surprising, noted Holcroft, that the 'Schools' could produce more power at the tender draw hook.

Difficulties in starting trains from No 7 up platform at London Bridge by 'Schools' during 1931 resulted in an investigation. The conclusion reached by the Locomotive Testing Section was that the type of piston valve used with a solid head was at fault. This had been derived from the German Schmidt pattern with wide rings fitted to the Borsig-built 'L' 4-4-0s supplied to the SECR in 1914. However, the casting for the Schmidt derived 10in valve produced by Eastleigh foundry was not as resistant to wear as the Ashford product. After discussion with German manufacturers it was clear that a valve with a small amount of clearance and narrow

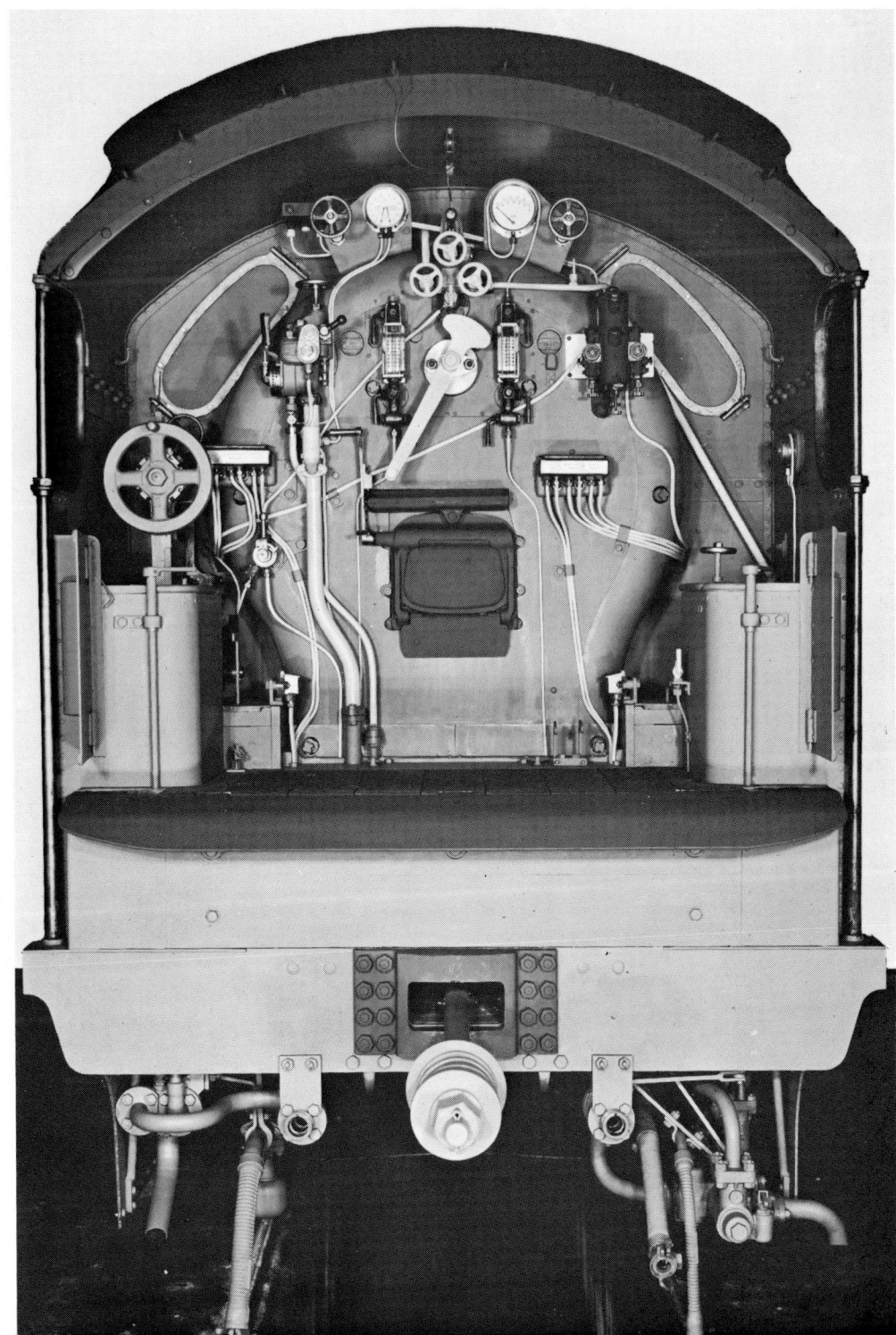

Right: The footplate of an 'Arthur'. *BR*

rings to prevent steam leakage had been found to be the solution in that country. Accordingly, these were adopted as standard for both 'Nelsons' and 'Schools' after 1935 and the lead altered; this, Holcroft believed, contributed to the 'blight which seemed to descend on the "Nelsons" after their earlier brilliance. The alteration did not matter so much to the "Schools" . . . customarily worked at 25% cut-off and part regulator opening, but the Western section working of the "Nelsons" with full regulator and short cut-offs was another matter altogether'.

Above: 'King Arthur' No E768 *Sir Balin* near Pluckley with a down boat train in 1929. It is paired with a six-wheeled tender. No 768 was used in the comparative engine working trials. *Lens of Sutton*

Below right: No E778 *Sir Pelleas*, the Nine Elms engine in the trials, on an up Bournemouth express near Pirbright Jn, c1929. *Lens of Sutton*

Right: 'Arthur' No E451 *Sir Lamorak* fitted with indicator shelter for the 1925 trials. *LPC/Ian Allan Library*

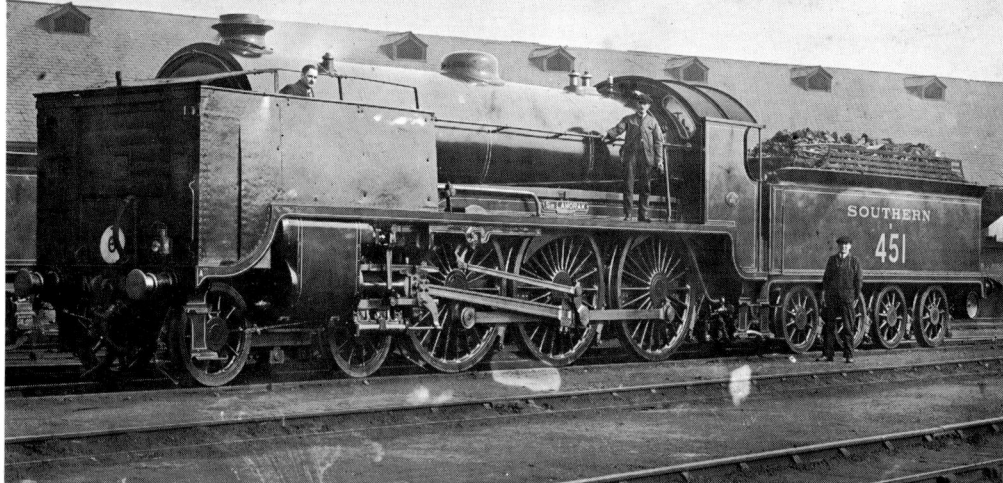

In early 1927, an indicator shelter was fitted to *Lord Nelson* for test running:

Left: At Nine Elms.
LPC/Ian Allan Library

Below: At Salisbury on 2 April 1927, ready to return to Waterloo with the 10.30am from Exeter.
Rev A. C. Cawston

Left: The footplate of a 'Nelson'. *BR*

Left: Firing a 'Nelson', with careful aim and a watchful eye for thin places in the firebed. *S. C. Townroe*

Below: 'Schools' No E909 *St Paul's* on shed at New Cross, fitted with indicator shelter for the London Bridge-Eastbourne test runs during 1931. *O. J. Morris/Lens of Sutton*

Bottom: 'Schools' No 916 *Whitgift* has just left Bromley South with a Victoria-Ramsgate train in the mid-1930s. *Lens of Sutton*

8
Modifications to the 'Nelsons'

Various engines of the 'Nelson' class were subjected to modification by Maunsell, not because improvements were by any means essential but because Maunsell was not wedded to theories and preferred to confirm them, or otherwise, by practical applications. It had long been a theory that smaller diameter driving wheels were necessary on heavily graded sections, as compared with easier routes, and in Drummond's time on the LSWR locomotives intended for working west of Salisbury were given 6ft diameter driving wheels instead of those of 6ft 7in in general use elsewhere on that system. In practice, the larger diameter wheel displayed no disadvantage, and, on a switchback route, was an advantage on the downhill and level stretches.

In Maunsell's tentative design for a 2-6-2 passenger locomotive a 6ft 3in wheel was proposed, and to clinch the argument about driving wheel sizes, 'Nelson' No 859 *Lord Hood* was fitted with 6ft 3in driving wheels. The locomotive was tried both on the Eastern and the Western sections, including some running between Salisbury and Exeter, in direct comparison with sister engines, but not the slightest difference could be detected in performance.

Another theory put to the test was in regard to the length of boiler tubes. The length of the boiler barrel of the standard 'Nelson' boiler had been decided by the length of tubes, 13ft 9in, stocked at Eastleigh for 'N15' and 'H15' boilers, although a longer barrel could have been used and the additional weight would have been borne by the bogie, and would not have increased the coupled axle weights. In theory, longer tubes would extract more heat from the flue-gases, and help to raise the temperature of the feed water which fed through clack boxes on the front ring of the boiler barrel. Someone suggested to Maunsell that adherence to a common tube length had been a case of penny-wise pound-foolish on the part of Eastleigh drawing office, so when the 11th engine, No 860 *Lord Hawke*, was built, the boiler barrel was increased by 10in. Again, the answer was a lemon; No 860 did not steam better than the others.

In theory, compound expansion increased the efficiency of the steam engine. Continental locomotive engineers had made a practical success of it whereas British engineers had not, with the exception of the Smith-Deeley Midland Compound 4-4-0. The principle still intrigued designers in spite of the limitations upon cylinder diameters imposed by the British loading gauge. A compound had been proposed for the first LMS express locomotive, and in 1931 Maunsell seriously considered converting a 'Nelson', with two 15½in diameter high-pressure cylinders and two 22in low-pressure cylinders. It was to be fitted with a proprietary make of poppet valve gear, of which the LNER was making extensive trial. Both projects were dropped, probably because Maunsell realised

that his department did not have the resources to carry out major development work.

In 1936, No 857 *Lord Howe* came out of Eastleigh Works with a new boiler which made the engine look longer and more massive than before. Within the round-topped boiler the front of the firebox projected forward into the barrel to form a combustion chamber, a feature which, according to evidence from other railways, made for more complete combustion of the gaseous components of the coal. Maunsell's proposed Pacific was being planned, with the intention that it would carry such a boiler.

No 857 was tried out on Victoria-Dover boat trains; it steamed more freely than the standard boiler, except when the engine had to be driven hard; clearly, the draughting was wrong and further experiments were needed with the blast-pipe and chimney. Dynamometer car recordings of the vacuum in the smokebox, and at grate level, and analyses of the flue gases would have proved invaluable, if these could have been procured. For some reason, no further interest was taken in No 857, with Maunsell's retirement in the following year.

Experiments with a four-beat crank axle on No 865 *Sir John Hawkins* have already been mentioned. The first really noticeable improvement in performance was observed in 1934 when No 862 *Lord Collingwood* was fitted with a Kylchap blastpipe and chimney, the joint invention of Kylala, the Finnish locomotive engineer, and M André Chapelon of the SNCF. The device improved the draught significantly, at the same time reducing the back-pressure on the exhaust steam. Despite favourable reports from the Locomotive Running Department, this improvement was not followed up immediately.

In 1938, some of the 'Nelsons' were fitted with recording speedometers, and examination of the paper rolls on which speeds were marked revealed quite a crop of 100mph bursts. By that time, Mr O. V. S. Bulleid had become CME and during his first 18 months on the Southern he made numerous footplate trips. He was particularly interested in the 'Nelsons' and made a series of memorable footplate appearances on the 'Golden Arrow'. He was convinced that the schedule between Victoria and Dover could be cut by higher speeds on rising gradients. On his instructions, No 862 *Lord Collingwood* was driven in full gear up Grosvenor Road bank out of Victoria, and then at 40-50% cut-off for the rest of the journey. Along the straight between Tonbridge and Ashford, with wide open regulator and both injectors working to keep the boiler water level in sight in the water-gauges, speeds were between 90 and 95mph. By the time he reached Dover the fireman, appropriately named Bull, was pretty well exhausted, but Bulleid was delighted. As Gresley's

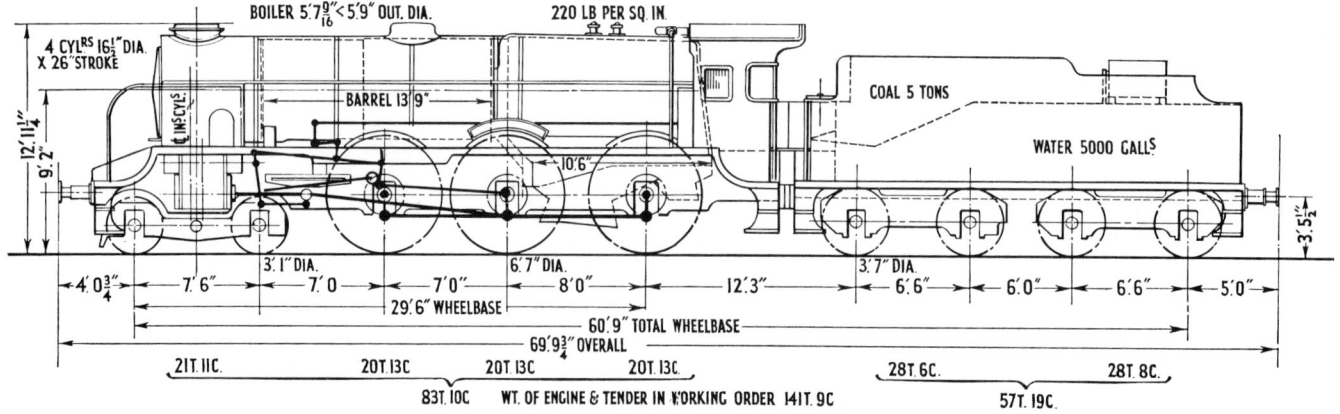

BOILER 5'7⁹⁄₁₆" < 5'9" OUT. DIA.   220 LB PER SQ. IN.
4 CYL͏RS 16½" DIA. X 26" STROKE
BARREL 13'9"
COAL 5 TONS
WATER 5000 GAL͏LS
12'11¼"   9'2"
IN͏ CYL͏S
10'6"
3'5½"
3'1" DIA.   6'7" DIA.   3'7" DIA.
4'0¾"   7'6"   7'0   7'0"   8'0"   12'3"   6'6"   6'0"   6'6"   5'0"
29'6" WHEELBASE
60'9" TOTAL WHEELBASE
69'9¾" OVERALL
21T.11C.   20T.13C.   20T.13C.   20T.13C.   28T.6C.   28T.8C.
83T.10C.   WT. OF ENGINE & TENDER IN WORKING ORDER 141T.9C.   57T.19C.

assistant on the LNER he had been on some hair-raising runs with the streamlined 'A4' Pacifics, and had accompanied the LNER 2-8-2 *Cock o' the North* to the SNCF testing plant at Vitry. His experience of improved front-end design led him to have the 'Nelsons' fitted with Lemaître five-jet multiple blast-pipes during 1938/39. Although a particularly clumsy chimney accompanied the modification, it clearly improved their performance. At the same time, he ordered Eastleigh to design new cylinders with 10in diam piston valves instead of 8in diam, and with improved steam and exhaust passages. Seven locomotives were so fitted in 1939/40, Nos 852/5/6/7/60/2/5. With the exception of No 863, which retained its original cylinders, the remainder were re-cylindered when renewal was necessary during overhaul. To cap this final modification, No 863 was none the worse without it!

A propos the straight, almost level 26 miles between Tonbridge and Ashford, a regular 'Nelson' driver who had been a young fireman in SECR days recalled the *joie de vivre* engendered by the effortless speeds which even the old Stirling engines could maintain there. The little wayside stations along the Weald were illuminated at night by oil lamps fixed to the platform fence, at about footplate height. The passage of a fast train was liable to blow them out, and the extinguishing draught could be increased by the fireman's leaning out with a firing shovel to act as a fan. After passing a station in this fashion, he and his driver would look back, to count the nightly 'score'. At other times, coal would be piled on the fire to create as much smoke as possible; the boat train would be enveloped in a thick, black cloud, whereupon the driver would chuckle: 'They'll think they're on the boat already, make it thicker and they'll think it's a bloomin' liner'.

The 'Nelsons' started life with the Urie pattern of double-bogie tender. This was Urie's improved version of the eight-wheel Drummond 'water-cart'; it did not leak nor melt its bearings. It was not, however, self-trimming although the fireman could easily climb back into the coal space as the footplate end was virtually open apart from a low partition fitted with a guillotine pattern of coal door. Two simple toolboxes were provided in each front corner. The final version designed just prior to World War 2 had a sharper slope to the bunker floor to induce the coal to tumble forwards, and sides were raised to increase the depth of the bunker. The capacity of five tons of coal and 5,000 gallons of water remained the same as earlier tenders. At the footplate end, vertical cupboards, including a 'clean one for clothes', provided a draught and dust screen. In Maunsell's time, there was some swapping of various patterns of bogie tenders, partly in connection with the Maunsell 'S15' 4-6-0 freight

locomotives, and the provision of tenders for the 'N15x' rebuilt LBSCR Baltics.

It must be mentioned that the tender was not only a vehicle for coal and water: it provided considerable braking power and carried vacuum reservoirs. When working loose-coupled freight trains down long, falling gradients, a big bogie tender played an important part in controlling the train. The handbrake could be screwed on and left on for many miles without overheating the wheels and brake blocks, with the engine brake in reserve to stop the train. A tender had other uses. The stocks of stores at the locomotive depots were supplied by regular stores vans, but items required more quickly were transported on tenders. Large objects such as connecting and coupling rods were loaded on the flat space over the back part of the tender, and small parcels were carried in the toolboxes. By this method, stocks of parts could be kept at the largest depots, and a part wanted by a smaller depot could be put on the next engine going in that direction. There were other consignments of a less official and more perishable nature: Devonshire cream, fresh fish from Folkestone or Padstow, turkeys at Christmas. They might well bear the official printed label marked OCS — On Company's Service — which could also be translated as 'Old Cadger's Society'. In the days when Nine Elms men working the overnight goods to Weymouth lodged at Dorchester, so the story went, a live pig bought in Dorchester market found its way back to London on the back of a tender, and survived!

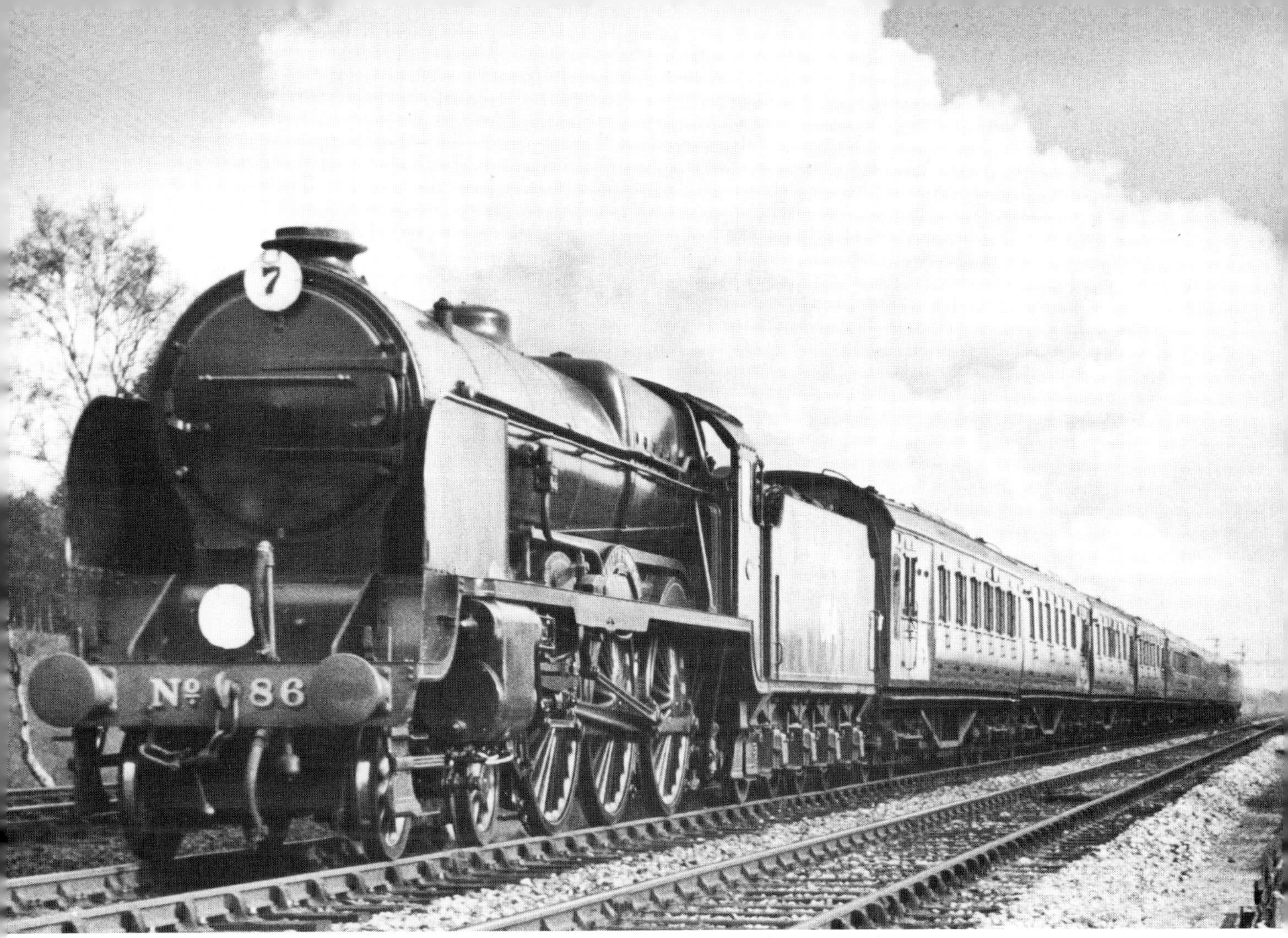
7
No 86

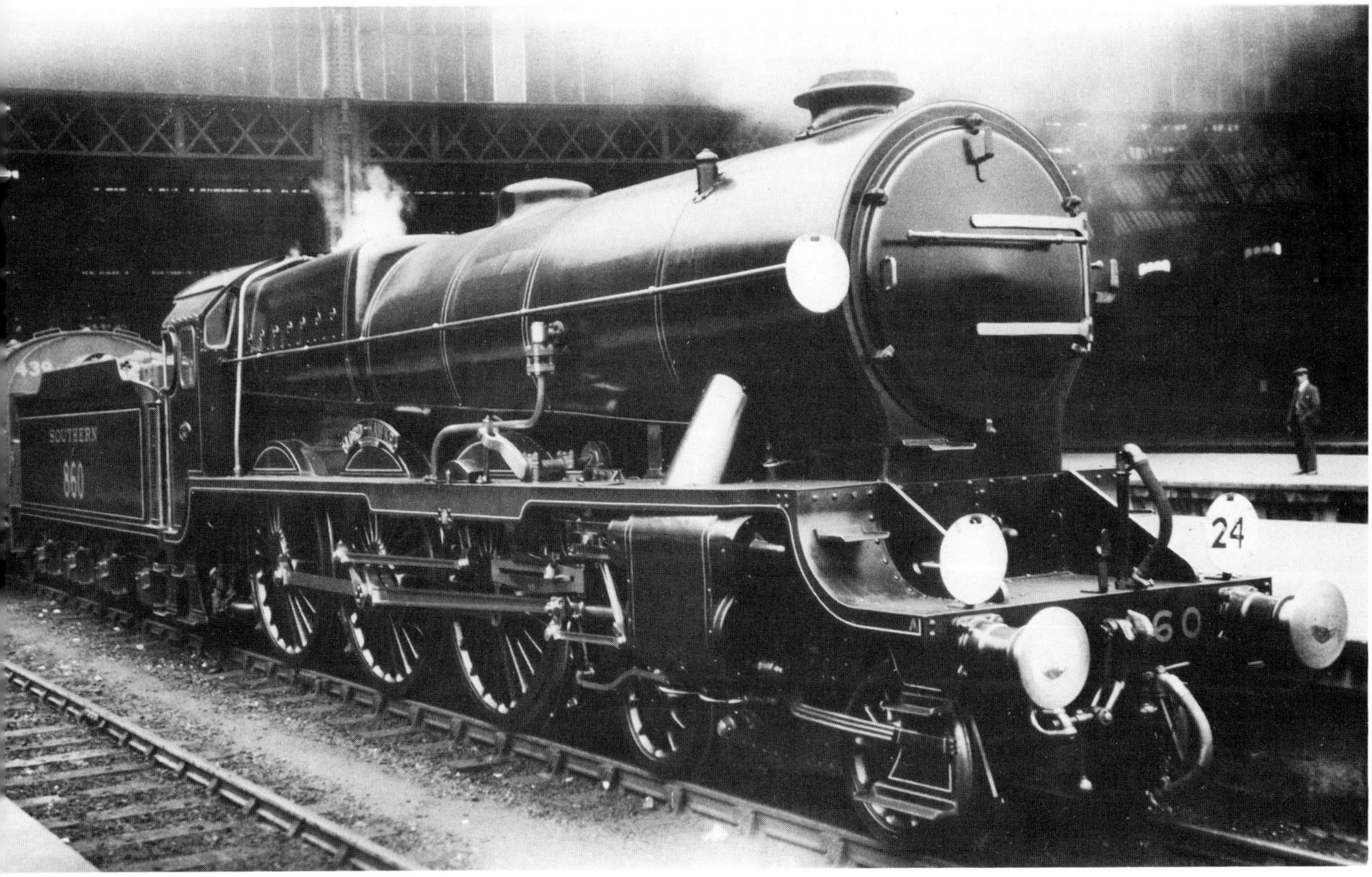
SOUTHERN
860
24

Left: No 859 *Lord Hood*, on an up boat train for Victoria, passes Shorncliffe in the mid-1930s. *Rev A. C. Cawston*

Top: No 865 *Sir John Hawkins,* c1936. *T. G. Hepburn/Rail Archive Stephenson*

Above: No 857 *Lord Howe*, at Eastleigh in June 1937, after receiving the large boiler. *O. J. Morris/Lens of Sutton*

Below: In 1938, *Lord Howe* heads a Victoria-Ramsgate train between Shortlands and Bromley South. *Lens of Sutton*

Above: No 862 *Lord Collingwood*, as fitted with Kylchap blastpipe and chimney in 1934.
LPC/Ian Allan Library

Right: No 865 *Sir John Hawkins* with the down 'Bournemouth Belle' in 1938. Fitted with Kylchap blastpipe and chimney.
Rev A. C. Cawston

Below right: No 855 *Lord Blake*, with Lemaître exhaust and early pattern wide chimney, on the straight section east of Tonbridge, near Paddock Wood, 1939.
Rev A. C. Cawston

Above left: With regulator closed, No 861 *Lord Anson* takes an up boat train through Tonbridge in 1939. Fitted with Lemaître exhaust, and paired with self-trimming tender.
Rev A. C. Cawston

Left: The improved chimney is carried by No 852 *Sir Walter Raleigh*, at the head of the down 'Bournemouth Belle', near Hersham, 1939. Self-trimming tender and malachite green livery.
C. R. L. Coles

Below: Southampton, 1939. No 851 *Sir Francis Drake* with the royal special, on the return of King George VI and Queen Elizabeth from their tour of North America.
S. C. Townroe

9
The Design of the 'Schools'

When the civil engineers had completed, in 1852, a branch of the South Eastern Railway from Tunbridge Wells to St Leonards they could not have imagined what problems they had created for future generations, by their having chosen to construct it to a loading gauge even more restricted than that of the owning company's other lines. In due course, thousands of freight vehicles were to carry an inscription that they were not allowed between Tonbridge and Hastings and the owning company was building passenger stock specially for the line, six inches narrower in width than the normal coaches. Railway companies all over the country carried, in their appendices to the working timetables, details of the limited dimensions of vehicles which could be allowed, with the added warning 'No vehicle with Guards' Side Observatories can be accepted for this branch'.

The small double track tunnel at Mountfield near Battle was the major obstacle, and it became even smaller when the tunnel lining had to be reinforced by an extra layer of brickwork. The clearance between trains passing in the tunnel is so close that, on one occasion when an error occurred in the track alignment, at one point, the offside door handles were sheared off the two trains. A century after the opening of the line, various solutions were under serious consideration: enlargement of the tunnel, its even more costly conversion to a deep cutting or the installation of a specially controlled, single reversible line. The problem remains to this day, in association with possible electrification.

The Southern Railway succeeded in making the former SECR main lines suitable to carry 'Arthurs' and 'Nelsons', but they were far too large for the Hastings route, over which traffic had reached a state when better motive power was needed. A locomotive was required which would be powerful enough to haul the Charing Cross-Hastings trains to the same timings between London and Tonbridge as the Kent Coast trains hauled by the 'Arthurs', and of similar tractive effort.

When the proposition came under consideration in 1928 it was evident, in the first place, that to conform to the maximum permitted width, 8ft 6½in, over the Hastings line, an engine with two outside cylinders large enough to provide sufficient power was out of the question: the width over the cylinders would be too great. A two-cylinder engine, whether with outside or inside cylinders, would not be acceptable to the civil engineer with an axleload of 21 tons; if adopted, it would have to have a lesser axleload on the coupled wheels to allow for the two-cylinder hammer-blow, on which the Bridge Stress Committee had commented adversely. There would also be less weight for adhesion, and there was not much level track between Charing Cross and Hastings. Clearly, a multi-cylinder engine was the answer, and three cylinders of 16½in

diameter — the same as the 'Nelsons' — could be fitted within a width of 8ft 5⁷⁄₁₆in.

For adhesion a six-coupled design, and nothing less, would have been the obvious choice, had it not been for the Hastings line. A shorter frame would have less throw-over on curves and thus more easily kept within the restriction on width, and a four-coupled engine would be more suitable for the sharp curves between Tonbridge and Hastings. Added to which, the four-coupled engine was cheaper to build and maintain; its internal resistance was lower (more free-running than a six-coupled) and less power was spent in propelling itself owing to its lighter weight. These advantages were to be amply demonstrated later, when the 'Schools' class proved such a success everywhere. Finally, a four-coupled engine suited the existing turntables — a lesser consideration, perhaps: nevertheless, a new turntable cost as much as a new locomotive. A 'Schools' could turn on a 50ft diameter table; 'Arthurs' and 'Nelsons' required 60ft and 65ft tables respectively.

Taking everything into account, the decision was made in favour of a four-coupled, three-cylinder engine with 6ft 7in wheels and a boiler pressure of 220lb. The tractive effort at 85% boiler pressure worked out at 25,130lb: almost the same as an 'Arthur' but weighing the equivalent of one coach less. With 21 tons on each coupled axle — the power to weight ratio was 598lb/ton. This was a high ratio and close to the limit desirable to avoid excessive proneness to wheelslip. The 'Schools' were to need careful handling to avoid it.

In order to simplify construction and the provision of spares, much of the new design was identical with the 'Nelsons': the wheel sizes, the outside cylinders, the motion parts and many other details. Even the front cab windows were the same, turned upside-down to suit! When it came to the boiler, the 'Nelson' pattern could not be followed. To conform to the Hastings gauge the cab had to be reduced in width over the cornices and therefore the upper cab sides had to be canted inwards. A cab of this shape dictated a round-topped firebox rather than a Belpaire type, which would also have made the boiler too heavy. The boiler was virtually an 'Arthur' boiler reduced in length. The grate area was ample with 28.3sq ft; the 8ft 3½in length of grate was easy to fire. The short boiler barrel — 2ft less than the 'Arthur' — affected the length of the superheater tubes with the result that the superheat temperature was lower than the optimum by current standards. In all other respects, the boiler pressure, the valve gear, the steam pipe and port areas and the balancing, the 'Schools' design could hardly have been better if it had been conceived 25 years later. The multiple-jet blast-pipe was the one later development and was fitted to 21 engines.

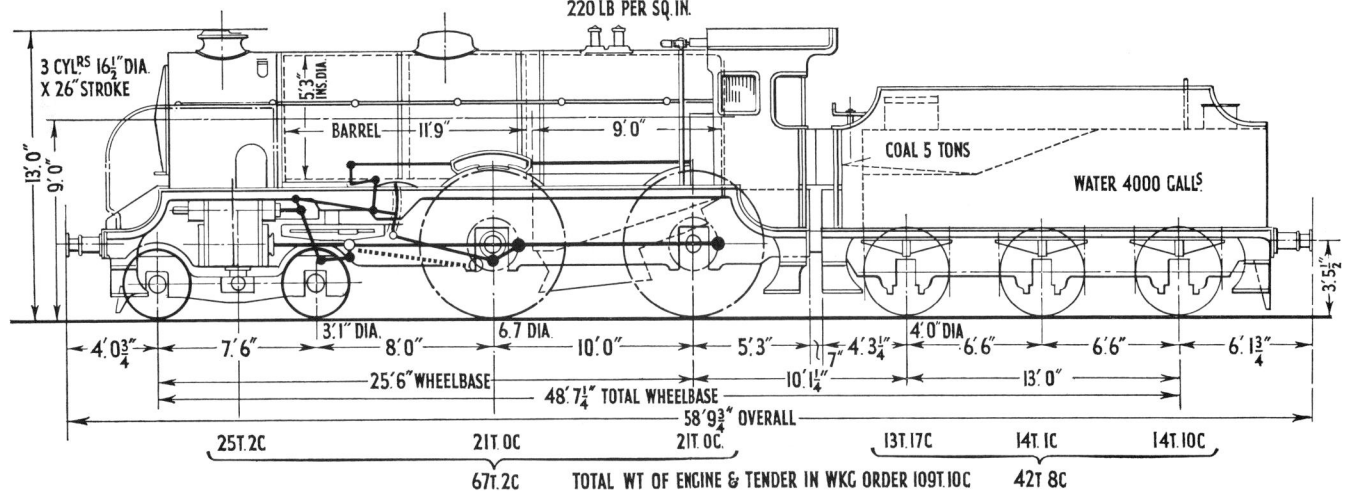

3 CYL^{RS} 16½" DIA. X 26" STROKE

220 LB PER SQ. IN.

13' 0"
9' 0"

5' 3" INS. DIA.

BARREL — 11' 9"

9' 0"

COAL 5 TONS

WATER 4000 GALL^S

3' 5½"

4' 0¾" — 7' 6" — 3' 1" DIA. — 8' 0" — 6' 7 DIA — 10' 0" — 5' 3" — 4' 3½" — 4' 0" DIA — 6' 6" — 6' 6" — 6' 1¾"

25' 6" WHEELBASE

48' 7½" TOTAL WHEELBASE

10' 1¼"

13' 0"

58' 9¾" OVERALL

25T. 2C   21T. 0C   21T. 0C.   13T. 17C   14T. 1C   14T. 10C

67T. 2C   TOTAL WT OF ENGINE & TENDER IN WKG ORDER 109T. 10C   42T 8C

Above: A 'Schools', in original condition, but as fitted with smoke deflectors.

The tenders carried 4,000 gallons of water and five tons of coal on six wheels. From No 910 onwards they were made more comfortable by arranging a bank of tool and clothes lockers across the footplate, which also gave better weather protection. Even better in this respect was a tender, first fitted to No 932, on which the sides were raised at the footplate end to match the cab sides. Similar improvement was made to all the 'Nelson' tenders.

For the new 4-4-0s, officially Class 'V' in the SR alphabetical classification, names were sought which would be a change from the sort of subjects already covered by named locomotives in the country, and preferably having some connection with the Southern. Considerable business was done in school traffic; there were numerous public and private boarding schools in the South, which at the beginning and end of term chartered special trains, or coaches attached to ordinary trains, to and from London. Consequently, the names for the engines were of well-known public schools, but rather than confine the list to those on the Southern system, which could have involved some invidious preferences, those chosen were a representative selection of schools both south and north of the Thames. Wherever possible, a new engine was taken to the station near the school for exhibition to the boys. A press photograph of one such occasion showed boys clambering all over the engine; a couple of them polishing the nameplate provided the caption 'Keep the name bright'.

The first engine left Eastleigh in March 1930. A batch of 10 had been ordered to cover the London-Hastings service but as it happened the Civil Engineer required more time to bring the Tonbridge-St Leonards section up to standard and permission for the 'Schools' to use the line was upheld until the following year, 1931. This proved fortunate as the 10 engines were completed and put into service during 1930, and had the opportunity of showing their paces on the Eastern and Western section main lines, with some startling results. No 909 *St Paul's*, for example, on an ordinary run from Salisbury to Waterloo, took 12 coaches weighing 420 tons full, over the 83.8 miles in a net time of 93¾ minutes. The climb to Grateley, 11 miles, took 20min 20sec; Worting Junction, 33½ miles, was passed in 44min 52sec, and Surbiton, 71.8 miles, in 78min 45sec. The average speed from Worting Junction to Surbiton was over 68mph. From a 4-4-0, this was great stuff, and soon every engineman was keen to try out a 'Schools'.

On the Dover and Ramsgate route, they began to work the

80min Folkestone Flyers, in place of the 'L1' 4-4-0s. Along the straight between Tonbridge and Ashford, the 'Schools' could cover the 26.4 miles in under 19 minutes with nine coaches.

On that fast length there were pronounced dips in the track beneath the overbridges. As has already been mentioned, when the South Eastern Railway was built, the depth between the formation and the sleepers allowed for a layer of ballast which was in time to prove quite inadequate for the traffic. Unless the formation was to be excavated at great cost, increasing the depth of ballast involved a rise in track level except where fixed structures such as overbridges limited the permissible alteration in rail height, hence the dips. At these places, the 'Schools' were prone to bounce quite alarmingly owing to their short wheelbase and a centre of gravity near the middle (the driving) axle. The bogie axleboxes were actually striking both top and bottom stops when bouncing occurred, the movement being described as not unlike the contemporary Austin Seven crossing a hump-backed bridge! The trouble was overcome by fitting stiffer coil springs to the bogie axleboxes.

It was because of the restricted clearances on the Eastern section that an enamel notice-plate was fitted in the cabs of all Maunsell engines, warning drivers to take great care when leaning out. The coaches, too, had notices over the windows to the same effect, with wording in French *Ne pas se pencher au dehors*.

Before long, the new engines were being described as 'the finest the Southern had ever built', a phrase which recurs in the recollections of retired staff. They were right, from the word go, and 10 of them were put into service without any need to return to workshops for modifications. Later, during overhauls, the gravity sanding was replaced by steam sanding, partly to improve the adhesion and partly because at slow speed the gravity system supplied so much sand that it interfered with vital track circuits, particularly at Waterloo, Charing Cross and Victoria where drivers of departing trains were inclined to be liberal with it.

The appeal of a 'Schools' did not rest entirely on its ability to rival larger locomotives in performance. The number of successful 4-4-0s in existence testified to the popularity of the type in British practice: indeed, the 4-4-0 was regarded by many as being the optimum size of locomotive from a handling and servicing point of view. To take an analogy with the automobile world, for reasons not easy to define there are some in which a driver instinctively feels at one with his machine, and so it was with steam locomotives. A 'Schools' was most pleasing to handle. The driver was well placed in relation to the front and rear buffers to judge the engine's position to a nicety when coupling up, and his view ahead did not suffer from the length of the boiler. With a quick operating regulator a cautious and slip-free start could be made, waiting until the train was well on the move before giving the engine full steam. From that point the engine seemed to canter away with long strides, softly chittery-chattering at the chimney top and at the open firehole door. The originals with Maunsell chimney had no vulgar bark; almost as much noise was audible from the clank of the nickel-steel coupling and connecting rods.

Oddly enough, neither the 'Schools' nor the 'Arthurs' and 'Nelsons' acquired nicknames, like 'Mongolipers' for Maunsell 'N' class and 'Maggies' for the 'Z' class. Drummond's 'T9' class 4-4-0s earned the name 'Greyhounds' for their free-running at speed, and certainly the 'Schools' could have been similarly described.

The bracketing of some station names with those of adjacent schools indicated the importance to the railways of school traffic before the age of the motor car. The LBSCR had 'Christ's Hospital (West Horsham)', 'Shoreham for Lancing College' and 'North Dulwich for Dulwich College'. On the Somerset and Dorset Joint line there was 'Chilcompton for Downside', whilst on its Reading branch the SECR built 'Crowthorne for Wellington College'. On Southern territory there were more public schools than the 40 'Schools' class engines and 28 of them were included in the list. Apart from commencing with the most-publicised, Eton, the names were selected in no particular order, and after the first 10 engines had been seen at work there were plenty of comments, and suggestions as to future naming! To make the choice less parochial and to minimise the risk of any ill-feeling that might follow the inevitable omissions of some Southern schools, Nos 919-930 were given the names of schools elsewhere. Amongst the names of the last nine engines were schools which qualified for precedence on grounds of age: indeed, King's School Canterbury (No 933) had its origins in the 7th century AD before Winchester, 1394, and Eton, 1440. Westminster, 1560, and Harrow, 1571, were two out of the many schools in the country which were founded in the 16th and 17th centuries, and it would have added interest if the engines had carried the names of the older schools only, with their foundation years shown on the nameplates, thus emphasising their historical significance in the growth of education.

During their last years, the 'Schools' were used for Royal trains. On one such occasion, when the train was about to leave Victoria for Epsom Races, the following exchange of pleasantries was heard between the Duke of Edinburgh and the Southern's Superintendent of Operation:

Prince Philip (leg-pulling): 'Do you really think your engine will get there?'.
S.O.O.: 'Sir, if Her Majesty's horse is half as good as our engine, it will come in first today!'.

Train journeys by members of the Royal family and by eminent persons used to be more frequent than today, and Southern men were often privileged to be in attendance, on formal and informal occasions. Winston Churchill was always good for a friendly wave and, sometimes, for amusing repartee. One day when a small crowd had gathered to see him off by train (he was Prime Minister at the time) the clapping was marred by a rude 'boo'. 'Winnie' turned to face the interrupter and said with a chuckle, 'Ah, I don't mind that noise a bit — after all, there are few countries left in the world where a man can say "boo" to a head of state without being arrested!'.

Below left: No 938 *St Olave's* at Grove Park with the 2.25pm Charing Cross-Hastings, 3 August 1938.   *O. J. Morris/Lens of Sutton*

Early days with the 'Schools':

Above right: No E900 *Eton* on display at Windsor and Eton Riverside, when new. Spring 1930.   *Lens of Sutton*

Right: No E904 *Lancing* on show at Lancing, when new in 1930.   *Lens of Sutton*

Below: No E900 *Eton* passes Dunton Green with an up Folkestone train in the autumn of 1930, before the class was allowed to work over the Hastings line.
F. R. Hebron/Rail Archive Stephenson

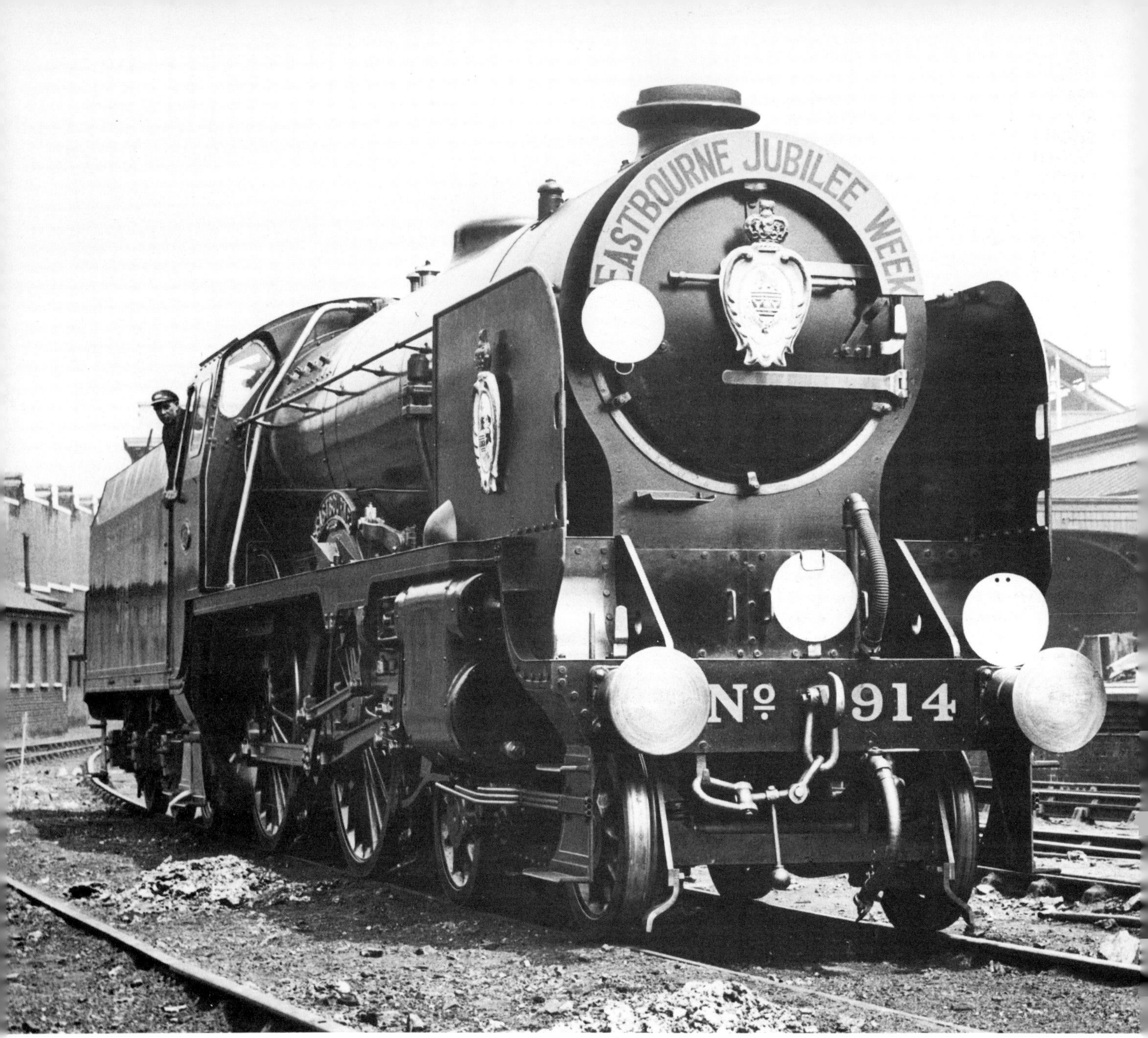
EASTBOURNE JUBILEE WEEK
Nº 914

SOUTHERN
923

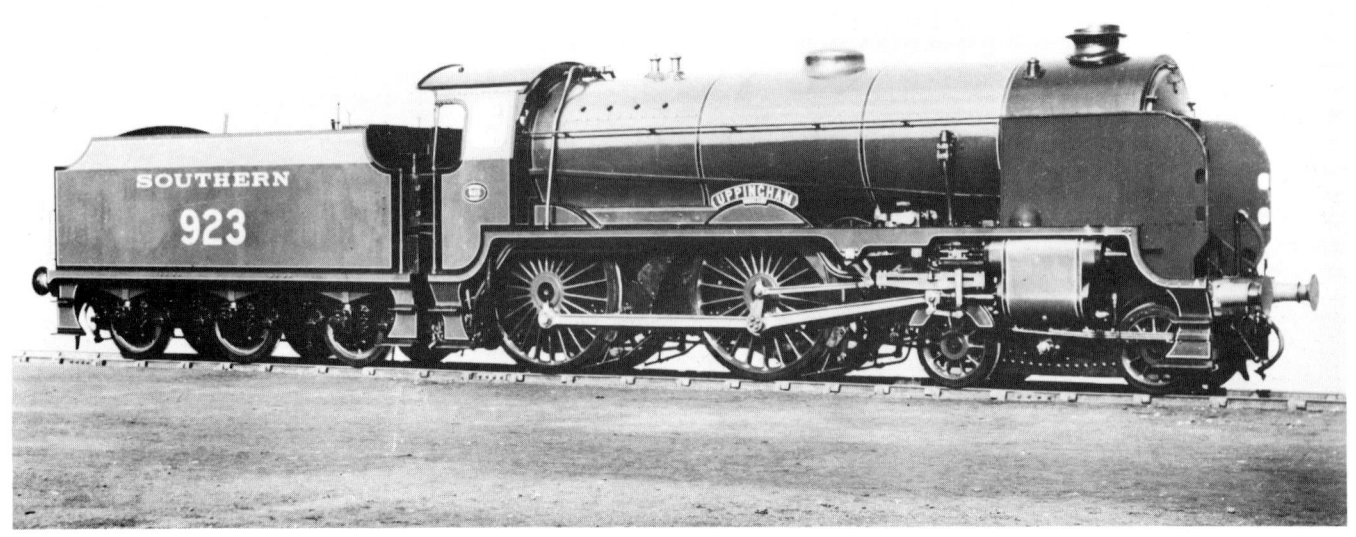

Left: No 914 *Eastbourne* in the engine yard at Victoria, before working the 1.10pm to Eastbourne. The locomotive is specially decorated for the Jubilee celebrations of the Borough of Eastbourne, in June 1933.   *Lens of Sutton*

Below left: No 923, when new in 1933, and carrying *Uppingham* nameplates. The school objected, and the engine was renamed *Bradfield*.   *O. J. Morris/Lens of Sutton*

Above: No 900 *Eton* at Cannon Street with a Hastings train, in the mid-1930s. 'Arthur' No 800 is alongside.
Real Photographs Co (R4331)

Below: No 915 *Brighton* making good progress near Orpington on a down VIP special from Victoria, c1936.
O. J. Morris/Lens of Sutton

Above: No 937 *Epsom* approaches Frant with the 2.25pm Charing Cross–Hastings, 5 May 1937. *Rev A. C. Cawston*

Below: No 932 *Blundells* waits to leave Waterloo with an express to Portsmouth, 1937. *S. L. Redshaw*

Right: No 903 *Charterhouse* at Chislehurst with the 3.25pm Charing Cross–Hastings, 9 August 1938. *O. J. Morris/Lens of Sutton*

Immediately prewar 'Schools' duties:

Left: No 935 *Sevenoaks* on an up Hastings express, June 1938.   *BR*

Below: No 917 *Ardingly* on a down Folkestone train at Ashford (Kent), 1938.   *BR*

Right: No 925 *Cheltenham* brings an up Bournemouth express through Clapham Junction, 1938.   *C. R. L. Coles*

Below right: In malachite green livery, with large buffer beam numerals, No 928 *Stowe* at Byfleet Junction, with the down line from Virginia Water coming in to the right, on a heavy down Bournemouth train, 1939.
C. R. L. Coles

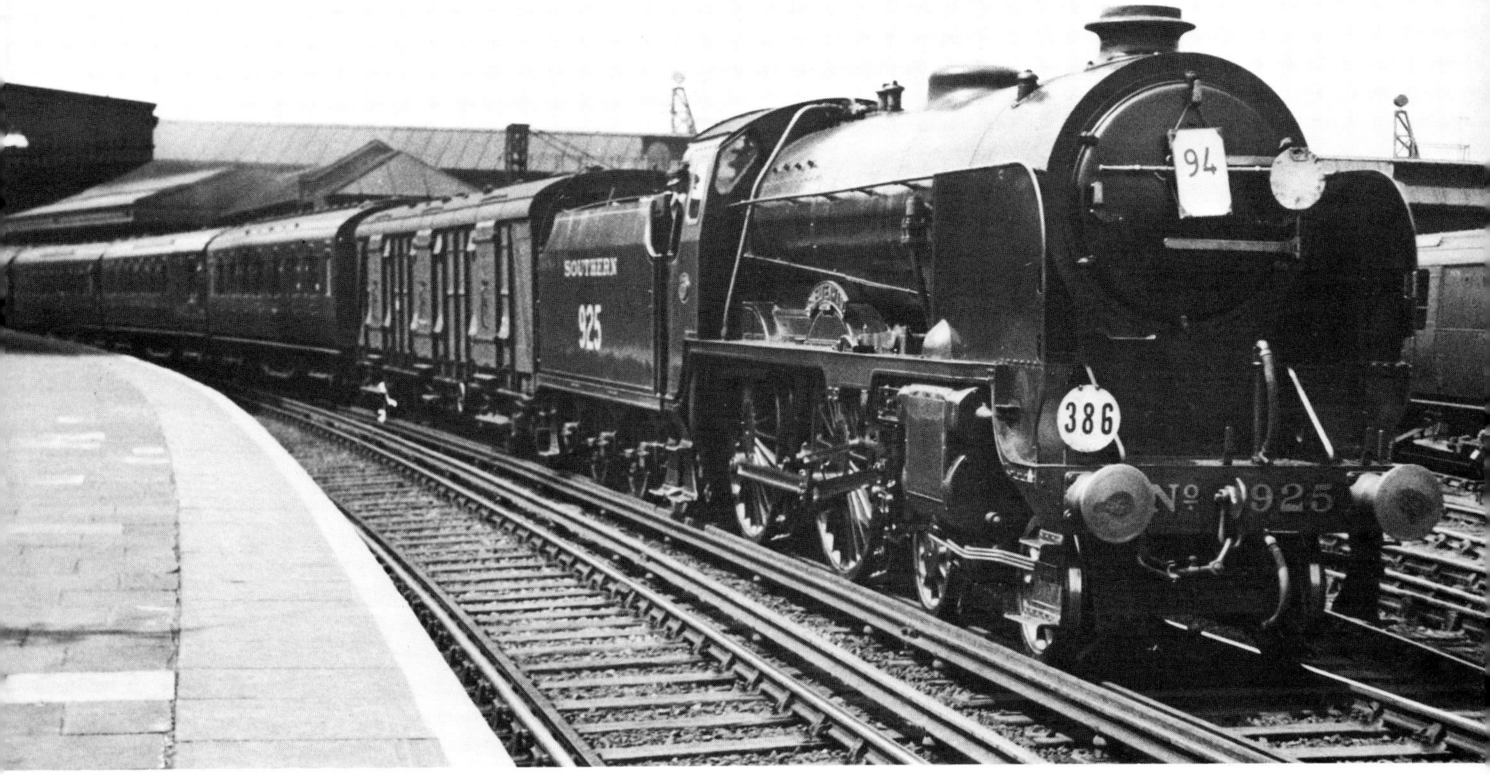
94
SOUTHERN
925
386
No 925

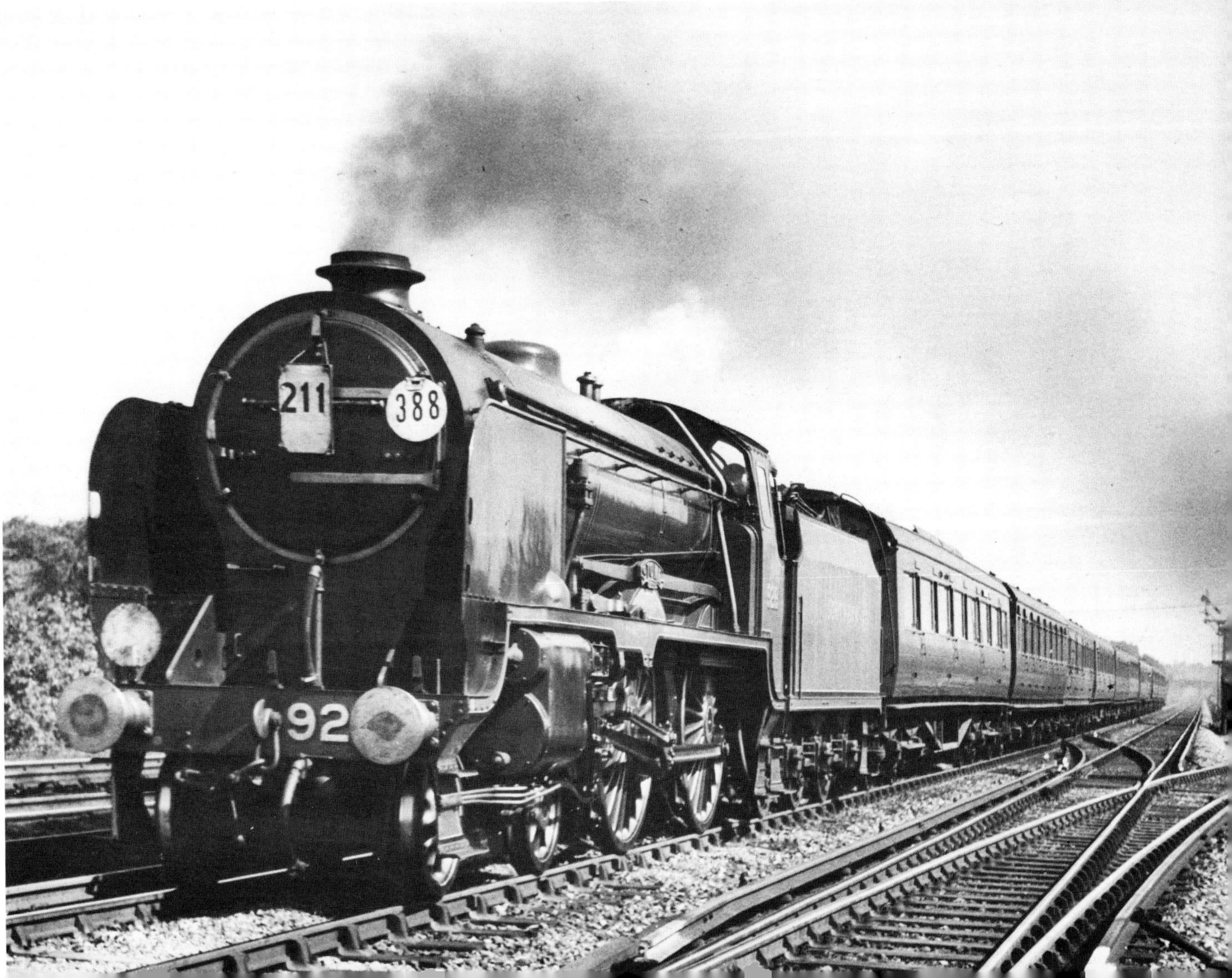
211
388
92

10
The Southern Workshops

Britain was the birthplace of the steam locomotive. As a heavy industry dependent upon ready supplies of iron, coal and steel, the principal locomotive building firms were to be found in the north, where smoke, noise and grey skies were part of the environment. In contrast, the locomotive, carriage and wagon workshops built by the predecessors of the Southern Railway were enviably situated; Ashford Works in a market town in Kent — the Garden of England — Brighton Works at a popular seaside resort, and Eastleigh on a rural site in the Itchen Valley. Lancing, an off-shoot of Brighton exclusively for carriages, was on the South Coast. All three workshops had replaced the original ones in South London, at Battersea, New Cross and Nine Elms.

The most modern workshops when completed in 1911 were those at Eastleigh, on a site of 92 acres. With plenty of space available, the sections productive of dirt and fumes, the forges and the foundries, were housed separately from the erecting bays. Being away from the residential area the only people to be disturbed by the thumping of a 35ton steam hammer and by the racket of pneumatic hammers in the boiler shop were the employees in the adjacent railway houses. The 'Schools', 'Nelsons' and the 'Arthurs', except for the 30 of the last type built in Glasgow, were products of Eastleigh, in an era when riveted construction had not given place to electric welding, untrustworthy as it was deemed, and when the use of oxy-gas for cutting metal was novel, as also was the use of motor trollies for carrying materials instead of a small army of labourers pushing wheelbarrows. Although the buildings were modern, most of the machine tools were elderly; one, an Armstrong-Whitworth screwing machine dated 1865, was in continuous use until 1935.

The time-honoured procedure for overhauling a locomotive was for it to be dismantled and then re-erected by one gang, the members of which took turns to accompany the trial run, ending up at some country station where it would be put into a siding to cool a warm axlebox, while the crew took refreshment in the local. After trial, the locomotive spent several weeks in the painting shop. This leisurely procedure was changed in 1931, following the lead of Crewe Works and its belt-system of rapid overhauls. Thereafter, each stage from stripping to re-erection was performed by specialist gangs, each confined to one routine operation and paint was applied in the erecting shop while assembly was taking place, regardless of footprints, finger-marks and dust. The change was not popular with the shops staff, but thereafter the complete overhaul of a 'King Arthur' was reduced from three months to 19 days. Not that the locomotive was ready for work on the 20th day, for it was likely to be shunted to the running shed minus floorboards, firebars and other parts.

It happened from time to time that a locomotive ex-works

would, after return to its home depot, develop some fault, such as a loose cylinder or leaking boiler, for which the works was responsible. Such instances were liable to spark off an exchange of acrimonious correspondence between the respective head offices of the Locomotive Running Department and the Chief Mechanical Engineer's Department; the latter, in keeping with the defensive attitude of railway departments generally, would express disbelief or a counter-accusation of maltreatment by the drivers and depot staff. In retaliation, the works would find fault with the next locomotive received for overhaul from the complainant depot, by reporting the boiler as badly scaled up. Proverbially, the pot was ever apt to call the kettle black.

To act as the intermediary between the two departments, Maunsell appointed a determined character, Tommy Brand, to have charge of all locomotive repairs. No locomotive was sent to works without his approval. In BR days, each Region had a Shopping Bureau with elaborate records, wall charts and what-have-you. Tommy, in his time, with his little black notebook, was a walking shopping bureau. He had been a locomotive fitter and a depot foreman on the LBSCR, and knew all the tricks of the trade. For a fitter to be torn off a strip by Mr Brand for causing a locomotive failure was a worse punishment than any paper reprimand.

An edict went forth, in Maunsell's reign, that a locomotive derailed, wholly or partially, must be sent to works before return to service for a precautionary check of weight distribution and spring adjustment by means of a weighbridge. To save time, the depots were allowed to arrange this direct either with Eastleigh or Ashford Works. The door was thereby opened to some quiet collusion between depots and works, so when a newly repaired locomotive did give trouble, it could be sent back to works 'for weighing' without undue publicity: the fact that the works kept the locomotive for several days, rather longer than for a simple weighing operation, was neither here nor there!

Eastleigh, like other large railway workshops, supplied a whole host of items for every department: signal and track components, office furniture, station barrows, tablet pouches, horse harness; in the words of an eminent Works Manager, an order for a million mousetraps would be welcomed. The first automatic carriage washing installations were designed and made there, and the gasworks continued to provide gas for restaurant car kitchens long after carriage lighting changed over to electricity, the gas being distributed to outstations by special gas wagons.

When the last 'Schools' class had been built, there were predictions that, with the rapid progress of electrification on the Southern, Eastleigh would get no more orders for new steam locomotives. Indeed, had it not been for World War 2, electric trains might have been running to Southampton and Bournemouth in the 1940s. In 1935, it began to look as if some relics of the steam era would be worthy of preservation, and the idea was approved by Maunsell. The oldest locomotive on the Southern, the ex-Isle of Wight Railway 2-4-0T *Ryde* built in 1864, had been standing idle at Eastleigh Works as nobody had the heart to scrap such a veteran, along with Dugald Drummond's single-wheeler inspection saloon, and together they were placed in the disused paint shop to form the nucleus of the Eastleigh Museum. Other relics were discovered in odd corners: an original Giffard injector, a Beattie flywheel steam feed pump, a pair of early wooden-centred coach wheels and a variety of nameplates and locomotive builders' plates. It was proposed to add the old Bodmin & Wadebridge coach which for many years stood in the centre of the concourse at Waterloo. However, in 1940 the urgent call for scrap metal for war purposes resulted in the disappearance of all but a few small items, including the elaborate LBSCR Royal Train decorations, and these were eventually taken over by the BR Curator of Historical Relics.

After the Grouping, Eastleigh became the sole supplier of all iron and brass castings. The latest pattern of continuous casting plant of French manufacture was installed in due course, largely to cope with the thousands of brake blocks consumed by the frequent stopping of the electric suburban trains, and a metallurgical laboratory was set up, to replace the rule-of-thumb methods which had prevailed in the making of castings. An amusing illustration of the latter arose when Maunsell ordered a thorough investigation into the wear of cylinders and piston rings. It came to light that the cylinders of the 'Arthurs' Nos 448-457 built at Eastleigh wore less than those of any others, and analysis of the cast iron proved it to have an unusual phosphorus content, making the iron hard and wear resistant. The foundry foreman was asked to explain, and after searching through a dog-eared notebook he was able to discover that a large batch of scrap permanent way chairs had been melted down at the time the cylinders had been cast. A chair of similar age was then examined in the laboratory and found to have an identical phosphorus content!

In 1846 the directors of the South Eastern Railway decided to purchase 185 acres of land at Ashford, Kent, on which to lay the foundations of a 'Locomotive Establishment'. By 1850, there had been constructed two separate workshops for locomotives and for carriages and wagons, together with a complete housing estate. Known as Newtown, it was a model village of its kind, and comprised 132 railway houses each provided with the modern form of lighting by a railway gasworks. Ashford was limited in size to the building and repair of medium-size locomotives and continued to function until nearly the end of steam. After grouping, the carriage work was transferred to Lancing and to Eastleigh.

Brighton Works, founded in 1852, had been built on the side of a hill, with the main station on one side and with a goods yard below. Over the years extensions had been added at different levels, inconvenient for moving material from one section to another, and there was no road access to the erecting and machine shops. When, in its last years in the 1960s, space was rented to a firm assembling light cars, these had to leave the works on rail wagons. Maunsell decided to dispense with the use of Brighton and the locomotive repair work was divided between Eastleigh and Ashford. Brighton Works stood almost empty from 1934 until 1940 when it was reopened to provide for additional war work and to maintain repair facilities in the event of bomb damage at the other workshops.

Lancing had been built in 1912 to deal with carriages and wagons, to relieve the congestion at Brighton. In Southern days it was the centre of all the carriage overhauls, leaving Eastleigh Carriage Works to concentrate upon new construction. A complete overhaul was achieved in 25 working days, and 2,500 coaches were dealt with annually. Lancing was closed in 1965.

The transfer of the repair of the ex-LBSCR locomotives to Eastleigh and Ashford in 1932 had an odd sequel. On commencing work on the first arrivals, the receiving works asked to be provided with the necessary drawings, in order that the dimensions of the working parts could be repaired in conformity with designed dimensions. The reputation of Brighton suffered a severe blow when it was discovered not only that many drawings were missing but, worse, few of the engines bore much resemblance, other than outwardly, to such drawings as did exist!

Besides its comparative cheapness to build, the steam locomotive was economical in spares; all cast iron, bronze, brass and white-metal could be recovered and reused. Practically all the spare parts could be made at Eastleigh and Ashford, at short notice if necessary: there were few problems of purchasing parts from outside manufacturers. Spare parts were transported to and from the depots by carrying them on the backs of tenders. The method was well organised, to ensure that the injector from Ashford for an 'N' class at Exeter and the brake valve from Eastleigh for a 'Schools' at Ramsgate were changed over from engine to engine en route to their destination. Oil was recovered by a special washing plant at Eastleigh Works to which all dirty cloths were sent. Every engineman was supplied daily with one new and one washed cloth, to be returned after duty. The washed cloths were then used by the engine cleaners, and eventually found their way back, with the dirty new ones, to Eastleigh. The recovered oil was found suitable for wagon bearings and suchlike.

The growing Electrical Department called for specialised workshops to deal with electric motors and control equipment, and these existed at Durnsford Road, Selhurst and Peckham Rye, and Slade Green in addition to the facilities at the main carriage workshops. A smaller specialised workshop at Stewarts Lane dealt with the lighting equipment on steam hauled coaching stock.

Left: Wheeling a Urie 4–6–0, using the two 50-ton Vaughan cranes in the erecting shop, Eastleigh Works, late 1930s. *BR*

Above: The exterior of Eastleigh Locomotive Works, late 1930s. Urie 'Arthur' No 748 on the extreme left. *BR*

Below: 'Arthur' No 800 *Sir Meleaus de Lile* ex-works, in the mid-1930s. *James R. Clarke/Lens of Sutton*

Bottom: 'Schools' No 936 *Cranleigh*, when new at Eastleigh in June 1935. *O. J. Morris/Lens of Sutton*

11
The Locomotive Running Department

The locomotive depots as they existed in 1937 are listed herewith, and the number of locomotives allocated to each one, in July of that year. The home depots of 'Arthurs' (N15), 'Schools' (V) and 'Nelsons' (LN) are also shown.

London Area

Bricklayers Arms (121) N15, V
Situated in the well-known goods yard, in the old SER buildings. New repair shop added 1934. Inconvenient location for light engines to and from Charing Cross, Cannon Street and London Bridge. 36ton breakdown crane.
Sub-shed: *Ewer Street (Southwark)* for turning, coaling and watering.

Stewarts Lane (141) N15, LN
Longhedge. Old SER and LCDR buildings; convenient for Victoria. Absorbed (1934) former LBSCR *Battersea Park* roundhouse depot. 20ton breakdown crane.

Nine Elms (123) N15, LN
Spacious ex-LSWR buildings in large goods yard, serving Waterloo. 36ton breakdown crane.

Hither Green (45)
Modern SR building (1933) near marshalling yard. Absorbed some freight locomotives ex-*Bricklayers Arms*.

New Cross Gate (64)
Old LBSCR buildings, unsuitable for largest locomotives.

Norwood (48)
Modern SR building (1935) near marhsalling yard. Absorbed *West Croydon* and some freight locomotives ex-*New Cross Gate*.

Feltham (70)
Modern LSWR (1922) building in marshalling yard, replaced *Strawberry Hill*. 20ton breakdown crane.
Sub-shed: *Ascot* closed 1937.

Kent

Gillingham (52)
Old LCDR buildings.
Sub-depot: *Faversham* (31).

Ramsgate (41) N15, V
Modern SR depot (1930) replaced *Margate*, *Ramsgate Harbour*, and *Deal* depots. 15ton breakdown crane.

Dover Marine (50)
Modern SR depot (1928) alongside beach, replaced *Dover Priory* and *Harbour* depots.
Sub-shed: *Folkestone Junction* for harbour branch locomotives.

Ashford (55)
Modern SR building (1931) replaced depot in main works.
36ton breakdown crane.
Sub-shed: *Canterbury West. (Maidstone East* and *Maidstone West* closed 1933.)

Tonbridge (53)
Old SER building, restricted site.

Tunbridge Wells West (21)
LBSCR building.

Sussex

St Leonards (32) V
LBSCR building at West Marina.
Sub-sheds: *Hastings* for turning, coaling and watering; *Bexhill West* for Crowhurst branch.

Eastbourne (25)
Best ex-LBSCR depot, spacious layout. Declined after 1933 electrification.

Newhaven Town (17)
Small LBSCR depot for boat traffic and port shunting.

Brighton (82)
LBSCR buildings. Awkward site. 36ton breakdown crane.

Bognor Regis (18)
LBSCR building. Home depot of Atlantics on Mid-Sussex line.
Sub-depot: *Littlehampton* (9).

Horsham (33)
LBSCR semi-roundhouse.
Sub-depot: *Three Bridges* (23).

Surrey

Redhill (28)
SER depot at strategic junction.

Guildford (89)
LSWR buildings, including semi-roundhouse. Cramped site.
Sub-sheds: *Ash* and *Bordon* (Hants).

Berkshire

Reading (17)
SER building.

Hampshire

Basingstoke (20)
LSWR building.

Eastleigh (105) N15
LSWR buildings and enginemen's dormitory (1902). 36ton breakdown crane.
Sub-depots: *Andover Junction, Southampton Docks* (17).
Sub-sheds: *Winchester* (*Chesil* was GWR), *Southampton Terminus, Lymington.*

Fratton (72)
Portsmouth. Roundhouse formerly joint LBSCR and LSWR. 36ton breakdown crane.
Sub-depot: *Gosport.*
Sub-shed: *Midhurst.* Coal stage at *Hayling Island.*

Bournemouth Central (48)
LSWR building, modern engine hoist. Cramped site near station. 20ton breakdown crane.
Sub-sheds: *Hamworthy Junction, Swanage.* (*Branksome* was LMS.)

Isle of Wight (27)
Ryde: Main repair works, modern running shed.
Newport: Old IWCR buildings.

Dorset
Dorchester (14)
Early LSWR building with dormitory house.
Sub-shed: *Weymouth* LSWR building demolished 1939. (Large locomotives used *Weymouth* GWR depot for turning.)

Wiltshire
Salisbury (59) N15
LSWR building. 36ton breakdown crane.

Somerset
Yeovil (19)
Early LSWR building with turntable at Yeovil Junction.
Sub-shed: *Templecombe Upper.*

Devon
Exmouth Junction (112) N15
Modern (1924) buildings replaced former *Exeter (Queen Street)* depot.
Workshop: 20ton breakdown crane.
Sub-sheds: *Seaton, Lyme Regis, Exmouth, Okehampton, Bude.*

Barnstaple (18)
Old LSWR building.
Sub-sheds: *Torrington, Ilfracombe.*
(*Barnstaple Pilton Yard*) (5) Lynton & Barnstaple depot closed 1935.)

Plymouth Friary (21)
LSWR building.
Sub-shed: *Callington* (Cornwall).

Cornwall
Wadebridge (7)
LSWR building.
Sub-shed: *Launceston.*

In the 1930s the salary paid to the man in charge of a locomotive depot ranged from £180 to £350 per annum according to the size and importance of the place. He was granted a percentage in addition for emergency calls, but was paid no overtime. He had to be available at all hours, day and night, except for one day in the month, when he could be absent provided a colleague at a neighbouring depot would cover any calls. He had to live within easy distance of the depot, and he had to leave word where he could be found if he went to a cinema or visited friends. One simple way of being summoned was by a special engine whistle code: an arrangement which suited ardent fisherman Tom S., often to be found in a boat about a mile offshore!

The greater proportion of depot buildings were pre-1900 and conversion from gas to electric lighting was not complete. Electric lamps on leads were gradually replacing the open-flame tallow-pot oil lamps used for working underneath an engine, or inside the boiler; a type of lamp in use in Ancient Egypt, its smoky flame causing one's clothes to reek, and a cigarette to taste of soot and paraffin. There was no heating in the sheds. Most of them were designed with one closed end where engines were berthed for repairs. The open end was permanently open for movements in and out; if there were any doors left, they had been clobbered so often as to render them inoperative! A few sheds were through sheds open at both ends, wherein the continuous draught at least carried away the smoke. As no depot building was large enough to accommodate all its allocated stud of engines under cover, the staff were accustomed anyway to work in the open in all weathers. Boilersmiths were more fortunate, as a locomotive firebox was a snug, if cramped, place to work in on a cold day, and a favourite hiding place for a quiet game of cards. Work in a smokebox, however, was the filthiest and most unpopular task of all, especially as the washing facilities were limited to buckets of hot water drawn from an engine. Such luxuries as washrooms and clothes-drying rooms awaited the passing of the Factories Act of 1937.

The cynic would say that the conditions were tolerated because the railwayman had a secure job in times of high unemployment. To some extent that was true, of some men, but the majority found running shed life congenial. Open day and night, seven days a week, direct supervision was minimal and lenient, provided everyone 'mucked in' at the busy times. There was a strong loyalty, not to 'the Company' whose image was ever that of Scrooge, but to the depot: the feeling that the guv'nor must not be let down. Men off duty would not demur at being called to cover a mate who had gone sick. Drivers would nurse an ailing locomotive back home rather than leave it at another depot. With the aid of hosepipes, brooms and buckets of whitewash, the oldest of sheds could be kept clean and tidy. As ever, it was the teenagers who would run wild; a bevy of engine-cleaners armed with 'sockers' — cleaning cloths soaked in oil — was potentially explosive. They were best put to work on engines in different parts of the shed so that one gang was kept out of range of another. Newly appointed welfare officers unacquainted with the genus engine-cleaner were shocked to find cleaners' mess-rooms devoid of glass in the windows. In the 1880s locomotives were commonly fitted with the Ramsbottom safety-valve, operated by a lever in the cab. The author's grandfather recalled a lad who would grab another's cap, put it on the safety valve and, with a touch on the lever, shoot it up into the rafers, from which place, if the cap lodged there, the victim had to retrieve it.

A cleaner tempted to show off by moving an engine faced instant dismissal: cases had ended in tragedy. It was in 1859 that an engine escaped from the LBSCR shed at Petworth and ran some miles along the line, collecting a pair of crossing gates before being stopped. A cleaner was suspected of tampering with it. Thereafter, running sheds were provided with trap points to catch runaway engines.

No depot was complete without its allocation of cats: office cats, stores cats and half-wild ones with kittens in coal stacks. Harold Attwell, one of Maunsell's testing staff, recalled that a cat walked out of the coal when an 'Arthur' was passing Woking on a Waterloo-Salisbury express. Pussy, presumably a Nine Elms resident, was consequently 'reallocated' to Salisbury shed.

Conditions at motive power depots deteriorated after World War 2. With shortage of labour, pits and pathways were too often piled high with uncollected ashes; buildings went in need of attention, in some cases deferred pending a reconstruction scheme. Nine Elms was intended to be replaced by a new steam-cum-diesel depot at Clapham Junction; Bournemouth was to move to enlarged premises inside the Branksome Triangle; Tonbridge was to be rebuilt at the West Yard, and so on. Understandably, expenditure was withheld owing to the uncertain future of steam but an atmosphere of neglect took hold.

Now, with a few exceptions, little remains of those former hives of activity; steam locomotive fitters and boilersmiths are a diminishing race. The good fitter was a versatile mechanic but the smith specialised in locomotive-type boilers, now scarce. One of his impressive arts was to take a light hammer and tap, one by one, a thousand stay-heads inside a firebox to tell which stays were sound and which were broken in the waterways.

The 'Nelson' firebox was in shape virtually the same as the Ashford 'N' class but enlarged, yet whereas stay breakage with the latter was no problem, the 'Nelsons' suffered severely from it. Evidently, there was some unevenness in the expansion and contraction stresses which overloaded the stays in certain areas of the firebox.

The trouble was minimised by a change from copper to monel-metal stays and by using flexible stays in the throat-plate area.

A summary of the periodical and mileage examinations applicable to the 'Arthurs', 'Schools' and 'Nelsons' is given on the following page. The frequency and extent of such examinations or 'preventative maintenance' was a matter upon which locomotive engineers seldom agreed. During Maunsell's regime the temptation to add to the list because of one or two failures was resisted, and the philosophy of 'leaving well alone' prevailed, and was justified. The number of fitters to be employed at a depot was calculated according to the requirement of the types of engines allocated; one fitter was allowed for every six engines of 'Arthur' and 'Schools' class, and one for every five 'Nelsons'. One boilersmith for 10 engines was a rough average. For comparison it may be mentioned that it became necessary to have a fitter for every three of the unmodified Bulleid Pacifics, but even so, their availability was lower than the 'Nelsons'.

The multi-cylinder 'Schools' and 'Nelsons', unlike the 'Arthurs', could be allowed to run for 30 to 36,000 miles before the valves and pistons needed to be extracted, and, even then, the renewal of valve and piston rings was to ensure another period of reliable running rather than because they were near the limits of wear.

The boilers of the 'Schools' were not at all troublesome, so that taken as a whole the maintenance of the 'Schools' was the easiest of all. The larger pistons and heavier motion parts of the 'Arthur' did not wear so well, and the thrust of the large outside cylinders gave the axleboxes a good deal of punishment; consequently an 'Arthur' would be likely to ride roughly after 20,000 miles or so. Unlike the 'Schools' and 'Nelsons', the axlebox guides were not fitted with adjusters (horn block wedges) to take up any knock, an omission which arose from the fear at the time the original 'Arthurs' were designed that a maladjusted wedge could lock an axlebox in its guide and cause a derailment. That this fear was groundless was proved by experience with the 'Schools' and 'Nelsons': the one alarming derailment of a 'Nelson's' leading coupled wheels has been mentioned in Chapter 6.

In the maintenance of 'Arthurs', no depot could rival Bournemouth in the 1930s when the inimitable Joe Elliott had charge there. Joe, who had started life as a fitter, contended that Eastleigh Works did not fit axleboxes properly and whenever a newly repaired 'Arthur' arrived, he had it put under the hoist for the axleboxes to be made a tighter fit. The process would be repeated as and when a driver reported axlebox knock, so that Bournemouth 'Arthurs' had a reputation for sweet running. To ensure that his 'Arthurs' would run the 111 miles from Waterloo to Bournemouth West with an ample margin of water in the 5,000 gallon tenders, Joe would renew the piston rings frequently; in fact, he reckoned that his methods of maintenance rendered superfluous the compilation of mileage records. The day came when, in connection with some mishap in the London area, he was instructed to send to Waterloo the complete records of one of his engines, for the information of a Ministry of Transport inspector. After some delay, the records were produced, all written in fresh ink. Suspicions being aroused, a few days later a high official arrived at Bournemouth without prior warning, demanding to see all the other records, after which it was Joe who went to Waterloo for a dressing-down.

A minor, but interesting alteration to the external appearance of the 'Arthurs', 'Schools' and 'Nelsons' was the removal, circa 1936/37, of the anti-vacuum valves on the smokeboxes. It was a fairly common practice everywhere to fit such valves, which were intended to admit air to the superheater and to the steam chest when coasting with regulator closed, to prevent the creation of a vacuum by the moving pistons which would draw ash, etc, from the smokebox into the cylinders. It had been noticed, particularly on the 'Arthurs', that slight carbonisation was occurring in the superheaters: this could only be the result of 'pumping back' from the steam chest: evidently, the anti-vacuum or snifting valves did not work. Practical tests proved this to be so: the valves either remained firmly shut, or, at low speeds, 'chattered'.

Another theory behind the fitting of these valves was that the air admitted to the superheater would prevent excessive temperatures when no steam was passing to absorb the heat. In practice, with the regulator closed and the blastpipe not in operation, the amount of heat passing round the superheater elements was reduced. So the valves on Maunsell's engines were scrapped without any untoward consequences, and one wondered when other designers would come to the same conclusion; in due course, many did so.

Another fitting on the 'Arthurs', 'Schools' and 'Nelsons' to be abandoned was the crosshead-operated vacuum pump, intended to maintain vacuum when running without the use of the steam-operated ejector, and so save steam. The pumps would also maintain vacuum if the steam pressure was seriously reduced. The reasons for removing the pumps were that they were found to require frequent attention and air leakages could cause failures of the brake system.

82

SR maintenance examinations of 'Arthurs', 'Schools' and 'Nelsons'

Average monthly mileage 4,000-6,000 miles

Period or mileage	Examine and test: in steam, as necessary
10-14 days	Wash out boiler. Examine all accessible parts of boiler including waterways and tubes, ashpan, firebars and smokebox
Monthly	Boiler water gauges Driver's brake valve Vacuum limit valve and drip valves Cylinder drain cocks and gear Steam heating equipment (in season) Manifold stop cock
Two-monthly	Injectors, live and exhaust steam Clackboxes Vacuum brake system, and hand brake Lubricators
Three-monthly	Test safety valves at full pressure Check pressure gauges against master gauge Renew firebox fusible plugs
Six-monthly	Measure and record tyre profiles and thickness Main frames and wheels Empty and clean out tenders
12,500 miles	Examine in position: Connecting rods and big-ends, coupling rods, crossheads, crank axles, valve gear, reverser, drawgear, bogie, buffers, springs Withdraw underfeed journal oil pads, all axleboxes
25,000 miles ('Arthurs') 36,000 miles ('Schools' and 'Nelsons')	Examine after dismantling: Connecting rods and big-ends, coupling rods, crank axles and crank pins, crossheads. Withdraw valves and pistons. Renew rings. Decarbonise ports and steam passages. Check cylinder relief valves, drain cocks etc Other parts for attention as reported by drivers. Brake blocks to be replaced as required by adjustments. Drivers to renew worsted trimmings and siphon corks
Annually	Boiler examination by Head Office boiler inspector. Tubes to be withdrawn as directed by boiler inspector, for examination for corrosion

In the wisdom of Sir Herbert Walker the management of the Locomotive Running Department and its staff of some 8,000 was vested in a chief officer who was independent, and not subservient either to operating or technical interests, which were liable to conflict. Internal policy, staff negotiations and disciplinary measures were in the hands of officers who had been trained at a locomotive works and had practical experience in charge of depots; however exalted, they were quite capable of putting on old clothes and taking a trip on the footplate. Bowler hats were a mark of rank and a protection against coal falling off tenders. It was an era noticeably free from militant action, for which some credit was due to an influential body of senior drivers who believed in settling grievances by constitutional methods, and to the locomotive inspectors, all ex-drivers, who were the diplomatic intermediaries between authority and the enginemen.

The senior inspector, John Watson, was an outstanding character. In his younger days as a driver at Nine Elms he had been invited to stand for election to the executive committee of his trade union and to declare certain lines of policy in his election manifesto. That did not suit John, who circulated a portrait of himself with the words 'J. Watson — Your Candidate'. He was elected at face value.

An advantage of the relatively small area of the Southern system was that Waterloo was within a day's journey from all parts. Officers and inspectors frequently met to discuss common problems, on an informal basis, with the station's 'Long Bar' as the meeting place. Locomotive men were reputedly a thirsty lot, but a sharp eye was kept for any abuses, and for any drivers booking on duty in an unfit state. All engines had a tray near the firehole on which a bottle of tea or cocoa was kept warm. Smoking on the footplate was against regulations. In practice, a little latitude was allowed provided no liberties were taken, and provided an engine was not left unattended when a driver slipped out for refreshment. It was hot work in high summer, and at one time on the LSWR enginemen were supplied during a heatwave with a cooling drink of water mixed with oatmeal, by arrangement with the refreshment rooms at the principal stations.

The most serious disciplinary cases were, of course, those of passing signals at danger. Decisions about a driver's future career, whether in the interests of safety he should be confined to shunting work, always involved a great deal of heart-searching, especially concerning an experienced man having an otherwise clean record. There could be no hesitation in fitting locomotives with smoke deflectors, clumsy as they might appear, if thereby one cause of signal errors could be eliminated.

A driver might call himself lucky if he reached retiring age without committing some minor offence such as forgetting to stop at a station; however, only a small percentage was involved in a longer list of errors which could eventually, by the totting-up process, result in a reduction to shed work. A considerable proportion could boast that they had never been late for duty. Some had to admit that, thanks to an accommodating signalman, their sins had not reached the ears of authority. A Brighton-bound driver in the middle of the night found himself diverted to the Eastbourne line at Keymer Junction; he was at fault for taking signals for, and the signalman for setting up, the wrong route. After stopping, he sent his fireman back to the signalbox, where the signalman was found asleep. After breaking a few more rules about wrong-line working and reporting of irregularities, the train went on its proper course and the delay was suitably covered up.

If the telephone system was rather ineffective the grapevine certainly was not, and naturally some tit-bits got relayed to management level, and the officers were wise to keep their ears open. Evidence obtained through the grapevine could hardly be used for disciplinary action, but it did sometimes reveal the truth.

Occasionally irregularities were reported by the public and one example had a sad ending. There were complaints of poaching on the Meon Valley line. Examination of signalbox records threw suspicion on a pick-up freight train and the length of time it had taken between two stations on certain days. An inspector then found a train stopped and unattended in mid-section, and on blowing the engine whistle the driver, fireman and guard came out of the woods, with rabbit-nets. The case was still *sub judice* when the driver took his own life. Rabbits on railway embankments were considered fair game when shot from the footplate.

Shortage of water in the boiler, with fusing of the lead plugs, was another serious crime, in view of the risks involved. The fireman may have been at fault, but on principle it was the driver who had to take the rap. There were quite a few cases of damaged fireboxes each year from this cause, but in only one instance, involving a 'Nelson', did the crown of the firebox collapse and the fireman was blown on to the tender and killed.

Inspecting Officers of the then Ministry of Transport had the right to investigate all mishaps involving injury or risk of injury to the public and cases of injury to the staff, whether serious or slight. Their activities, although limited to making recommendations for preventive action, had a wholly beneficial influence and were always conducted with fairness and impartiality. They held footplate permits and could, by arrangement, ride on any engine they wished.

A steady flow of applications from members of the public for footplate trips was received at Locomotive Running Headquarters. Some of them were difficult to refuse: for example, the person who wrote 'I am about to retire after holding a first-class season ticket on your railway for 25 years, and I would like to make my last journey on the engine!' Requests usually had to be declined, as the official view, supported by the Ministry, was that the presence of a stranger might, by his getting in the way or speaking at the wrong moment, interfere with the vigilance of the engine crew. Drivers were forbidden to let anybody, railwaymen included, ride on the engine without a permit. It was not unknown, of course, for the rule to be broken by some kind-hearted driver. One such was persuaded by a keen amateur to let him ride from Charing Cross to Ashford but while he was on the engine the suitcase he had left in the train was stolen, so the cat was out of the bag and the driver got three days' suspension from duty.

It was only necessary for a driver to receive a verbal caution from somebody in authority, for a warning to circulate rapidly through the jungle telegraph. For example, a certain superintendent rode in a train from Waterloo to Reading, and on alighting he commented to the driver that he heard no whistle warnings given as required at public crossings. So far as he was concerned, that was the end of the matter, but within 48 hours a formal request was submitted through the staff committee at a depot many miles away, asking for the lineside whistle boards in that area to be repainted. Posting admonitory notices in the depot notice-cases never had the same effect.

The summer months in the years up to 1939 were hectic ones for the locomotive department. Extra trains to cope with holiday traffic began in May, and the summer timetable was introduced a month earlier than the other group companies. Leave for the enginemen was spread out between April and October to minimise the number of men absent at one time. Additional cleaners, to permit the upgrading of permanent cleaners to firemen, and firemen to drivers, were taken on for the period and stood off during the winter. Engine repairs were brought forward or deferred in order to have the maximum number available. Gone are the Saturday queues at Waterloo which filled the station concourse and started outside in the road below; no longer are empty trains kept in readiness in every available siding within a 30-mile radius of London, nor spare locomotives at vantage points such as Tonbridge, Redhill, Horsham, Guildford and Basingstoke where assistance might be required.

All the principal trains would be run in two or more portions. The 11am Waterloo-West of England, for example, had four relief trains departing before and after the advertised time, and the choice of locomotive for each train required careful judgement. On hand for these trains there would be the weekday 11am engine, a 'Nelson', a Scotch 'Arthur', a Salisbury 'Arthur', a 'Paddleboat' and a Feltham 'S15' temporarily uprated from freight work. These would have to be shuffled so that the early departures would be certain to show the others a clean pair of heels. The driver who had been given the 'Paddleboat' would spot E. S. Moore, the Divisional Locomotive Superintendent, standing on the end of No 11 platform, climb off the engine, and expostulate about the load of the train, the weather, the inexperience of the fireman, the doubtful quality of the coal and the condition of the engine, E. S. Moore would listen patiently, remove his pince-nez glasses, studiously clean them and, when the flow of words ceased, grunt: 'I expect you'll do your best'. The driver, having relieved the pressure of his feelings like the release of steam from the safety valves, would grin and get his train away in good style.

There were 'Black Saturdays' when some little incident would cause delays to escalate. A driver would discover, just before starting time, that the regulation minimum of $19\frac{1}{2}$in of vacuum could not be held with the small ejector, and a posse of carriage examiners and station staff would frantically search for the cause of the leakage. An 'Arthur' once started off and then, with the train barely out of the platform, a coupling parted, whereupon a coil of wire binding, unravelling from the torn vacuum hose-pipes, short-circuited the live rail. No wonder E. S. Moore kept hanging on the wall of his office the poker-work motto: 'No sooner have you made ends meet, than somebody moves the ends'.

The most complicated exercises in locomotive diagramming were those connected with annual events such as Ascot and Epsom Races and the Aldershot Tattoos, to which, in steam days, trains converged from all points of the compass. After arrival, and within a limited time before the homeward journeys, every locomotive had to run light to one or other of the nearer locomotive depots for servicing. They then had to be returned to their trains, which were marshalled in correct sequence of departure on one of the running lines. They were field days for the supervision staff and for the breakdown crews who were held in readiness at key points. Long practice in coping with those events was to prove invaluable when the Southern was called upon, in 1940, to cope with over 385,000 troops, of several nationalities, landed at South Coast ports following the fall of Dunkirk and the collapse of France. Coaching stock of all four Group companies was mustered to form 200 trains by which the men were dispersed all over the United Kingdom. On that occasion, many drivers, firemen and guards were on duty continuously for 24 hours at a stretch. At one of the locomotive depots at a key point, Redhill, so many engines were being serviced that the yard became for a time completely blocked with mountains of ashes. For all the veteran Southern locomotives which were pressed into service, it was their finest hour!

Above: Nine Elms: 'N15'
No 740, when new in 1919.
Lens of Sutton

Left: Nine Elms: a particularly
characteristic view, with
'N15' No E754 *The Green
Knight* on the ash-pit, c1930.
Rail Archive Stephenson

Below: Battersea: 'Arthur'
No E801 *Sir Meliot de Logres*,
28 October 1928. Running
foreman in bowler hat,
extreme right.
O. J. Morris/Lens of Sutton

Right: Bricklayers Arms: 'Schools' No 921 *Shrewsbury.* Lens of Sutton

Below: New Cross: No E908 *Westminster,* **24 October 1930.**
O. J. Morris/Lens of Sutton

Left: Eastbourne: No 914
***Eastbourne*, c1934.**
Lens of Sutton

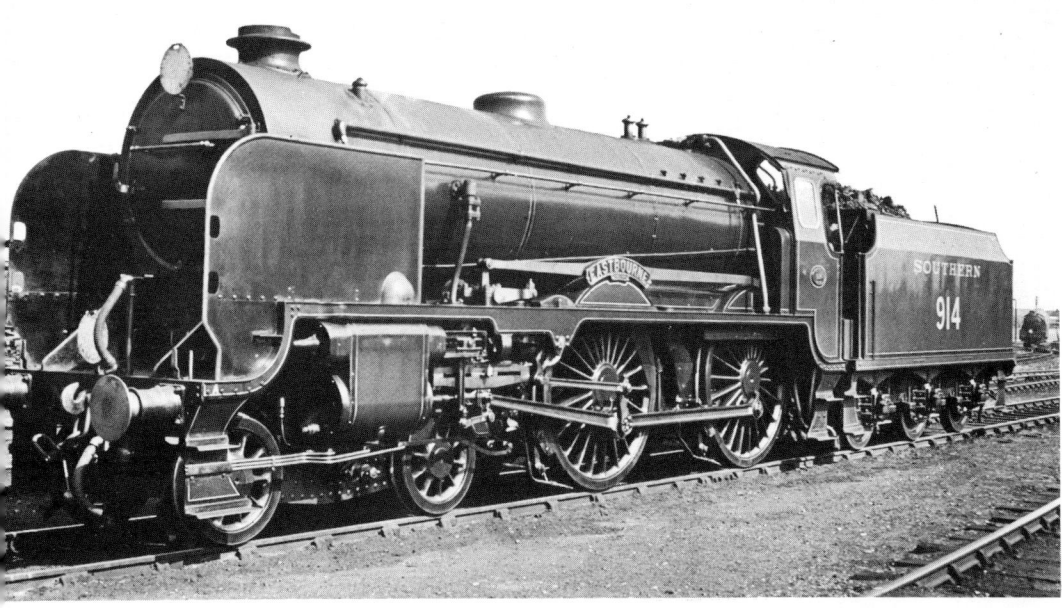

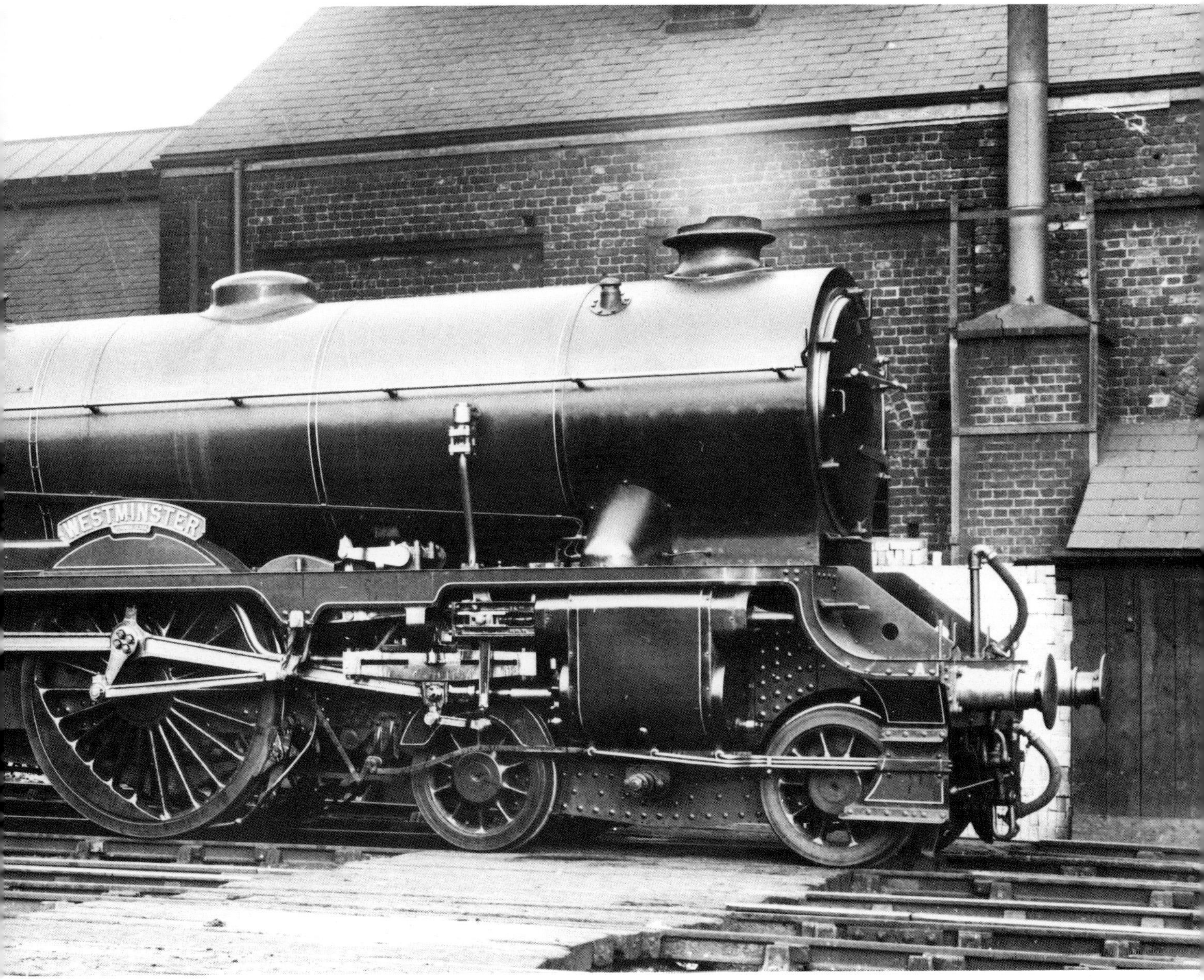

Above: Urie 'Arthur' No 740 *Merlin*, c1937. Snifting valves still in place. *C. R. Gordon Stuart/Lens of Sutton*

Below: Eastleigh: No 784 *Sir Nerovens* in the mid-1930s. Note the stacked fire-irons showing at the leading end of the tender. *Lens of Sutton*

Above: Yeovil Junction: E777 *Sir Lamiel* is turned, sometime in the early 1930s.
C. R. Gordon Stuart/Rail Archive Stephenson

Left: No E783 *Sir Gillemere*, with its experimental smoke deflector, at Oxford GWR shed, 9 April 1927.
H. C. Casserley

Below left: Bournemouth: No 914 *Eastbourne* in malachite green livery, recently released from Eastleigh Works with Lemaître blastpipe and wide chimney. A 1938 scene with Bournemouth fitters Alf Saunders and Cecil Knott about to open the smokebox door. *S. C. Townroe*

12
'Arthurs','Schools' and 'Nelsons'
Performance to 1939

At every depot there were a few speed-merchants amongst the drivers, ready to attempt an unofficial record when egged on by provocative argument in the mess-room or by some private enthusiast who made it known that he was travelling in the train with stopwatches. They would have liked the opportunity of trying out Southern engines on the main lines to the North where there was greater scope for uninterrupted high-speed running than on their home ground, an opportunity which one or two drivers were able to enjoy to the full during the locomotive exchanges of 1948, though not with any of Maunsell's engines. Occasionally, train running logs published in the *Railway Magazine* revealed that liberties had been taken with the schedules and, if minutely analysed, with speed restrictions. To these displays, higher authority turned a blind eye whenever they chanced to read the popular railway press. The *Railway Gazette* catered for professional railwaymen and did not publish information which did not bear the stamp of officialdom.

Although it had occurred a quarter of a century before, the disaster at Salisbury in 1906 when an up Plymouth boat special was wrecked by excessive speed still lingered in the memories of former LSWR staff, and a Board Minute which required all trains to stop at Salisbury was still in force. All down trains were likewise restricted at Poole, because of the sharp curve preceded by a steep down gradient. Members of the Chief Civil Engineer's Office travelled the system to detect track irregularities, and to check up on the observance of speed limits. Their presence in a reserved compartment was often spotted by the guard in time to give the driver the tip, but firm action was taken against drivers who were caught. Special watch was kept on sharp curves following complaints by gangers that the track was being pushed out of alignment by somebody unable to tell the difference between 15mph and 35mph.

The curve at the west end of Tonbridge station was a good deal sharper than it is now, and as non-stop trains approached at high speed in both directions with a long bank to follow in the up direction, drivers were always tempted to rush it. The 'Arthurs' and 'Nelsons' had thinner flanges on the centre pair of coupled wheels to ease the negotiation of curves; nevertheless at other than slow speeds, those engines were apt to go round with a series of jerks as if the curve consisted of a series of short straights. With the introduction of flange-oilers or greasers, fitted to the rail, the effect was greatly reduced as well as the wear of rails and flanges.

In 1927 the 11am Waterloo-West of England was given the title of the 'Atlantic Coast Express', which was abbreviated to the 'ACE'. The 'Arthurs' proved capable of keeping the 86-min schedule to Salisbury, 83.8 miles, with ease. This irked some eager drivers at Nine Elms, one of whom, Fred Stickley with his favourite 'Arthur' No 777 *Sir Lamiel* (colloquially known as the 'Austin 7' or 'Pile of 7s'), ran to Salisbury in under 75min. Officialdom was *not* amused. The story went that Stickley was summoned to headquarters and severely reprimanded by the Locomotive Running Superintendent. On leaving that dignitary's office, somewhat crestfallen, he was then escorted along the corridor to the Chief Mechanical Engineer's office and warmly congratulated for proving what a Maunsell 'Arthur' could do. But the 86min schedule remained.

The same locomotive, No 777, was involved in a fine run in the up direction with the 'ACE', as reported in the *Railway Magazine* for June 1936. The 90min allowance for Salisbury to Waterloo was cut by $17\frac{1}{4}$min. Over the $65\frac{1}{2}$ miles from Grateley to Wimbledon, the average was 79.6mph; over the $33\frac{1}{2}$ miles from Worting Junction to Esher, 82.7mph. Maxima were $88\frac{1}{2}$mph at Andover and 90mph at Byfleet.

During the 1930s accelerated schedules were introduced on the other Group companies, culminating in the high-speed running of the 'Silver Jubilee' on the LNER. The Southern kept to a policy of regular-interval expresses at speeds well within the capability of the locomotives. Waterloo applauded when *Punch* published a cartoon in which a passenger, alighting from his train unexpectedly before time, was seen making a bee-line for the buffet in order to put the time saved to good purpose.

Drivers were not entirely deprived of opportunities for speed, as the Southern schedules did not have built-in recovery times, and drivers were instructed to regain time.

The Urie 'Arthurs', as might be expected, never did anything very spectacular. In 1930, Nos 736-755 were distributed thus: Nine Elms 9, Eastleigh 2, Bournemouth 2, Salisbury 2, and Exmouth Junction 5. They were generally used on the semi-fast services, and on Southampton boat trains, van trains and specials. They worked passenger trains on the Portsmouth direct line until electrification, after which Nine Elms transferred five to Eastleigh.

The Eastleigh 'Arthurs', Nos 448-457, had a settled existence at Salisbury. It was Southern practice to keep particular engines to the same depot as far as practicable, and thus to encourage a depot to look after its own, for anybody's engine was likely to become nobody's care. These 'Arthurs' worked the main line in both directions and with particular success over the switchback Salisbury-Exeter section, over which the non-stop trains like the 'ACE' were allowed 96min for the 88 miles. Two minutes more were allowed in the up direction. The load for the schedule was 11 bogies, and the Salisbury 'Arthurs' could take 14 bogies when pressed.

The following examples of good runs may be quoted from

Cecil J. Allen's articles on British Locomotive Practice and Performance which appeared in the *Railway Magazine*:

TABLE 1

No 452 with 10 coaches, 345 tons full, non-stop

	Mileage	Time (min-sec)
Salisbury-Templecombe	28.5	32-20 start to pass
Templecombe-Yeovil Jct	10.8	9-25 pass to pass
Yeovil Jct-Axminster	22.0	19-55 pass to pass
Axminster-Sidmouth Jct	14.7	18-50 pass to pass
Sidmouth Jct-Exeter Central	12.0	11-35 pass to stop

The net time was 92min and a top speed of 80mph was exceeded at Gillingham, Sherborne, Axminster and Broad Clyst.

TABLE 2

No 453 with 13 coaches, 450 tons full, non-stop

	Mileage	Time (min-sec)
Salisbury-Templecombe	28.5	31-53 start to pass
Templecombe-Yeovil Jct	10.8	9-19 pass to pass
Yeovil Jct-Axminster	22.0	20-32 pass to pass
Axminster-Sidmouth Jct	14.7	19-23 pass to pass
Sidmouth Jct-Exeter Central	12.0	18-40 pass to stop

Note: Signal checks at Axminster and approaching Exeter.

TABLE 3

No 451 with 11 coaches, 375 tons full, non-stop

	Mileage	Time (min-sec)
Exeter Central-Sidmouth Jct	12.0	16-12 start to pass
Sidmouth Jct-Axminster	14.7	14-20 pass to pass
Axminster-Yeovil Jct	22.0	23- 6 pass to pass
Yeovil Jct-Templecombe	10.8	11-20 pass to pass
Templecombe-Salisbury	28.5	29-57 pass to stop

For comparison in 1926, Urie Arthur No 747 worked the up 'ACE' with 350 tons full, thus:

TABLE 4

	Mileage	Time (min-sec)
Exeter Central-Sidmouth Jct	12.0	15-50 start to pass
Sidmouth Jct-Axminster	14.7	15-40 pass to pass
Axminster-Yeovil Jct	22.0	21-55 pass to pass
Yeovil Jct-Templecombe	10.8	12-20 pass to pass
Templecombe-Salisbury	28.5	31-25 pass to stop

The train was stopped by signals at Templecombe. Allowing for that, the net time was 93min. It was on this journey that Mr Allen clocked 90mph for the first time on the Southern.

Reviewing locomotive performance between Salisbury and Exeter in a 1950 *Trains Illustrated*, Mr Allen was to comment:
'By the middle 1930s, the "King Arthurs" were at the zenith of their achievements. Speeds had risen: the fastest booked time from Salisbury to Exeter, indeed, had come down to 93 minutes for the 88 miles, by a curious flyer which appeared in the timetable to originate at Salisbury in the small hours at 3.6am, but which actually began its journey with newspapers at Waterloo at 1.30am. On the fastest runs the "King Arthurs" had a nominal load limit of 355 tare tons, but in the height of the season this figure was often exceeded, and still these capable 4-6-0s "could take it."
'The finest "King Arthur" run west of Salisbury of which I have ever seen details was one made in 1934 by No 768 *Sir Balin*, in charge of Driver Young, who had behind his tender 13 bogie vehicles, crammed with passengers and luggage, weighing 421 tons tare — 66 tons or two full coaches over the limit — and not less than 460 tons gross. With this tremendous train Young achieved the brilliant feat of running the 88.0 miles in 90min to the second, a gain of six minutes on schedule. He was favoured with a clear road throughout, and there were some tremendous downhill speeds to provide the necessary impetus for the climbs. So the train was whirled through Gillingham at 82mph, Sherborne at 85, Axminster at 86½, past Milepost 158 (after Honiton) at 82, and through Broad Clyst at 82; in comparison, the lowest speeds over the summits were 42mph at Semley, 50 up Templecombe bank, 54 up Sutton Bingham bank, and 37 at Hewish, while Young triumphantly took his train into Honiton tunnel, after the long 1 in 80 of Seaton bank, at 26½mph. It required 23min 50sec to get from Salisbury up the 17.5 miles to Semley, but the ensuing 69.4 miles up hill and down dale through to Exmouth Junction were run in the astonishing time, with this load, of 63min 55sec. Twice the express was near to making "even time" from the start, for Seaton Junction, 64.2 miles, was passed in 64min 30sec, and Exmouth Junction, 86.9 miles, in 87min 45sec. Such a run as this would be quite sufficient to earn the "King Arthurs" a place among the locomotive "immortals" '.

It was the practice in Southern days to change engines at Salisbury in both directions. The pros and cons of doing so were often debated; whilst ostensibly through working would have improved the daily mileage run by some engines, instances were limited whereby the round trip could be made in the day and so balance the out-and-home engine workings. The same difficulty was encountered, in securing long-mileage daily duties for the main line diesel-electric locomotives in the 1950s. Lodging turns, and hence through working of engine crews, had been abolished, so Salisbury had become a changeover point for enginemen. The change of engines as well, was in keeping with the principle of keeping engines and crews together on the top-link duties. If thereby the maximum possible mileage was not obtained out of the engines their appearance and condition gained, and the enginemen got more satisfaction out of their work.
The early allocation of the 'Scotsmen', Nos 763-792, was, roughly speaking, the first 10 to Stewarts Lane, the second 10 to Nine Elms and the last 10 to Bournemouth. After 1933, approximately half of them were on the Eastern section and half on the Western. The small-tender 'Arthurs' No 793-806 from 1926 to 1933 worked on the Central section, where they were matched against the LBSCR Baltics (afterwards rebuilt to 'N15x' class) and proved the better engines. The 'N15x' class turned out to be no better than the Urie 'N15'. After the Central section electrification Nos 793-806 went to the Eastern section where they remained almost until their end. From 1926 until 1937 Nos 783-792 formed a team which operated most successfully from Bournemouth. The later numbers displaced by 'Schools' then went to Exmouth Junction.
As to performance on the Eastern section, Cecil J. Allen reviewed the efforts on what he called, the 'Dover Road', in a 1950 *Trains Illustrated*:

'Then came the strengthening of the track and underline bridges, in Southern Railway days, which at length permitted the introduction of 4-6 0 engines and considerable increases in loads. It was a tremendous change in 1927 for me to mount the footplate of *Lord Nelson* himself at Victoria one day in the summer of 1927, at the head of the then 10.45am Dover boat train — later to blossom out into the "Golden Arrow" — and to realise that behind our tender were nine Pullmans, a corridor first, and four six-wheelers, making up a total load of 460 tons. Owing to the presence of a special train for the President of France, we were shifted from the usual No 2 platform to the opposite side of the station, and that meant no banking assistance up the 1 in 62 to the Grosvenor Bridge. But Driver Stuckey took the precaution to sand his rails as the engine backed on to the train, and that meant a grand start, even though with no more than 40% cut-off and half-regulator to get us over the top. "Now come along, my beauty, come along," I heard him gently apostrophise his steed as he opened the regulator, and "come along" *Lord Nelson* most certainly did.

'Directly this hard work was over, cut-off came back to 25%, and between there and 30% it stopped for all the rest of the journey, with the regulator never more than two-fifths open. Even this moderate handling took us up to Penge Tunnel at 31½mph and Knockholt at 33½; with a time of 31min 5sec to this point, 17.6 miles, we had gained a minute on schedule, but two permanent way slowings as we ran down to Tonbridge put us ¾min behind time at Paddock Wood. Then followed some fine running for 30% cut-off and half-regulator took us along the straight at a speed which rose by Staplehurst to 70½mph, and at no point fell below 61½ until we were pulled up for a third permanent way check after Ashford. The 21.3 miles from Paddock Wood to Ashford, passed in 73min 25sec from Victoria, were run in 19min 40sec. From the Ashford slack we accelerated up the hill to 46mph at Westenhanger, and reached 66 before easing to 55 through Folkestone Junction. Eventually we stopped at Dover Marine, 78 miles, in 98min 10sec from Victoria, dead on time; the net time was 94min. I was greatly impressed with the smooth and quiet running of the big 4-6-0, as also with the perfectly even draught in the firebox that is obtained with the 135-degree crank arrangement of a four-cylinder engine.

'Next came the era of the "King Arthur" 4-6-0s and the speedy 'Schools' 4-4-0s on the Folkestone, Dover and Deal service, together with the 76min timings in each direction between Waterloo and Folkestone Central, 69.1 miles — a remarkable timing indeed in view of the necessarily slow running between Waterloo and London Bridge and the climb from either direction to Knockholt. Brilliant running was needed, in the up direction particularly, for the working book actually demanded less than "even time" from the Folkestone start to passing Tonbridge — 40.4 miles to 39½min.

'The fastest start I have ever known in this direction was by "King Arthur" 4-6-0 No 803 *Sir Harry le Fise Lake*, hauling an eight-coach train of 270 tons gross. Unfortunately the correspondent who sent me the details had not taken any records of his speeds, but as the averages on the three stages Smeeth-Ashford-Chart-Pluckley worked out at 78.2, 71.1 and 75.0mph, it is clear that Ashford must have been approached at about 80. The 4.5 miles from Folkestone Central to Sandling Junction were climbed in 7min 21sec; the 9.3 miles on to Ashford took 7min 51 sec, the 21.3 miles from there to Paddock Wood 17min 27sec (*average* 72.6mph for 30.6 miles on end), and Tonbridge was passed in 37min 45sec, 1¾min early. The climb of 12.9 miles to Orpington was then taken easily in 19min 24sec and with the unusual luxury of a perfectly clear road into London, *Sir Harry* passed

London Bridge, 68 miles, in 70min 24sec, and drew up at Waterloo in 73min exactly. Even inclusive of the Waterloo stop, the overall time to Charing Cross was no more than 76min 48sec, 3¼min less than the old 80min non-stop schedule.

'A run timed by Mr O. S. Nock is a remarkable example of what one of the Schools can do when fully extended. The load this time was not eight bogies but eleven, making a total of 390 tons; the engine was No 917 *Ardingly*. Up the rising gradients from the start the engine gradually accelerated to 47½mph at Sandling Junction; then came 76½mph through Ashford, 69 at Chart, no less than 79 at Headcorn, 70½ at Marden, and 75 at Paddock Wood; over 30.9 miles from Smeeth to Tonbridge an average of 72.6mph was kept up, and this with nearly 400 tons of train. So Ashford, 13.8 miles, was passed in 17min, Paddock Wood, 35.1 miles, in 34min 30sec (just inside "even time"), and Tonbridge in 39min 9sec, a shade ahead of schedule. The climb to Knockholt was a tax with such a load, but *Ardingly* kept up 35½mph on the 1 in 122 to Sevenoaks Tunnel, and did not drop below 34 on the 1 in 144 in the tunnel; then came 61 through Dunton Green and a minimum of 44 at Knockholt summit. From Tonbridge to Knockholt had taken 17min 42sec. "Down the hill" speed mounted to 75mph at Grove Park; once again there was a clear road, so that London Bridge was passed in 72min 36sec, and the stop effected at Waterloo in 74min 49sec, just over a minute early. This was a grand performance indeed'.

The first depots to have 'Schools' were Dover and Deal in the May and June of 1930. In September Deal was closed with the opening of the new Ramsgate depot. It had a band of main line drivers who had been working the accelerated Folkestone-Charing Cross trains in great style with the 'L1' 4-4-0s and they proceeded to show what could be done with 'Schools'. In the same year Eastbourne, another depot with a reputation for able drivers and well-kept engines, introduced 'Schools' to the fast trains to and from Victoria. In 1931, Ramsgate had Nos 900-903/05/06, Eastbourne Nos 904/07-09 but in July the latter were sent to St Leonards to start the 'Schools' on the Tonbridge-Hastings route. Their success already obvious, an order for 20 more was agreed upon. By the end of 1933, all the first 10 had been sent to St Leonards, and Nos 910-923 were at Ramsgate.

When the first batch of 'Schools' was being built, scrapping was taking place of some of the lower-powered 4-4-0s. All 43 of the Brighton 'B2x' class were to be cut up, 10 of the Ashford 'B1' class, and the Ashford 'F1' class was steadily diminishing. Likewise on the Western section the Drummond 'C10' class of 10 engines was eliminated, together with 49 of Adams' express 4-4-0s. Whilst many of them had become surplus to requirements, others had reached the limit of economic repair, and their place had been filled by remaining 4-4-0s. Before the second batch of 'Schools' was finished, a case had been made for increasing the batch to 30, making 40 'Schools' in all. Nos 924-933 were earmarked for the Western section, and Nos 934-939 were given to Bricklayers Arms to supplement the others already working on the Eastern section.

Nos 924-933 were allocated to Fratton depot for working the Portsmouth-Waterloo trains. They were suited to the size of the roundhouse at Fratton, and at the end of the up journey to Waterloo they could be turned there, on a turntable formerly on the north side, and serviced in the sidings on the south side of the station which went by the familiar name of The Beach, thus avoiding the light run to Nine Elms depot. The Beach is now a berth for electric stock.

Prior to the arrival of the 'Schools', Maunsell's 'U1' class three-cylinder 2-6-0s had been tried on the Portsmouth line with rather poor results — surprisingly, because on paper they were slightly more powerful than the 'Schools' and with six wheels of 6ft 0in diameter they should have had an advantage on the 1 in 80 gradients. On the other hand, their boilers were inferior in pressure, grate area and heating surface, and could barely sustain the non-stop run down to Woking, let alone the harder work south of Guildford. On the Maunsell Moguls the leading bissel truck was connected to the frame with a Cartazzi slide, a device with two opposite-sloping wedges on each mating face which provided a self-centring action. It also allowed the Moguls to sway rather freely at the front end, which on the 'U1' was in the form of a box above the buffer beam known as the 'piano'. When running downhill from Buriton Tunnel to Havant on reverse curves, the view from the footplate of the 'piano' rocking from side to side was a little disconcerting.

The 'Schools' rode sweetly through curves and climbed the gradients even better than the 'Arthurs'. On non-stop trains between Waterloo and Portsmouth in both directions, a 'Schools' was allowed 90min with a maximum of 11 coaches.

In 1937 electrification of the Portsmouth line via Guildford displaced the 'Schools' from Fratton. The freight and van trains continued to be worked by steam, as elsewhere, and the number of locomotives rendered redundant was not such as to warrant any scrapping, surplus locomotives being put into store. This was just as well, as the events of 1939 onwards were to prove.

Nos 924-933 were then sent to Bournemouth. The trains on the Bournemouth services were heavy, especially in the summer, and included some non-stop express over the 108 miles to Bournemouth Central. Only three speed restrictions below 60mph existed: 40mph at Worting Junction on the down line; 15mph at Northam curve, Southampton; and 40mph over the old bridge and causeway crossing the River Test at Redbridge. The 'Arthurs' at Bournemouth had been great favourites with their drivers, and the tenders carried 5,000gal against the 4,000gal of a 'Schools'. Even with a load limit of 10 coaches, the water supply was only marginally sufficient for non-stop working. Once again, 'Arthurs' and 'Schools' were to be matched, this time under more difficult conditions; moreover the traffic department had a habit of adding a couple of extra coaches at short notice. The Bournemouth men took up the challenge, and in the *Railway Magazine* for September 1939, Cecil J. Allen was able to say 'the phenomenon of Southern locomotive performance is the place that has been taken by the "Schools" which display tractive powers by no means inferior to the "King Arthur" 4-6-0s, and not far short of those of the larger "Lord Nelson" engines'. He went on to quote specimen runs such as:

TABLE 5

No 926 Repton, *14 coaches equal to 490 tons full; one stop, at Southampton*

	Mileage	Time (min-sec)
Waterloo-Surbiton	12	18- 9 start to pass
Surbiton-Woking	12.4	13- 7 pass to pass
Woking-Basingstoke	23.4	28- 3 pass to pass
Basingstoke-Winchester	18.8	18-58 pass to pass
Winchester-Southampton	12.6	14-59 pass to stop*
Southampton-Bournemouth	28.8	35-44 start to stop

*Dead stop by signals at St Denys

TABLE 6

No 927 Clifton *with 15 coaches equal to 525 tons full*

	Time (min-sec)
Waterloo-Surbiton	17-53 start to pass
Surbiton-Woking	12-23 pass to pass
Woking-Basingstoke	25-18 pass to pass
Basingstoke-Winchester	18-2 pass to pass
Winchester-Southampton	14-24 pass to stop

The present-day timing of 67min from Waterloo to Southampton with 12-coach electric trains seems less remarkable than 88min with 15 coaches when it is remembered that the 3,200 rated horsepower of the Class 430 (4-REP) electric multiple-unit is nearly three times that of a 'Schools'! And the electric train runs on roller bearings instead of the plain bearings of prewar steam stock, and has electro-pneumatic brakes instead of vacuum brakes.

One slight concession made to the 'Schools' was the limit of seven coaches up the 1 in 50 Upwey bank between Weymouth and Dorchester; 'Arthurs' were allowed to take eight coaches, and 'Nelsons' 10 coaches, without a banking engine. Otherwise, apart from the 1 in 60 between Poole and Parkstone, the gradients were not difficult although continuous steaming was required up the 1 in 252 from Allbrook Junction to Roundwood summit.

The zenith of the 'Schools' was attained in 1938 when they were newly painted in light green livery, with coaching stock to match, for the 'Bournemouth Limited'. The train was as fine a sight as any of the famous trains in British railway history, and running non-stop in both directions between London and Bournemouth it was one of the longest runs regularly performed without taking water from track troughs. The 'Bournemouth Limited' was booked over the 108 miles between Waterloo and Bournemouth Central in 116min down and 118min up. Non-stop runs had commenced in 1899 and were never resumed after 1939. The 'Limited' ran to Weymouth, with a portion for Swanage and a 'Schools' berthed overnight at Dorchester depot to start the up working from Weymouth next morning. So for one glorious year there flashed across the Wessex landscape a train which reflected the bright greens of the New Forest in summer, and which even on dull days held a glint of the 'Sunny South'.

TABLE 7

	Surbiton-Basingstoke (35.8 miles) pass to pass
	Time (min-sec)
No 864 *Sir Martin Frobisher* (Lemaitre-fitted)	34-11
No 932 *Blundells* (original condition)	35-40
No 860 *Lord Hawke* (Kylchap-fitted)	35-54
No 860 *Lord Hawke* (original condition)	36-2
No 861 *Lord Anson* (original condition)	36-40
No 927 *Clifton* (original condition)	37-41
No 926 *Repton* (original condition)	41-10

With such talented rivals, the 'Lord Nelson' class may not appear to have held the pride of place befitting the largest Southern express locomotives, but there was no doubt in the minds of the locomotive running foremen who, when confronted with a choice, would put a 'Nelson' on the hardest and heaviest train. To illustrate the greater reserve of power in the 'Nelsons', the logs given of 'Schools' with 500ton trains can be compared with those of 'Nelsons' made by Cecil J Allen in the same period, 1937-39, taken over the 35.8-mile stretch between Surbiton and Basingstoke. The 60mph limit in the London area ended at Surbiton and thence sustained power output was required. Three 'Nelson' runs were with the 12 Pullman-car 'Bournemouth Belle', 500 tons, and that of No 861 with a 14-coach 'Crusader' special, 515 tons. 'Schools' Nos 926/27 were loaded as recorded above; No 932 was hauling 510 tons.

Writing in an article reviewing the performance of the 'Schools' class in a 1957 issue of *Trains Illustrated*, Cecil J. Allen was to single out No 932's performance with a 15-coach train of 510tons gross as 'the maximum achievement'. Over the 70 miles from Wimbledon-St Denys, hauling eight times its own weight, the 4-4-0 maintained an average of 61.5mph. To round off the comparisons, years later John Webber of Nursling clocked 31min 16sec with a rebuilt Merchant Navy on the 12-car 'Belle'. Engine No 35005 *Canadian Pacific* was hot-footing it with Driver E. Rabbetts of Bournemouth on the eve of his retirement.

Immediately before the outbreak of World War 2, 'Schools' were also responsible for some fine running between Waterloo and Salisbury. On the verge of retirement, Driver Silk of Nine Elms with No 931 *King's Wimbledon* on a 305 tons gross load ran from Waterloo to a signal stop at Grateley (72.8 miles) in 64min exactly. For 60.8 miles from Surbiton to Grateley the speed had averaged almost precisely 75mph. Also in 1939, in the opposite direction, Driver Rice with No 937 *Epsom* and a 12-coach load of 410 tons gross achieved a time of 55min 19sec for the 59.4 miles Salisbury-Woking at which point the train was brought to a stand by adverse signals. Reporting the run Cecil J. Allen commented, 'With an unchecked run, Waterloo would have been reached in 76¼min, or 8¾min less that the present (1956) schedule of the "Atlantic Coast Express". Such a feat would excite comment with a 95ton "Merchant Navy" Pacific; with a 67ton 4-4-0 it was beyond praise'.

Let that keen observer of locomotive performance, O. S. Nock, make the final and impartial comment on the heyday of 'Arthurs', 'Schools' and 'Nelsons'. 'The high morale of the Southern locomotive department,' he wrote,* 'was reflected not only in the fine tradition of enginemanship in the working of trains but in the smartness of turn-out of every passenger locomotive, at all depots from Ramsgate and Dover in the east to the smaller sheds in Devon and Cornwall, at a period when elsewhere in Britain standards of locomotive cleanliness were declining'.

Southern Steam, David & Charles, 1966.

Left: Urie 'Arthur' No E745 *Tintagel* leaves Waterloo with a Bournemouth train, c1929/30.
C. R. Gordon Stuart/Lens of Sutton

Above: Salisbury-based No 456 *Sir Galahad* comes past Esher with a down West of England express, mid-1930s. *Lens of Sutton*

Right: No 740 *Merlin* near Yeovil with the down 'Atlantic Coast Express' in the early 1930s; train almost completely made up of ex-LSWR stock.
F. R. Hebron/Rail Archive Stephenson

Below right: Salisbury's No 451 *Sir Lamorak* approaching Honiton Tunnel on the long 1 in 80 climb of Seaton bank with the down 'Atlantic Coast Express' in the 1930s. *F. J. Arthur*

Above: Nine Elms shed's No E777 *Sir Lamiel* passes Raynes Park with a Waterloo-Bournemouth train, c1930.
F. R. Hebron/Rail Archive Stephenson

Below: No 785 *Sir Mador de la Porte* at Bournemouth Central, c1936.   *T. G. Hepburn/Rail Archive Stephenson*

Above right: No 780 *Sir Persant* threads the New Forest near Lyndhurst Road with the down 'Bournemouth Belle', 6 October 1936.   *O. J. Morris/Lens of Sutton*

Right: Under the Kingston by-pass comes E788 *Sir Urre of the Mount* with an up express, c1929.   *Lens of Sutton*

Below right: Otterbourne cutting, south of Shawford: No 784 *Sir Nerovens* heads the 11.02am Bournemouth-Waterloo, 22 September 1936. At the rear of the train are through coaches for Newcastle, York and Bradford.
O. J. Morris/Lens of Sutton

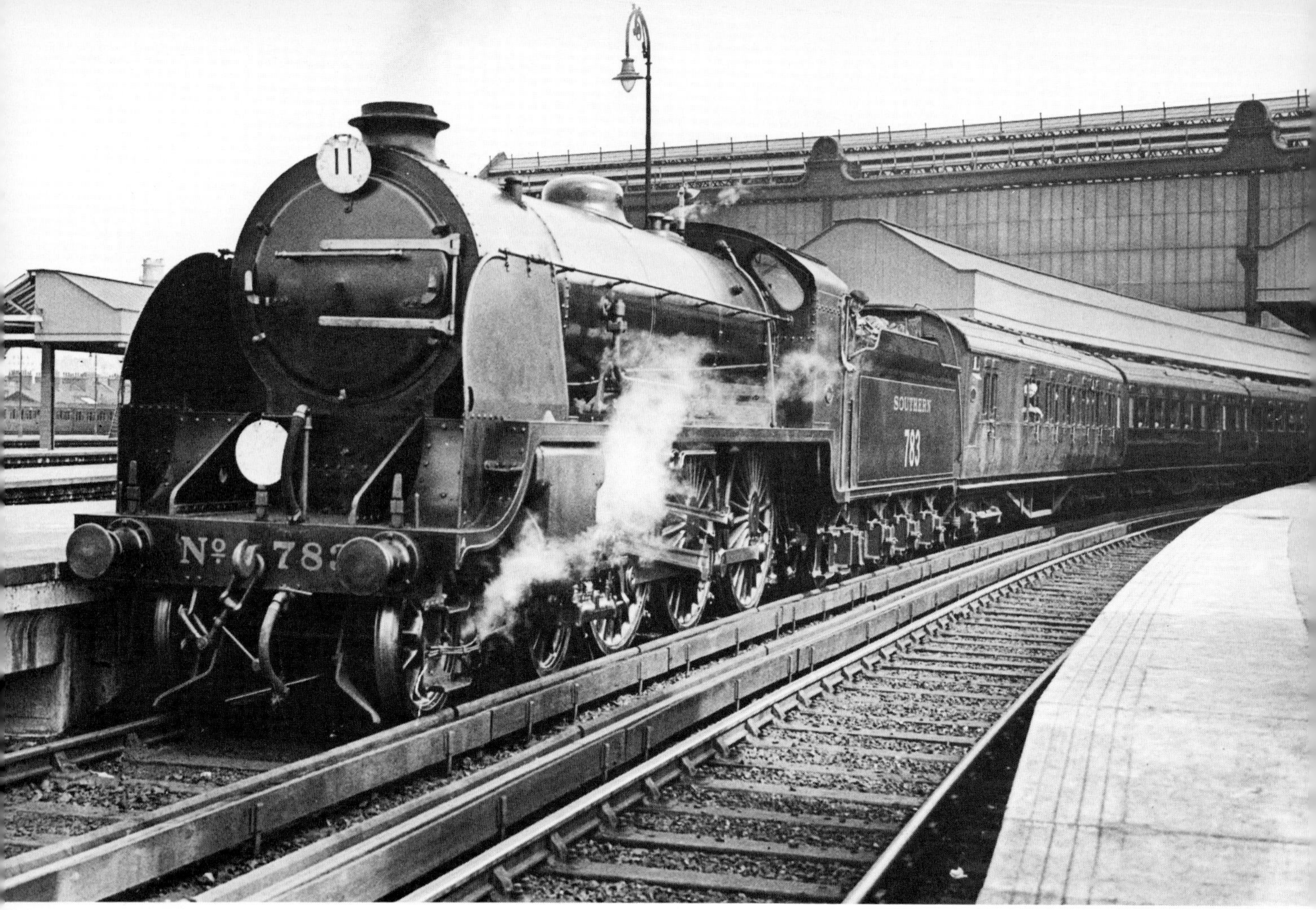
11
SOUTHERN
783
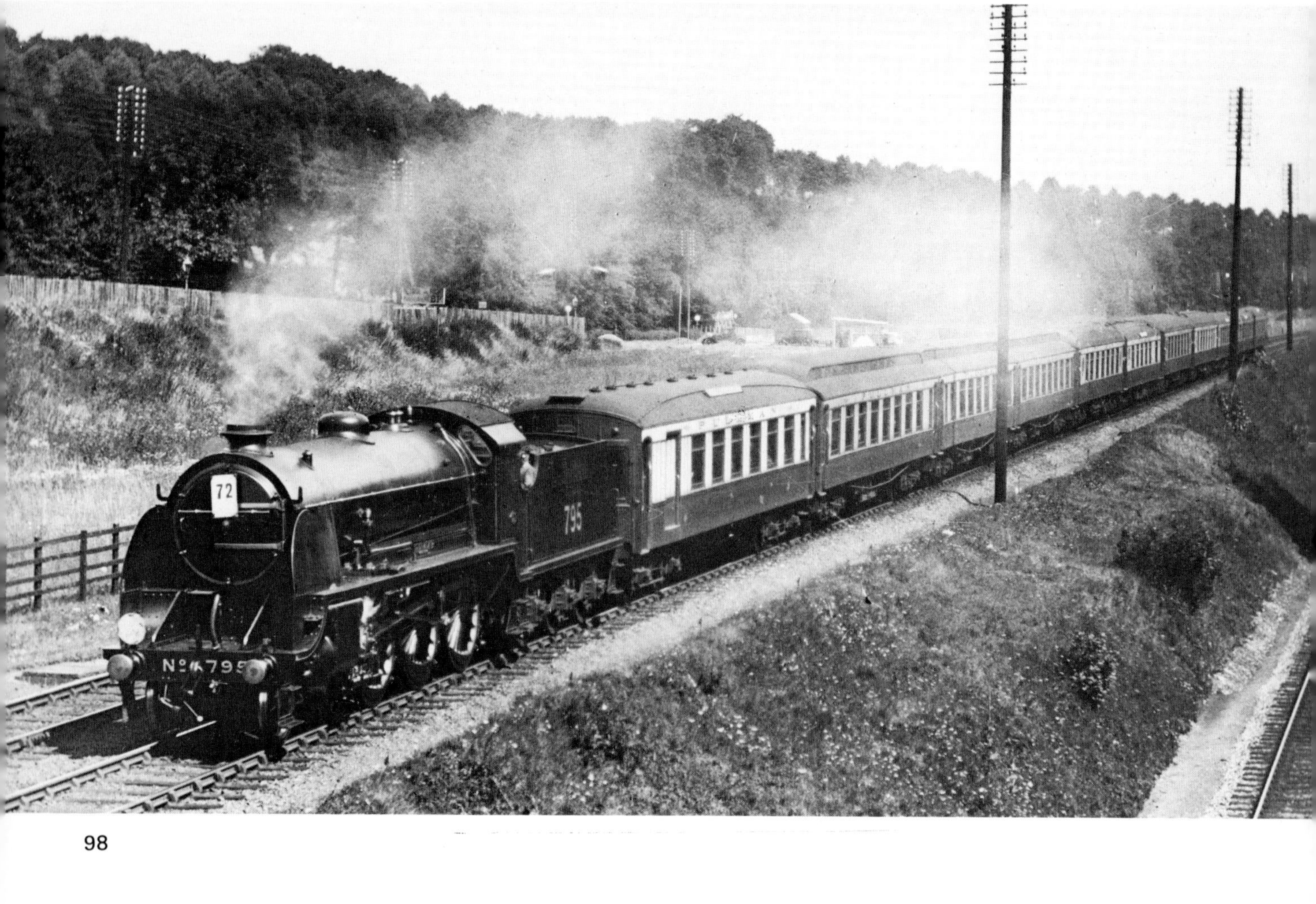
72
795

Above left: The 'Atlantic Coast Express' of 16 July 1937 leaves Waterloo behind No 783 *Sir Gillemere.* *John P. Wilson*

Left: Another premier train, the down 'Southern Belle', c1929. No E795 *Sir Dinadan,* near Horley. *Lens of Sutton*

Above: Pluckley: 'Arthur' No E769 *Sir Balan* speeds through with a down boat train, c1927. *Lens of Sutton*

Right: By now fitted with smoke deflectors, No E769 blackens Orpington as it approaches the station with the 11.10am Victoria–Dover Marine boat train, winter 1928/29.
F. R. Hebron/Rail Archive Stephenson

Above: A late 1930s view of No 805 *Sir Constantine* east of Shorncliffe with a London–Dover via Maidstone East boat train. *Rev A. C. Cawston*

Below: Dover Priory — No 800 *Sir Meleaus de Lile* drifts into the station with a Margate–Charing Cross train during the late 1930s. *Lens of Sutton*

Right: An interesting photograph: F. E. Mackay's study of *Lord Nelson* leaving Victoria, on Grosvenor bank with 10.45am Dover boat train. The occasion of C. J. Allen's footplate trip in the summer of 1927.

Below right: 'Arthur' No 763 *Sir Bors de Ganis* approaches St Mary Cray Junction with an up Ramsgate–Victoria express in the late 1930s. *Lens of Sutton*

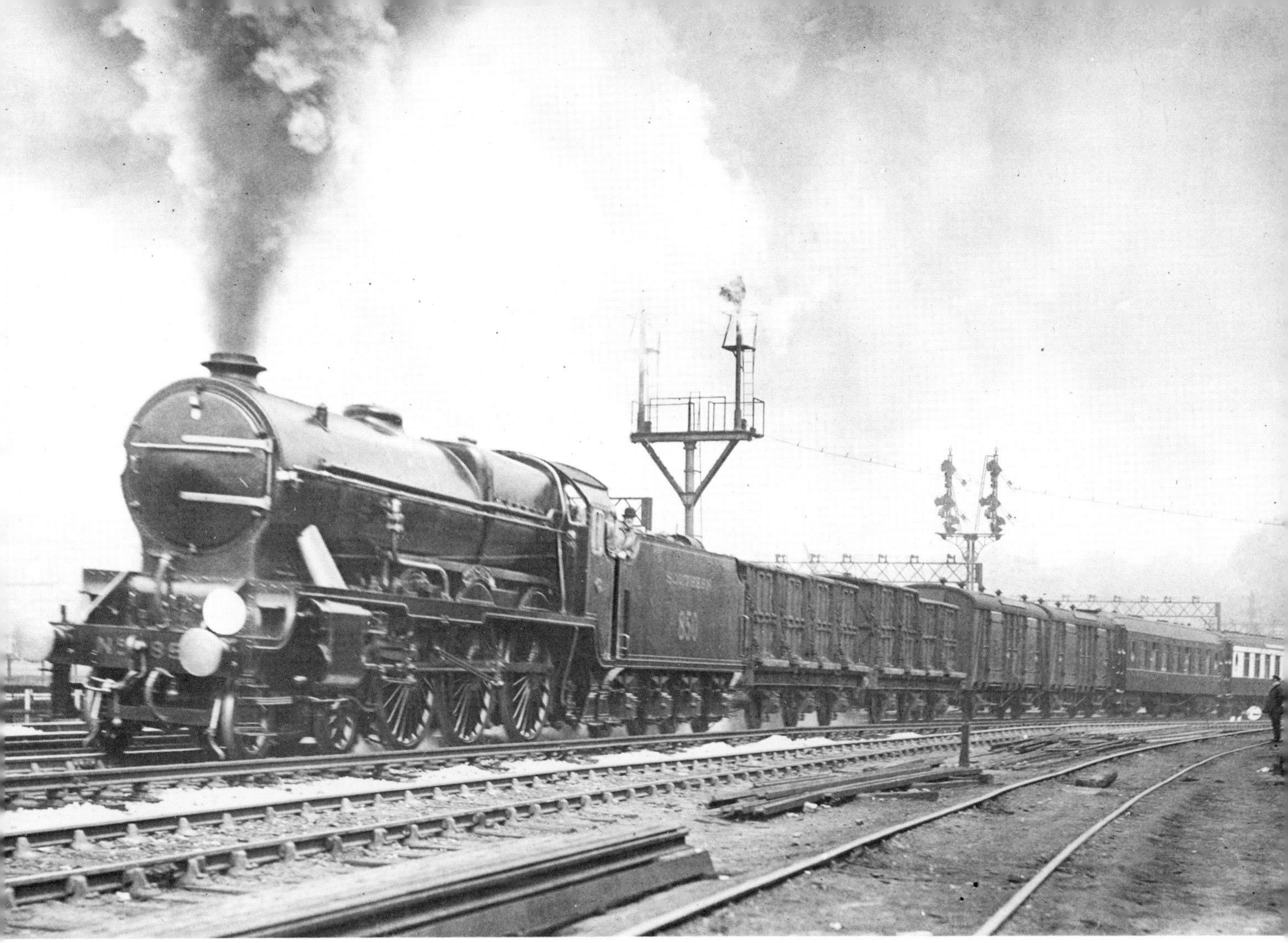
SOUTHERN
850

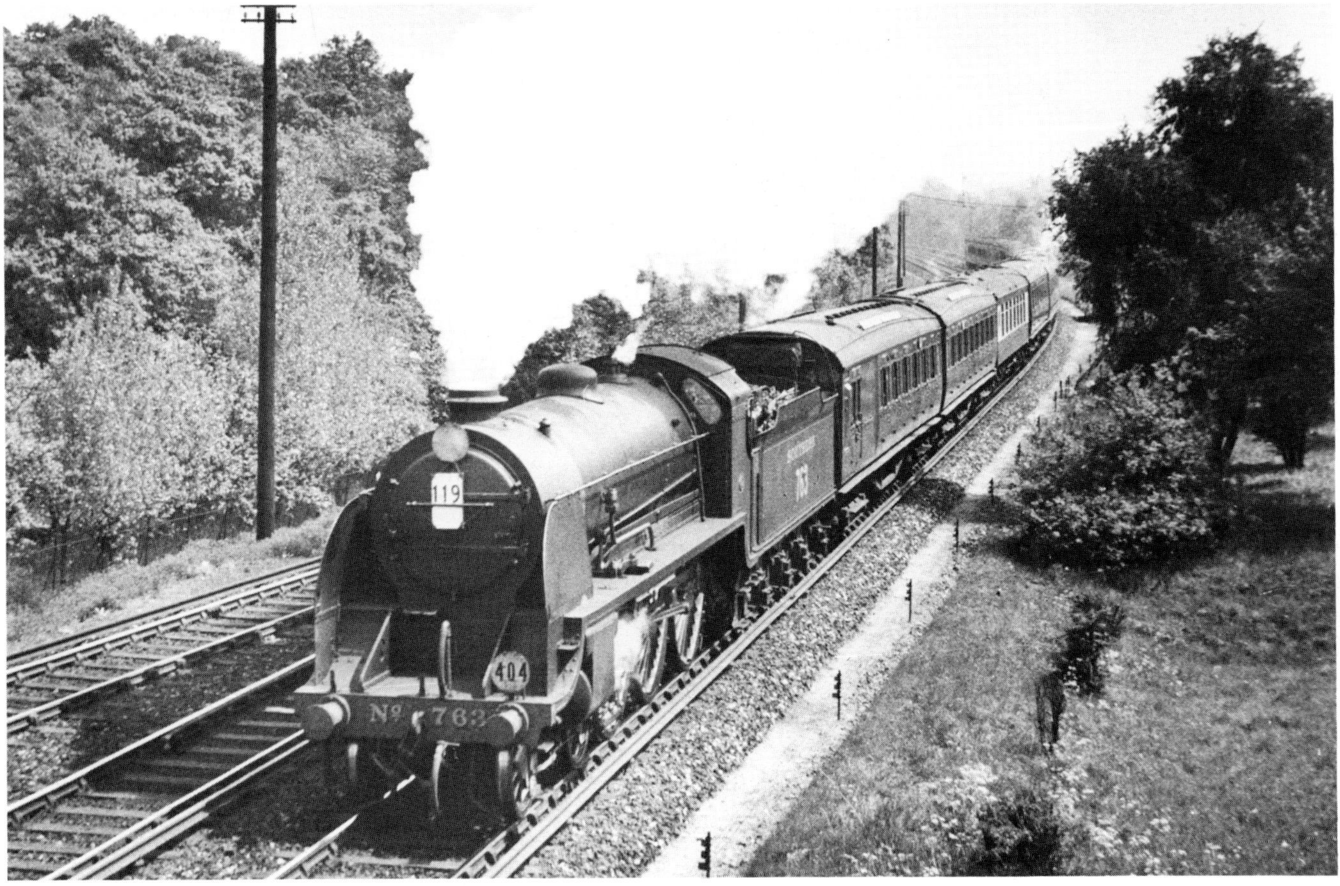
119
404
Nº 763

Above: No 857 *Lord Howe* passes Sydenham Hill with the down 'Golden Arrow', 11 September 1936.
A. W. Croughton/Lens of Sutton

Left: *Lord Nelson* in Thanet, leaving Birchington with a Kent Coast train, 1930s.
H. Gordon Tidey

Above right: No 861 *Lord Anson* passes Walton-on-Thames with the down 'Bournemouth Belle', 1938. *C. R. L. Coles*

Right: 'Schools' No E903 *Charterhouse* near Chelsfield with a down Folkestone express composed of Maunsell's 'Folkestone' corridor stock (with Pullman). Autumn 1930.
F. R. Hebron/Rail Archive Stephenson

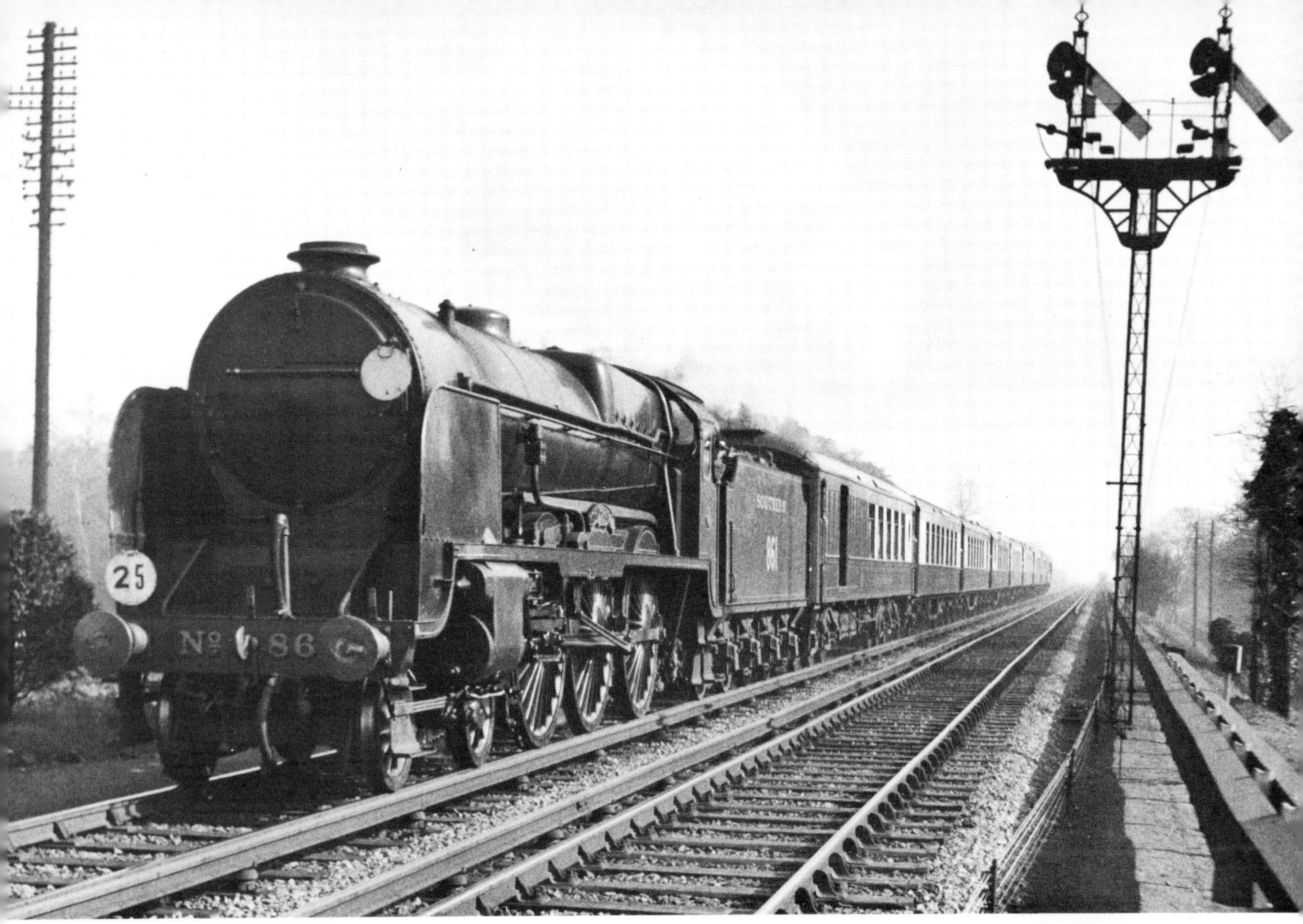
25

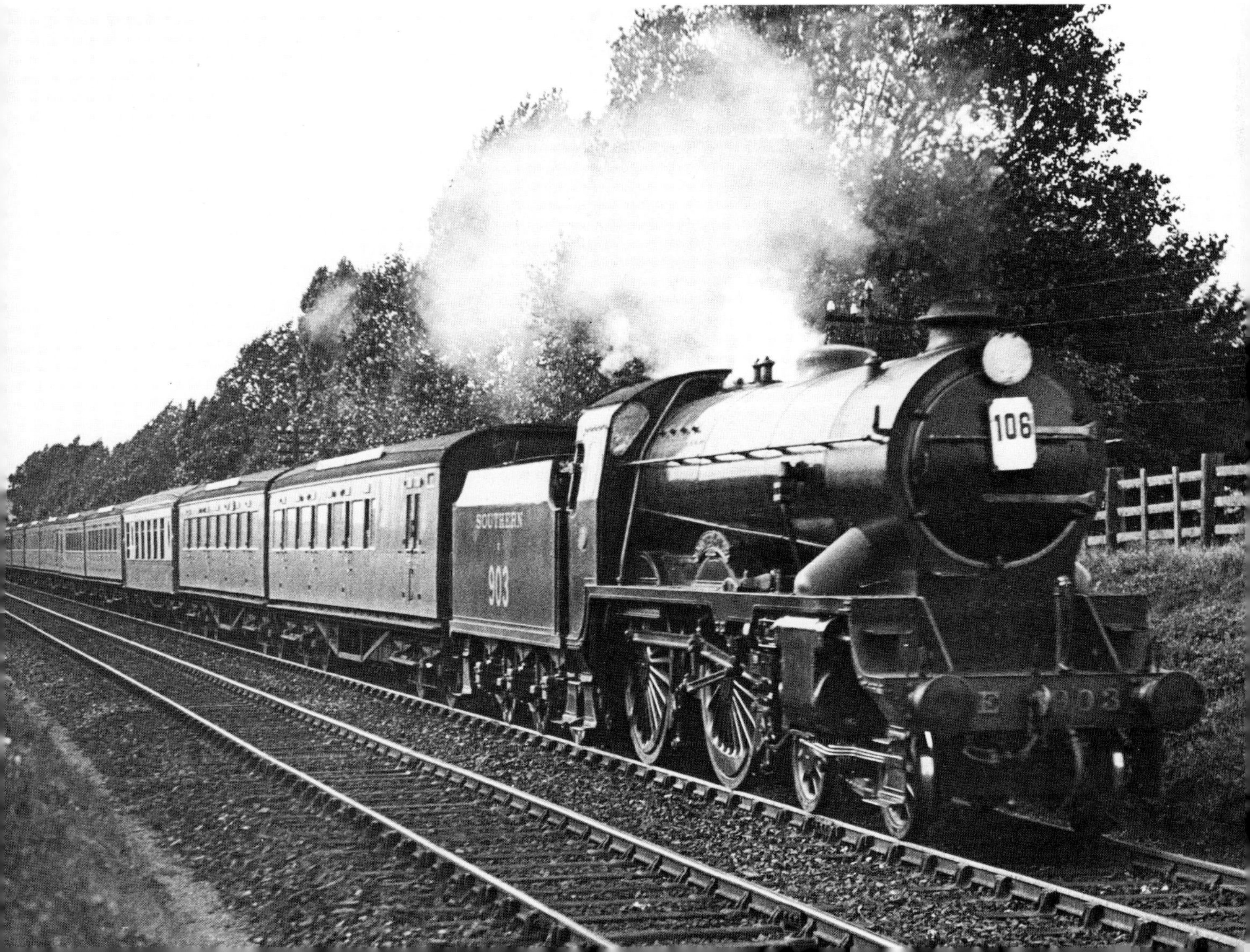
106
SOUTHERN
903

Above: No 915 *Brighton* sets out from Charing Cross with the 11.15am to Dover and Deal, 14 July 1937. A newish Maunsell corridor set (No 958) is behind the engine. *John P. Wilson*

Left: London Bridge: No 916 *Whitgift* calls with a down Hastings turn, mid-1930s. *Lens of Sutton*

Right: New cylinders and the ugly wide chimney are featured on No 937 *Epsom*, restarting from West St Leonards with an up Hastings express, 18 July 1939. *John P. Wilson*

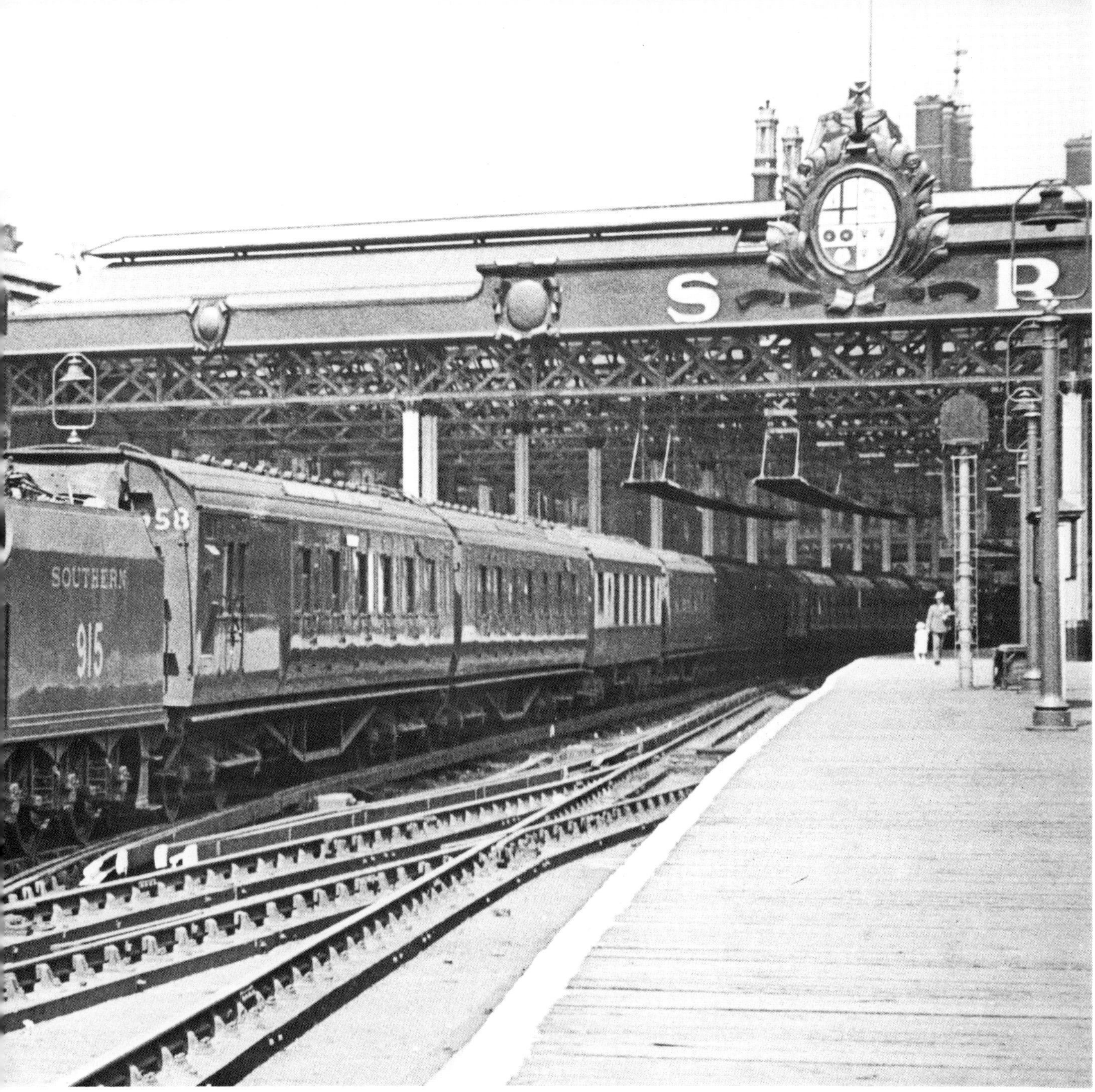
S
R
58
SOUTHERN
915

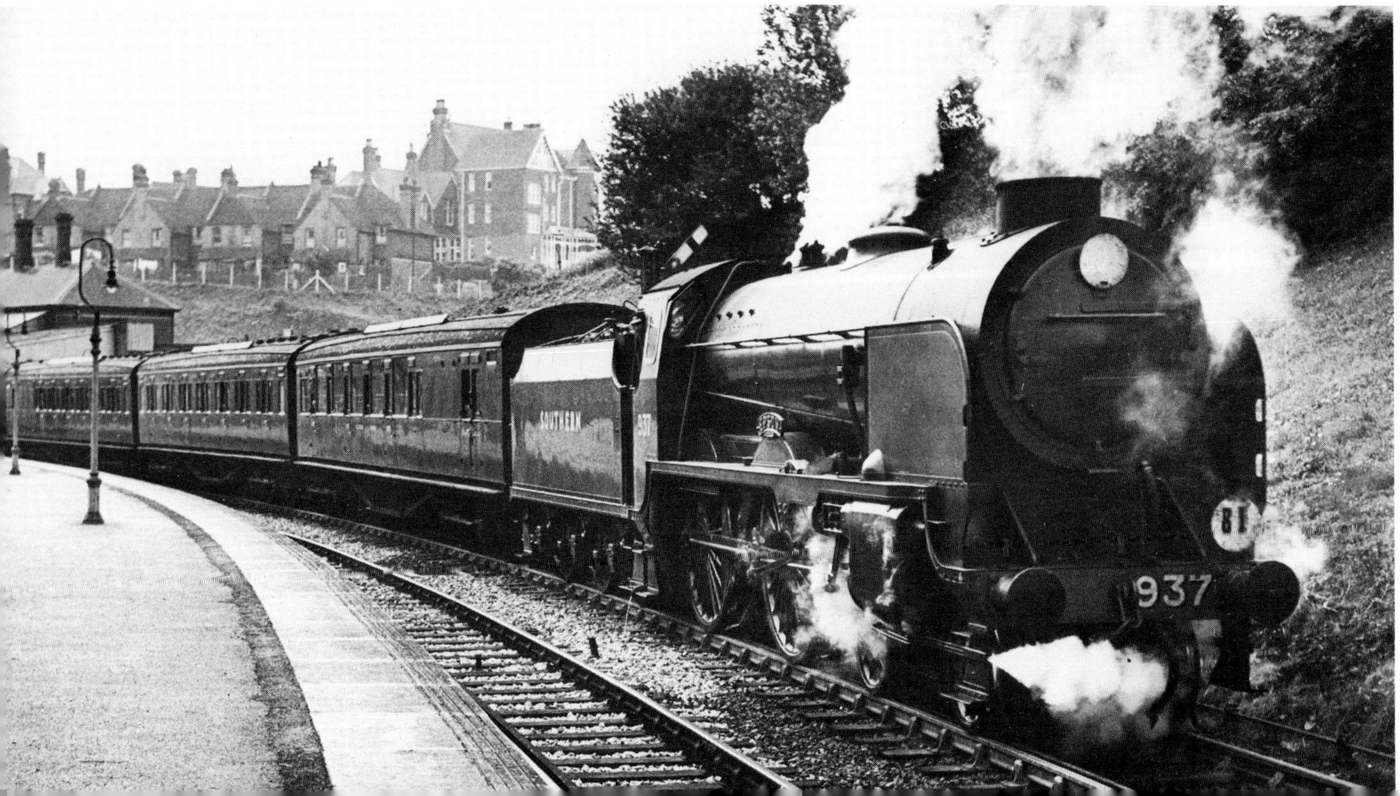
SOUTHERN
937

Above right: Brilliant malachite green livery is carried by No 929 *Malvern*, at Radipole Halt with a Bournemouth-Weymouth local, 1939. *Lens of Sutton*

Right: Lemaître-equipped No 931 *King's Wimbledon* restarts from Winchester City with a Waterloo-Bournemouth train, 20 July 1939. *John P. Wilson*

Below: Waterloo: No 927 *Clifton* at the head of a Bournemouth express in 1938. 'M7' 0-4-4T No 40 alongside. *O. J. Morris/Lens of Sutton*

13
The War and After

In the early summer of 1940 the Southern Railway found itself well and truly in the front line when the Nazis overran Belgium and France, and most of the territory became within a few minutes flying time of enemy airfields. Regular services were maintained everywhere, nevertheless, though on a reduced scale. Gone were the boat trains, excursion trains, Pullmans and most dining cars. For a time, there were for once some 'Arthurs', 'Schools' and 'Nelsons' out of use. Cleaning and maintenance declined as the running sheds were preoccupied with air raid precautions. Servicing engines in the blackout had to be carried on without lights, though hot ashes had to be dropped and firehole doors opened. Staff had to carry gas masks and steel helmets; during the invasion scare drivers asked to be provided with rifles on the footplate. Between July 1940 and August 1943 there were 58 daylight attacks on SR trains from the air, the majority in Kent. Only a few caused casualties; early on, Ramsgate driver Goldsack was killed by machine-gun bullets, and the CME promptly sought ways of protecting the enginemen.

A 'Schools' class was taken in to Ashford Works and the cab was lined inside with a layer of asphalt as some protection against bullets, but it made the cab extremely cramped and gave no protection from attacks from behind, so the idea was dropped. The trail of steam from the chimney of a moving engine enabled the pilot of an aircraft to spot a potential target, so for the second experiment 'Arthur' No 783 was fitted with three chimneys and three blastpipes in order to see whether the escaping steam would thereby be more quickly dispersed, instead of forming one long trail. It was not particularly effective in doing so; what it did do, was to bring down quantities of soot from hitherto undisturbed areas of tunnel roofs, effectively blacking out the front cab windows and much else. By that time, mid-1941, the menace had been reduced: enemy raiders did not have much chance of looking for moving targets, and preferred to drop their bombs on coastal towns and retreat quickly across the Channel. In one such attack on Deal, bombs fell on the station where a train was standing, killing Driver Cotton of Ramsgate, one of the expert 'Schools' class drivers.

In all, 189 Southern locomotives were damaged by enemy action, but only one, 'Paddleboat' No 458, was too badly crippled to be worth repair. No 458 was hit by a bomb at Nine Elms depot during the London blitz of 1940-41, as also was a 'Nelson', No 855, and 'Schools' No 934 was hit when standing on Cannon Street bridge. Few running sheds escaped air-raid damage: the most seriously hit were Bricklayers Arms, Stewarts Lane, New Cross Gate, Nine Elms and Fratton. Five shedmasters received the British Empire Medal.

In 1942, 10 Urie 'Arthurs' were able to be spared to help the North Eastern Area of the LNER, Nos 739, 740/2/4/7/8/9, 750/1/4. They returned to the Southern in 1943 when military traffic was building up in preparation for Overlord, the allied invasion of Europe.

With the return of peacetime the 'Arthurs', 'Schools' and 'Nelsons' found themselves relegated to the 'second division'. The Bulleid Pacifics had by then appeared on the scene. Instead of the narrow fireboxes of the Maunsell engines, which demanded considerable technique in firing, the Pacifics had large, square fireboxes; they were easy to fire and would steam liberally, almost regardless of the skill of the fireman and the quality of the coal. By then, the National Coal Board controlled the distribution of fuel, and the railways could no longer buy from collieries of their choice. The customer was not offered a menu: he had to eat what he was given, and it was usually hash. The best locomotive coals went elsewhere, some to export markets.

In 1946 the Government sponsored a scheme to convert a proportion of the Group companies' locomotives to oil-firing. On the Southern it was decided to turn over to oil in the Eastleigh and Exmouth Junction districts, convenient for sea-borne supplies and in substitution for Welsh coals in short supply, which those districts normally used. Thus it came about that a variety of locomotive classes operating in those districts had to be converted to oil, ranging from Urie 'Arthurs' to 'T9s'. 'Arthurs' Nos 740/5/8/9 and 752 belonging to Eastleigh were converted, and performed very well with a weir-type burner fixed at the front of the firebox. Two 'West Country' Pacifics so converted did not steam well with that arrangement, and trials with a burner in the centre of the grate were in hand when the Government ran into difficulties over oil supplies and the scheme collapsed. The first 'Arthur' converted, No 740, worked the 11.30am Waterloo-Bournemouth on 9 April 1947. Oil storage tanks, together with pumps and steam heating equipment to make the crude oil fluid for delivery to the locomotive tender tanks, were installed at Eastleigh and Fratton, and preparatory work had been put in hand at Exmouth Junction, Barnstaple, Plymouth and Wadebridge. But all in vain: by the autumn of 1948 all the Urie 'Arthurs' had been restored to coal-firing.

In the last year before nationalisation, 1947, the allocation of the 'Arthurs', 'Schools' and 'Nelsons' was approximately as follows:

'King Arthurs'
736-755: Nine Elms 4, Bournemouth 2, Eastleigh 9, Salisbury 3 and Exmouth Junction 2.
448-457: Salisbury.
763-792: Stewarts Lane 8, Nine Elms 9, Dover 5, Bournemouth 4 and Eastleigh 4.

793-806: Stewarts Lane 5, Ashford 6, Bricklayers Arms 2 and Hither Green 1.

'Schools'
Nearly all based on the Eastern Section at Stewarts Lane, Bricklayers Arms, Ramsgate, Dover and St Leonards. Locomotives Nos 928-30 were based at Brighton for working to Salisbury on the Brighton-Cardiff and Brighton-Plymouth through trains.

'Lord Nelsons'
All based on the Western Section at Nine Elms 5, Eastleigh 8 and Bournemouth 3.

On the Southern, the recovery from expanded wartime passenger schedules was probably quicker than on other Regions of the newly nationalised British Railways. That was particularly true of the Eastern section where increased residential traffic to and from London and later the introduction of heavier BR standard rolling stock (except of course on the Hastings line) meant that hard work was required. Despite the allocation of Bulleid Pacifics to the principal workings, the 'Arthurs' and 'Schools' continued to appear on SER and LCDR main line trains, often working in the same link as Bulleid Pacifics. On the Hastings line the 'Schools' class remained unchallenged until their replacement by diesel-electric multiple-units from 1957.

On summer Saturdays in particular the 'Arthurs' were to be seen at the head of a number of Kent Coast holiday workings, as well as boat trains to and from Dover and Folkestone. Writing in the September 1957 *Railway World*, the late Norman Harvey, an often percipient observer of Southern Region steam locomotives, provided an interesting example of an 'Arthur' at work on a secondary train, but one nonetheless producing some good running:

'One Saturday afternoon two or three summers ago I was standing on the up platform at Folkestone Central watching the heavy holiday traffic. A "King Arthur" class engine drew in on the 3.48pm from Deal, No 30769 *Sir Balan*, heading a train that looked rather out-of-place on the former South Eastern and Chatham Railway as it was composed entirely of LSWR bogie corridor main line stock. With *Sir Balan* at its head it reminded me forcibly of the Salisbury to Exeter expresses of 20 years previously. Although the 3.48pm was booked non-stop from Folkestone Central to Waterloo in the ample time of 89min, it was running about eight minutes late owing to the inevitable delays consequent upon the heavy summer traffic. The engine had already worked down from Victoria to Ramsgate via Chatham, and as these summertime "rounders" (as they are called by the enginemen) leave little time for disposal duties I wasn't sure how 30769 would fare. I decided to sample her work, however, and obtained an example of "King Arthur" performance at its finest, fully comparable with some of their best achievements on the Exeter road.

'The start from Folkestone Central in the Ashford direction is by no means an easy one. For nearly six miles to Westenhanger the line rises at an inclination which varies from 1 in 230 to 1 in 330, and it was symptomatic of the expert handling of 30769 that the summit was breasted in just under nine minutes from the start for 5¾ miles. Once over the top (at Westenhanger) the ensuing 29.4 miles of mainly downhill track to Tonbridge were run in 25min 5sec at an average of 66-67mph. There was obviously no case here of the dirty fire which I had feared, and the 4-6-0 ran freely up to a speed of nearly 80mph.

'So far as I could judge from the front of the train, steam was shut off after passing Marden and the engine allowed to coast into Tonbridge; by this point most of the late time had been regained, and the "Never-ready junction" let us though without even a sight of an adverse distant, only one minute behind time. Once round the sharp curve at the London end of the station No 30769 was opened out again and breasted well the four-mile pull up at 1 in 122 to the mouth of Sevenoaks Tunnel. Through the tunnel the gradient eases to 1 in 143 up, but often this lessening of the incline is of no help to enginemen owing to the dampness of rails. The minimum speed of 39mph past Weald Intermediate was quite creditable and a recovery to 42mph by the tunnel mouth showed that no slipping took place.

'The usually restrained running followed through Sevenoaks station, where the train was by now ahead of time, and a brisk recovery with a maximum of 60mph at the foot of the 1 in 160 downgrade to Dunton Green gave impetus for the pull up to Knockholt, mostly at 1 in 143. Speed didn't fall below 39mph in Polhill Tunnel, and 30769 was getting into her stride again through Orpington when the first adverse signals of the journey were sighted. Even so, 65mph was attained coming down to Grove Park before steam was shut off to observe the 60mph speed restriction that prevails in from Hither Green, and by London Bridge we were 4½min early. This was too good to last and a dead stand for signals ensued at Metropolitan Junction, where we had to await the clearing of a platform at Waterloo. Despite this setback 30769 pulled in 3½min early, and I estimate that she had come up from Folkestone Central in 75min net, or within the 80min allowance to London of the best non-stop expresses.

'Here I was able to secure the driver's name. He was Joe Brewer of the Top Link at Stewarts Lane. It transpired that Driver Brewer was an old LSWR man and it was fitting that my best run on a "King Arthur" should have come from a man trained in the exacting Drummond tradition'.

Norman Harvey contributed an interesting article to the June 1961 *Railway World* as a tribute to the 'Schools', having heard that the first members of the class were being cut up at Ashford. His tribute included some interesting and relevant details of the operation of the 'Schools' on the Eastern section in the postwar days, apart from the customary presentation of train running data.

Speaking of his prewar runs with 'Schools' to Hastings, Mr Harvey suggested that they had an apparent margin of about 20% in hand on the most exacting schedules then in force. He went on to comment:

'Years later, when I had the engines under close review in their daily workings from Bricklayers Arms Depot, I came to realise that there was less in hand perhaps than I had thought. Nearly all the work from that shed was done on Grade Two Welsh coal; and when the calorific value of supplies fell off their steaming qualities diminished. They were also sensitive to regular washing out — most Southern engines, to my LMS trained mind, seemed more sensitive here, although it had to be remembered that they were in the main older than the top link locomotives north of the Thames. But on the Eastern section they were worked exceedingly hard; the quality of daily work achieved over the difficult

Hastings line was borne out by the high standard of punctuality sustained for several years by the keen staff of St Leonards Depot.'

There then followed the opinion, 'most drivers seemed agreed that you could notch up a "Schools" to a very short cut-off indeed, and they would run best at speed with a mere cushion of steam in their cylinders'.

Norman Harvey went on to comment that the standard of running with 'Schools' on the SER main lines was higher than on the Chatham route:

'However, I would like to give an example of Schools performance over this route that is much more in line with their achievements elsewhere, the more so in that I had no chance to speak to the enginemen before we left London Bridge. The train was the 4.45pm from Cannon Street, worked by the Top Link at Stewarts Lane, and retimed to leave London Bridge (Platform 1) at 4.46pm, the engine and stock having come through from Ludgate Hill. All these business trains from the City to the Ramsgate line are booked slow road to Chislehurst; and nothing can be attempted until the Chatham route has been gained at St Mary Cray Junction. Thus, No 30916 was nearly 6min down at Chislehurst; it proved possible to recover three minutes of this by the time the first stop had been reached at Faversham (in 61min 53sec for 49.0 miles). A good steady run was given, with sectional times exactly kept from Swanley to Sole Street, and maximum (74mph) and minimum (48mph) speeds not being at all abnormal. Indeed, only 67mph at Cuxton Road might be regarded as restrained; and the maximum below Sittingbourne was not exceptional. But more than enough was done to better the schedule, and the station-to-station allowances below Faversham gave enough margin in hand to ensure a punctual arrival at the principal resorts. The load was a much more substantial one than I encountered before the war.'

The timings given by Mr Harvey were:
No 30916 Whitgift *with 10 coaches, 340 tons full*

	Mileage	Time (min-sec)
London Bridge-Chislehurst	9.4	16 40 start to pass
Chislehurst-Sole Street	14.5	16 10 pass to pass
Sole Street-Chatham	7.4	9 10 pass to pass
Chatham-Faversham	17.7	19 53 pass to stop
Unchecked throughout		

The best performance recorded by Norman Harvey with a 'Schools' on the Chatham route was with No 30922 *Marlborough* in the hands of Sam Gingell and loaded to 275 tons gross. The speeds of 42mph at Sole Street and 84mph through Farningham Road were reckoned to be 'more in line with the finest achievements on SE metals'.

What those achievements might be may be demonstrated by three runs from the 1950s, published in contemporary railway journals. In the down direction, Cecil J. Allen gave details of a trip on the 4.15pm 'Man of Kent' from Waterloo-Folkestone with No 30919 *Harrow* on 11 coaches of BR standard stock, 395 tons full. Paddock Wood, 34.1 miles from the Waterloo restart, was passed 3½min early in 38min 7sec. Then there was a check to 47mph east of Staplehurst but Folkestone was reached in 73¾min against a booking of 76min, or 71¼mins net. The 11.7 miles from New Cross to Knockholt were covered in 13¾min, at an average of

50.7mph over gradients including stretches of 1 in 120/142. In his valedictory 'Schools' article Norman Harvey featured a good effort on the 3.25pm Margate-Charing Cross, non-stop Ashford-Waterloo, with No 30933 *Kings' Canterbury* on 361 tons tare. Leaving Ashford on time, the train was delayed by signals to Tonbridge where it was eight minutes down. Time recovery began at once, with minima of 37mph at Weald Intermediate and, better, 50mph at Knockholt. By Hither Green the lateness had been reduced to four minutes, but signal checks affected the final section although the net time overall was no more than 62min for 55.4 miles. In 1960 Cecil J. Allen published a run when No 30914 *Eastbourne* achieved a similar 62min net time on a 395ton gross load. Speeds of up to 82mph were reached between Ashford and Tonbridge, but then came a signal stop at the latter. As a result, the speed before Sevenoaks Tunnel was no greater than 34mph, but the maximum at Knockholt was 50mph. A Ramsgate crew were in charge.

It was on the Hastings line trains that the 'Schools' probably sustained their first postwar performances until diesel multiple-units took over almost completely in June 1958.

Generally, the more spectacular exploits of the 'Schools' on the Western section have gained undue attention at the expense of consistent, hard slogging for over 25 years between London and Hastings. This is a little surprising as the class was designed to suit that route with its limited loading gauge and sharp and frequent curvature. Fortunately, Mr F. S. Bond, a regular traveller between London and Tunbridge Wells between 1949-58, kindly made available to the editor of *Railway World* material from the 351 runs he recorded with one of the hardest Hastings line workings, the 5.06pm Cannon Street to Hastings. This sheer volume of logs is invaluable in painting a picture of everyday working of great competence, highlighting the exceptional and illustrating the considerable skill of Southern footplatemen.

In the years preceding dieselisation the 5.06 was worked by a St Leonards 'Schools'. Until 1951/52, St Leonards crews were in charge during the winter months and Bricklayers Arms men in the summer. Thereafter men from 'The Brick' worked it throughout the year. Taking mid-1955, for example, the 'Schools' allocation relevant to the Hastings line was as follows: St Leonards, 30900-10/20; and Bricklayers Arms, 30924-39. Of these, 30900/1/7/9/20/4/9-31/3/4/7-9 had Lemaître blastpipes and wide chimneys. Although both St Leonards and Bricklayers Arms had duties involving two round trips to Hastings in a day for their 'Schools', the two locomotives from St Leonards covering the Cannon Street commuter trains worked out and back only.

As to the formation of the 5.06, before 1939 the train included a Pullman car and was booked to reach Tunbridge Wells Central (33.3 miles) in 45min, thence non-stop to Crowhurst. From 1945 until June 1957 it consisted of 10 corridor coaches and a Pullman buffet car, taring 358-361 tons. The train was always packed — with people sitting on camp stools or standing in the corridors — and, postwar, the time to Tunbridge Wells had been lengthened by 2½min. The new timetable introduced following the Cannon Street signalbox fire of April 1957 resulted in the 5.06 (now 5.05) contracting to eight vehicles of 262 tons tare, including two of the uncomfortable SECR non-corridor coaches. This period also saw substitutions by 'U1' 2-6-0s on at least three occasions in September 1957, one of the class managing to reach Tunbridge Wells three minutes early on the new schedule in 46min from Cannon Street.

The scheduled timings of the 5.06, and other business trains on the Hastings line, do not appear very demanding until one gives second thought to the gradients on the route and takes note of the service speed restrictions. Out of Cannon Street there is a succession of curves, junctions and speed restrictions to New Cross. The climb to Knockholt summit involved hard work for steam locomotives made more difficult by pathing problems at peak times, the runs with the 5.06 showing that the penalty for brisk running was crippling checks on the worst parts of the ascent. Then, there is the second summit at Sevenoaks Tunnel, the six-mile descent from which gives up trains starting from Tonbridge a hard time. Onwards to Tunbridge Wells the sting is in the tail as, having threaded Tonbridge at 20mph, Hastings line trains face a severe climb following the sharp curve away from the main line including an immediate half-mile at 1 in 53/47. This section involves the train gaining 235 vertical feet in four miles, not unlike the ascent to Peak Forest from Millers Dale on the former Derby to Manchester main line. It is an interesting comment on the excellence of the 'Schools' design that a four-coupled locomotive could be trusted to perform consistently on a route with these obstacles.

Taking Mr Bond's carefully detailed logs, there were two particularly fine performances. In July 1950, No 30900, with Driver Bond at the regulator, covered the 10.4 miles from New Cross to Chelsfield in only 11min 45sec — with a minimum of 46mph at Elmstead Woods and 60 through Orpington. Despite further checks the net time was, in Mr Bond's experience, the 'blue riband' for the 5.06 of $42\frac{3}{4}$min. In October 1956 No 30907 made an excellent run, the climb to Knockholt being taken with a minimum of $50\frac{1}{2}$mph and no more than 2min 59sec spent between Orpington and Knockholt station. There were checks before and after Sevenoaks. A quite remarkable climb by No 30907 away from Tonbridge saw a steady increase of speed up the bank and a record time of 8min 48sec between Tonbridge and Tunbridge Wells. The overall time was 46min 48sec, net time $43\frac{1}{2}$min. Just to show how good these performances were the Hastings diesel unit working the 6.4pm ex-Cannon Street was booked in 45min.

With limited space at hand it is only possible to highlight other interesting runs and to suggest that an aggregate of all the best station to station times recorded by Mr Bond on the 5.06 gives an 'ideal' time of about $39\frac{1}{2}$min to Tunbridge Wells. The records also point to an overall net time on a typical run of between $43\frac{1}{2}$-$44\frac{3}{4}$min. What is of particular interest is that with 12 best runs the honours were shared evenly between the Lemaître and single blastpipe equipped 'Schools'. The recovery from checks on the heavily graded sections in the suburbs showed just how free steaming the 'Schools' could be. A good example of this was noted with No 30930 which was checked to 5mph after Hither Green, passed Elmstead Woods at 39mph and cleared Knockholt summit at 47mph. A maximum of 75-80mph past Hildenborough was not unusual.

In the up direction, the climb from Tonbridge was made more difficult by the sharply curved stretch away from the junction with the Redhill line. Even so, Mr Bond's best runs with 'Schools' show a remarkable uniformity of performance with 37-41mph attained after Tonbridge by trains not calling there and 31-35mph sustained up to the summit at the north end of Sevenoaks tunnel — taking a typical 11-coach 350/360ton train. The lighter off-peak Hastings trains of around 260/290 tons tare which stopped at Tonbridge could be expected to sustain minima of 41-43mph on the climb up to and through Sevenoaks Tunnel. One double-headed run saw the ascent taken at a steady 52mph in the course of recovering 10 minutes between Tonbridge and Waterloo!

This, then, is further evidence of the fine work of these 4-4-0s which, it should be remembered, weighed only 67 tons of which only 42 tons were available for adhesion. In later days they may have disgraced themselves on the Uckfield line by stalling on the climb out of Lewes but, in Mr Bond's experience, even in conditions of frost and snow, they never failed on this score during his 350 runs with the 5.06 from Cannon Street, despite having a trailing load, tender and train, of 420tons. The load was tons gross.

The difficulties of the Hastings line did not cease at Tunbridge Wells, and Norman Harvey was to give some interesting details of the working of Lemaître multiple-jet blastpipe equipped No 30934 St Lawrence on the 1.2pm Cannon Street-Hastings on an October Saturday in 1955. The driver was Harry Cummins of Bricklayers Arms.

'From Tunbridge Wells, the 1.2pm ran fast to Crowhurst, through the glorious scenery of the Sussex Weald. On starting No 30934 had full regulator and 60% cut-off, notching back to 30% as soon as the train was under way. At Frant the regulator was on the first valve, with cut-off unchanged to Battle. The switchback road to Wadhurst was taken in style with a maximum of 76mph. No 30934 passed Frant in 5min 55sec; Wadhurst in 9min 10sec. Stonegate was passed in 14min 10sec; Etchingham in 17min 10sec; Robertsbridge in 19min 5sec; Mountfield in 21min 56sec and Battle in 24min 49sec. Cummins pulled up in Crowhurst station in 27min 45sec from Tunbridge Wells Central, as against 32min booked.

'The maximum speed on the long sweep below Stonegate was 75mph and the final stretch of 1 in 100 up to Battle breasted at a minimum of 56mph. For this fine work the regulator had been advanced to two-thirds open. The engine was steaming perfectly all the way down, and the experience of Fireman Hewitt stood us in good stead.' The details of locomotive working were supplied by a Mr R. E. Saberton who was riding on the footplate on this occasion.

Twenty-five years after their displacement from the Hastings line, it is good to recall just what was expected of the locomotives and crews, day in and day out, on one of the most taxing assignments in the London area, certainly as regards steam-operated commuter services.

In 1947, the supply of new 'spamcan' Pacifics was in full spate as Mr Bulleid continued to produce them in what seemed an unending stream. Soon there would be enough for every main line depot, and thereby reducing the Maunsell engines to more menial tasks. In that last year of Southern I was installed as Running Shed Superintendent at Eastleigh. My colleagues were grumbling about the extra work the Pacifics were causing, and it was only a matter of time before some of them would be allocated to Eastleigh depot. Then I had an idea. Eastleigh had half the 'Nelson' class already, the other eight being divided between Nine Elms, five, and Bournemouth, three. Why not have them all?

There were obvious advantages in having the whole class at one depot and the suggestion was acted upon. Eastleigh engines worked a few Waterloo-Bournemouth trains and their major task lay with traffic in and out of Southampton Docks, particularly in the days of the big ocean liners. The *Queen Mary* and the *Queen Elizabeth* could each demand up to eight boat trains and other passenger ships added their quota, almost daily. The Union Castle line sailed for South Africa every Thursday at 4.0pm; there was the French ss *Ile de France* and the ss *United States*.

So it came about that from 1948 until their demise the 'Nelsons' became identified with Eastleigh motive power depot. Mechanically, they were free from any weak points, but to keep them steaming well the shift foremen made it a rigid rule to put them in for a boiler wash every 10 working days. Not so much for de-scaling — less frequently needed after the adoption of briqette water treatment — as for cleaning tubes, especially superheater tubes, tubeplates, brick arches and firebars. Leaking fireboxes and tube ends, which were troublesome in their early days, were infrequent and the leading boilersmith, a most conscientious man, kept an eye on the boilerwashers in case they should try to hurry the cooling-down of a 'Nelson' boiler with cold water.

Eastleigh was supplied with Welsh coal, for other than shunting engines; the wagon labels bore the names of collieries such as Aberaman, Bedwas, Bargoed and the unpronounceable Penrhiwceiber. The coal was rated as grade 2 but the 'Nelsons' made steam with it, without too much ash or clinker. Unlike the more volatile Midlands and Yorkshire coals it did not readily make much smoke, a help to the enginemen who had to move in and out of the Ocean Terminal and other sheds in Southampton Docks where smoke and blowing-off, despite being kept waiting, were obviously unwanted. Drivers of the new 'West Country' class not fitted with dampers soon had complaints to answer.

The 'Nelsons' were known to keep clean front ends; that is to say, when cylinders and steam chests were opened up for examination after 36,000 miles there was seldom much carbon deposit restricting the ports and passages, and causing piston and valve rings to become solid in their grooves. Some other types, notably 'S15s' and 'N' class, were quite the opposite and sometimes the piston valves were found immovable beyond the working stroke, so having to be driven out, first with a lead hammer and, failing that, a jack if there was a convenient jacking point. A good fitter was one who could assemble or dismantle without marking the parts but seized valves were the very devil. One could end up with a broken valve liner or worse. Carbonisation was the result of particles of ash drawn down the blastpipe when an engine was drifting with closed regulator. Some engines of the same class had more carbon than others. The reason for relative freedom from carbon in the case of the 'Nelsons' may have been due to the eight beats plus multiple-jet blastpipe. Anyway, the foreman fitter could take comfort from the fact that the 36,000 miles interval examination of the front end of a 'Nelson' was unlikely to encounter any snags, and if necessary, could be deferred without noticeable effect on performance.

Heated axleboxes, spring gear defects or broken parts of any kind were rare, hence the 'Nelson' class showed excellent availability; thus, when Nine Elms or Bournemouth had a shortage of usable Pacifics, they were able to borrow 'Nelsons'. Perhaps the most irritating faults lay with the vacuum brake system, with weak ejectors, leaks or twisted rolling-rings in the brake cylinders. A steam brake system would have been preferable for engine and tender. The exhaust steam injectors were untrustworthy, despite the improved models supplied by the makers in the postwar years. They were awkwardly placed and required a degree degree of precision in assembling the components that was best achieved on a bench in main workshops. Although it took half-a-day to remove and replace one, it was the quickest way to get an engine back into service with two good injectors. Mr Bulleid rightly chose not to have them.

At Eastleigh, as at other depots, there were usually some drivers who were, on doctor's orders, unfit for normal duties by reason of injury or illness. Some were able to do light shunting at places like Winchester and Redbridge; a few were not fit to drive at all but able to make themselves useful around the shed, happy to be kept at work among engines. Their experience in the making of trimmings was needed, as they regularly checked the dozens of trimmings on the 'Nelsons', thus ensuring reliable lubrication. Others went round the shed collecting lamps and disc boards and repainting them white. The photographs in this book betray a variation in the state of discs, a reflection of the availability of staff. Painting such things was, according to Staff Office, non-productive. Likewise, engine-cleaning came to be regarded as a part-time task for a pool of spare firemen, if there were any. In the early postwar years Eastleigh was able to keep the 'Nelsons' clean; on boat trains they got quite a lot of attention from overseas visitors. The drivers' committee, however, asked for priority to be given to cleaning parts inside the frames, to save soiling their overalls when oiling during preparation duties. We reached a compromise, on the basis that engines would be better maintained if the working parts were not repulsively filthy. Alas, as steam drew near its end, often the only part to be wiped over was the cabside number.

Noticeably absent from details given in the practice and performance articles appearing in the postwar railway journals are runs with 'Nelsons'. Their opportunities for work on principal express passenger turns were limited in view of the number of Bulleid Pacifics nominally available. One of their more important duties was on the 11.30am Waterloo-Bournemouth West express but this was easily timed and did not require much in the way of effort from a 'Nelson'. Their other workings were on secondary passenger trains on the Bournemouth line and on a couple of Waterloo-Salisbury slow trains. Only one snippet seems to have caught Cecil J. Allen's eye when a contributor to his *Railway Magazine* articles provided details of No 853 *Sir Richard Grenville* running from Dorchester to Wool (10 miles) in 10min 18sec start to stop, with a maximum of 86mph, on a 310 tons gross up Weymouth train in 1948. Better than average was a run detailed by Norman Harvey in the April 1964 *Railway World*. John Webber had much earlier recorded No 30864 *Sir Martin Frobisher* at the head of a 13-coach, 460ton gross Sunday train, non-stop from Southampton Central-Waterloo. A net time of 84½min was estimated for this run which included 53/54mph attained from Winchester to Roundwood box; maximum speeds east of Basingstoke were in the order of 65-70mph.

Up until 1946, the 'Arthurs', 'Schools' and 'Nelsons' had not been involved in any major mishaps. But in December of that year No 851 *Sir Francis Drake* and all 12 coaches of an up Weymouth train were completely derailed at speed approaching Byfleet station. The track beneath the train was torn up, but it came to rest upright and nobody was injured. The line was cleared quickly by the combined efforts of breakdown gangs from Nine Elms, Bricklayers Arms, Brighton and Guildford: it was the only occasion in Southern history when four steam cranes were seen together. Three months previously No 917 *Ardingly* and the coaches of a Victoria-Ramsgate train had been derailed at Catford: the only fatality was an RAF pilot who had survived the Battle of Britain. Both accidents were the direct result of poor track conditions attributable to dirty ballast and poor drainage, brought about by the maintenance difficulties of the war years. In 1947, No 453 *King Arthur* on an up Salisbury train ran into the rear of an up Bournemouth train at Farnborough because of a signalman's error. *King Arthur* lay slain on his side but both driver and fireman got away with a bad shaking.

In July 1952, No 30854 *Howard of Effingham* came to grief lying on its side at the bottom of an embankment at Shawford and, again, the driver and fireman scrambled out of the cab unhurt. At Shawford the up local and up through lines converge into one up line. The 'Nelson', with a Bournemouth-Waterloo train, was on the up local line. The junction points had been set, and the appropriate semaphore signal cleared, for an up boat train ex-Southampton Docks on the through line. The 'Nelson' driver mistook the clear signal as applying to him, with the result that *Howard of Effingham* ran off the end of the local line, though a sand drag and pitched down the embankment. Fortunately, the coupling between the tender and the first coach parted and the train and passengers did not follow. Within minutes the passengers transferred themselves to the boat train, which had stopped alongside when its driver saw what had happened; within an hour or so the empty Bournemouth train had been hauled away, and the drama was over, except for the recovery of the 'Nelson'. As it was out of reach of breakdown cranes, No 30854 was later jacked upright and winched up a temporary track laid at a slope of 1 in 13 on the side of the embankment. Ten days after the accident No 30854 was in Eastleigh Works, little the worse, and requiring only the removal of a few dents and a fresh coat of paint. In contrast, out of the 98 SR Class 33 diesel-electric locomotives which came along later, two were destined to be completely written off by accident damage.

In 1953 the first 'Arthur' to be scrapped was No 754; other Urie 'Arthurs' were withdrawn year by year until 1958,

when the last, No 738, disappeared. Their names, recast on new nameplates, were transferred to BR Class '5s' but lost something of their significance in the process.

The 'Arthurs', 'Schools' and 'Nelsons' were obsolescent in 1948 and quite obsolete alongside the excellent BR Class '5s', easily serviced and maintained. Some enginemen even preferred a BR '5' to a 'Merchant Navy' on the 'Bournemouth Belle'. With 140 Pacifics there was, on paper, little justification for keeping so many 'Arthurs' and 'Nelsons' but the number of Pacifics available for service on any given day fluctuated wildly, and the Maunsell engines had to be held in reserve to make up deficiencies. The appearance of the first modified Pacific, 'Merchant Navy' No 35018, in April 1956 marked the culmination of a long struggle with the shortcomings of the originals and, for the Regional officers involved, a long wait for approval from higher up. So the faithful Maunsell 'Arthurs', 'Schools' and 'Nelsons' were destined to linger on into the 1960s, outwardly somewhat decrepit but inwardly reliable to the end.

The inauguration of Stage 1 of the Kent Coast electrification in June 1959 marked the beginning of the demise of the 'Arthurs', 'Nelsons' and 'Schools'. Some of the 'Arthurs' displaced on the Eastern section were transferred, others scrapped. The 'Schools' moved to the Central and Western sections, and were to be found on Bournemouth line duties; to Salisbury and Exeter on slow trains; between Reading, Guildford, Redhill and Tonbridge and on London-Brighton via Oxted peak-hour trains. The electrification of the SER main line to Ashford, Folkestone and Dover in 1961 spelt the end for the Maunsell express passenger engines. Bulleid Light Pacifics were transferred to the Western section and, to the accompaniment of pressure from the British Railways Board to reduce the steam locomotive fleet, the 'Arthurs', 'Nelsons' and 'Schools' were withdrawn from normal service at the end of 1962. Even so, the familiar outline of a Maunsell 4-6-0 was still to be seen on the Southern Region until almost the end of steam in the South of England. The 'S15s' lasted until 1965/66.

Right: The vain attempt to reduce the visibility of a working steam locomotive in wartime: 'Arthur' No 783 *Sir Gillemere*, at Eastleigh, 7 January 1941. *B. W. Anwell*

Above: Early postwar Waterloo, 26 July 1947. Left is 'Lord Nelson' No 854 *Howard of Effingham*, to its right Urie 'Arthur' No 738 *King Pellinore*. Far right is 4–COR electric multiple–unit No 3138 on a Portsmouth service.   *C. C. B. Herbert*

Right: Surprisingly clean 'Schools' No 901 *Winchester* at Sevenoaks with a down Hastings train, c1945.
A. W. Croughton/Lens of Sutton

Above: Leaving Salisbury with a down express for the West of England is 'Arthur' No 30451 *Sir Lamorak*, in SR-style malachite green livery. Bulleid stock in the train.
Rev A. C. Cawston

Below: Winchfield, and No 30785 *Sir Mador de la Porte* heads a down Bournemouth express. Bulleid six-coach restaurant car set leads the train. 20 April 1949. *E. C. Griffith/Lens of Sutton*

Right: A fine sight as No 30772 *Sir Percivale* storms past Micheldever with an up Ocean Liner express in 1950. *F. R. Hebron/Rail Archive Stephenson*

Below right: The characteristic LSWR lower quadrant signals feature at Winchfield as No 30777 *Sir Lamiel* passes with a down Bournemouth train, 15 April 1949. *E. C. Griffith/Lens of Sutton*

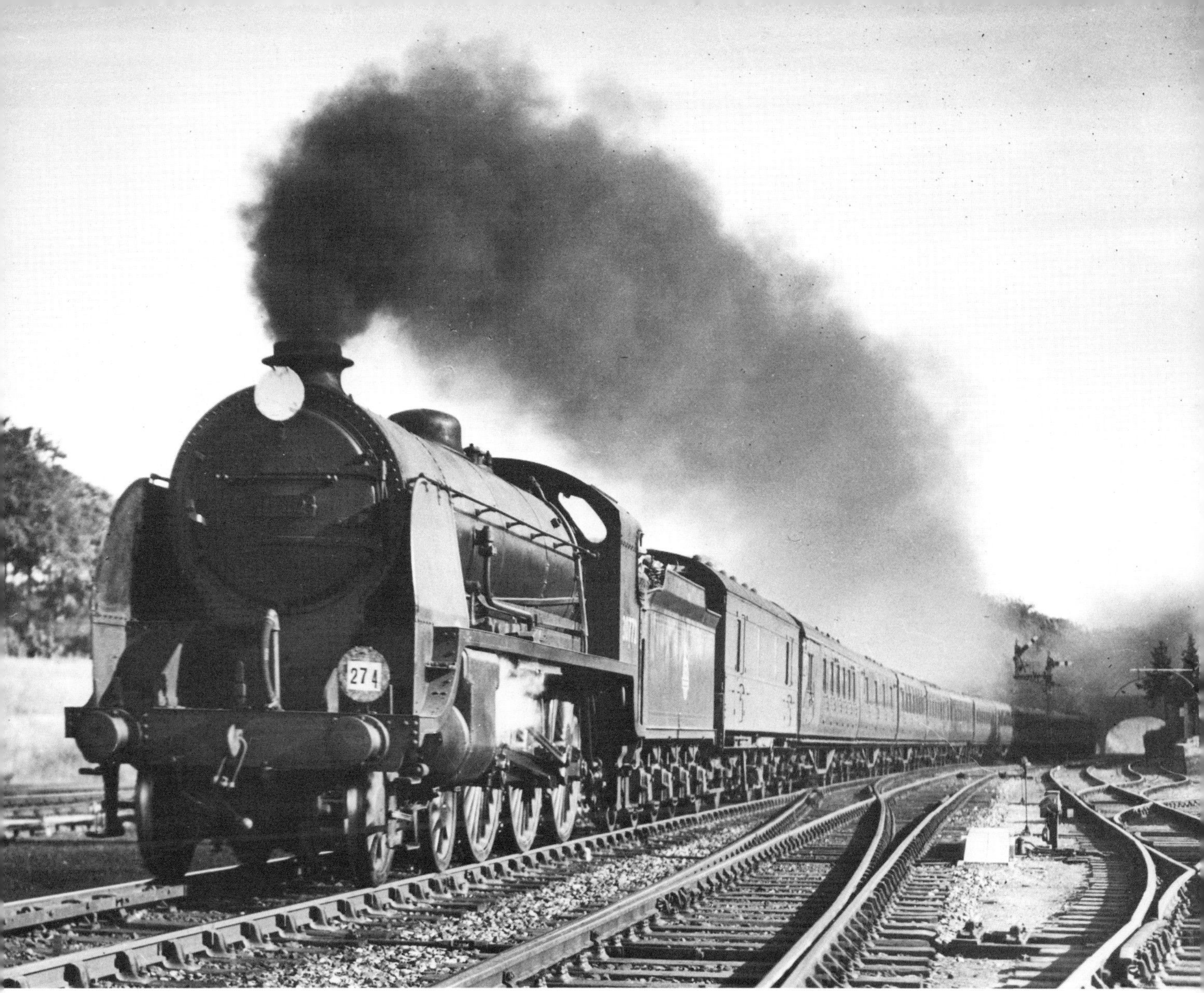
274

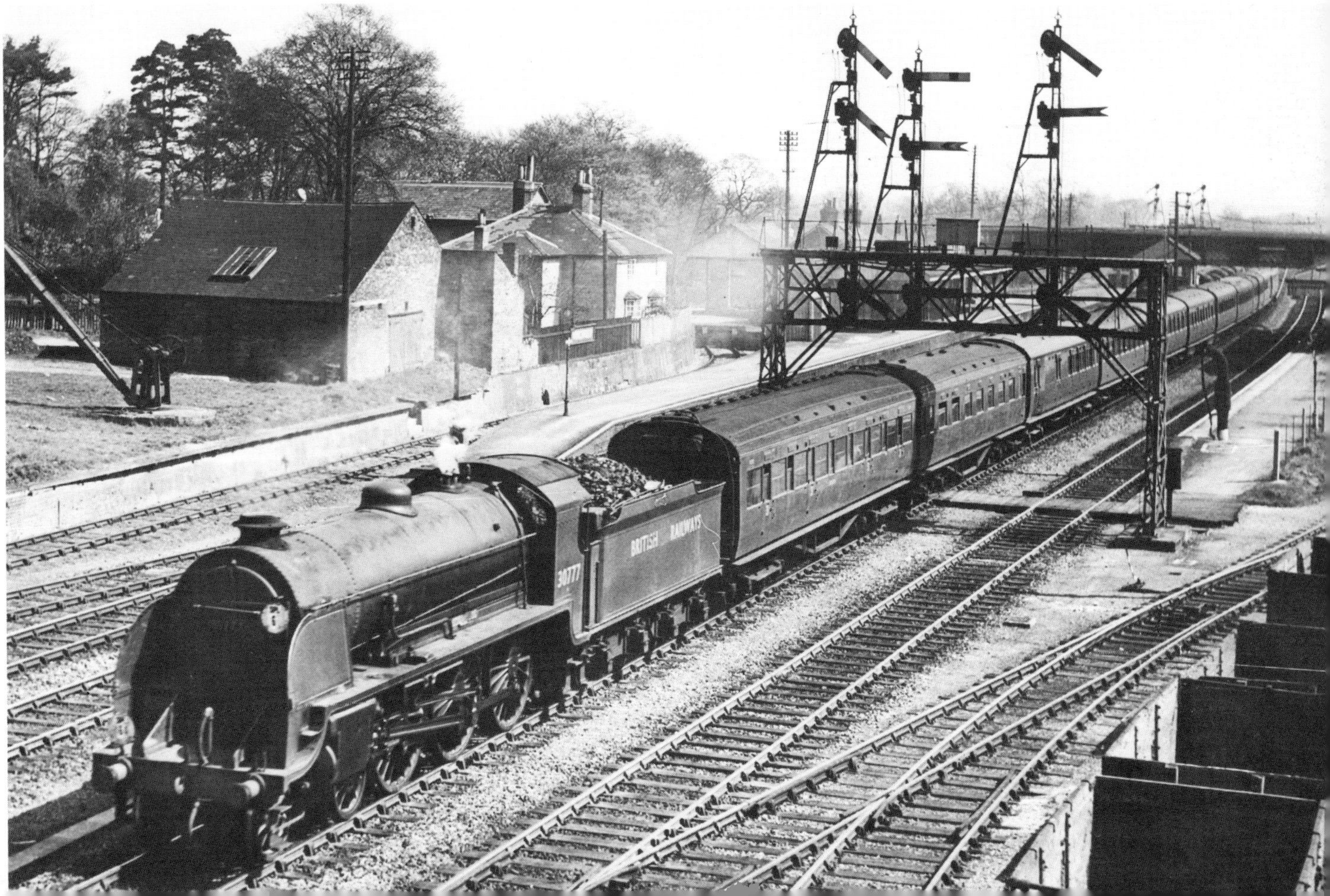
BRITISH RAILWAYS
30777

Right: 'Arthur' No 30779 *Sir Colgrevance* generates a smokescreen at Byfleet with a down troop train for Southampton Old Docks, 14 April 1950.
Rev A. C. Cawston

Below: Lemaître-equipped No 30736 *Excalibur* near Hinton Admiral with the Bournemouth-Birkenhead train, formed of ex-GWR stock. 3 September 1955.
D. M. C. Hepburne-Scott/Rail Archive Stephenson

Right: 'Schools' No 926 *Repton* heads a heavy express for Dover in early postwar days. *Rev A. C. Cawston*

Below: No 30924 *Haileybury* in Folkestone Warren with a down Margate train on 20 June 1949.
E. R. Wethersett/Real Photographs Co

A quartet of 'Schools':

Above: No 30919 *Harrow* passes Weald Intermediate signalbox at the head of a down slow train for Dover, 27 August 1958. *Noel Matthews*

Top right: No 30929 *Malvern* approaches Priory Tunnel with a Margate train, having just departed from Dover Priory. *T. G. Hepburn/Rail Archive Stephenson*

Above right: No 30918 *Hurstpierpoint* comes towards Factory Jn, Battersea with a Victoria-Ramsgate train in the early 1950s. *Lens of Sutton*

Right: The up 'Kentish Belle' is headed by a grimy No 30912 *Downside* as it leaves Whitstable on 16 August 1958. *S. Creer*

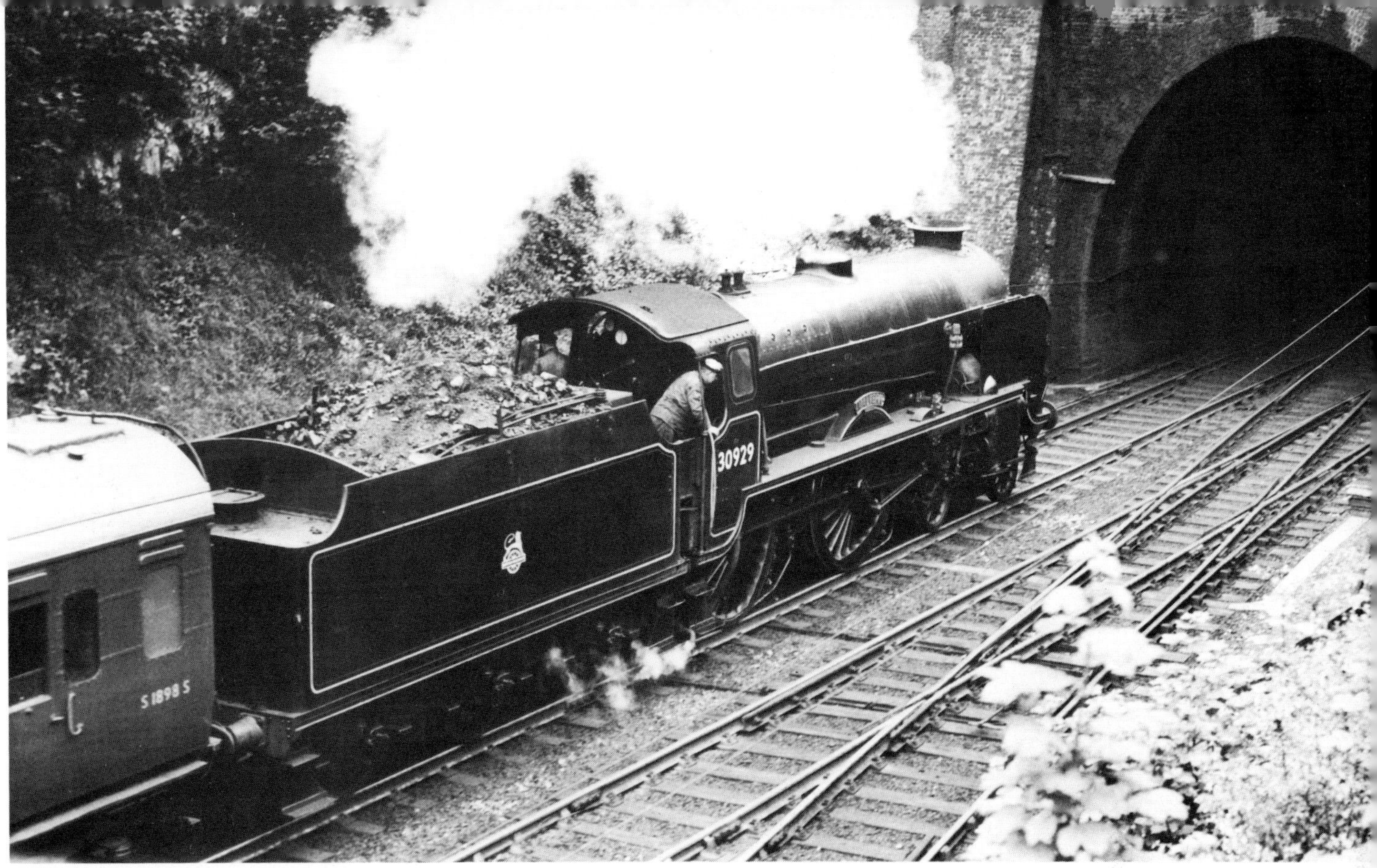
30929
S 1898 S

30918

KENTISH BELLE
485

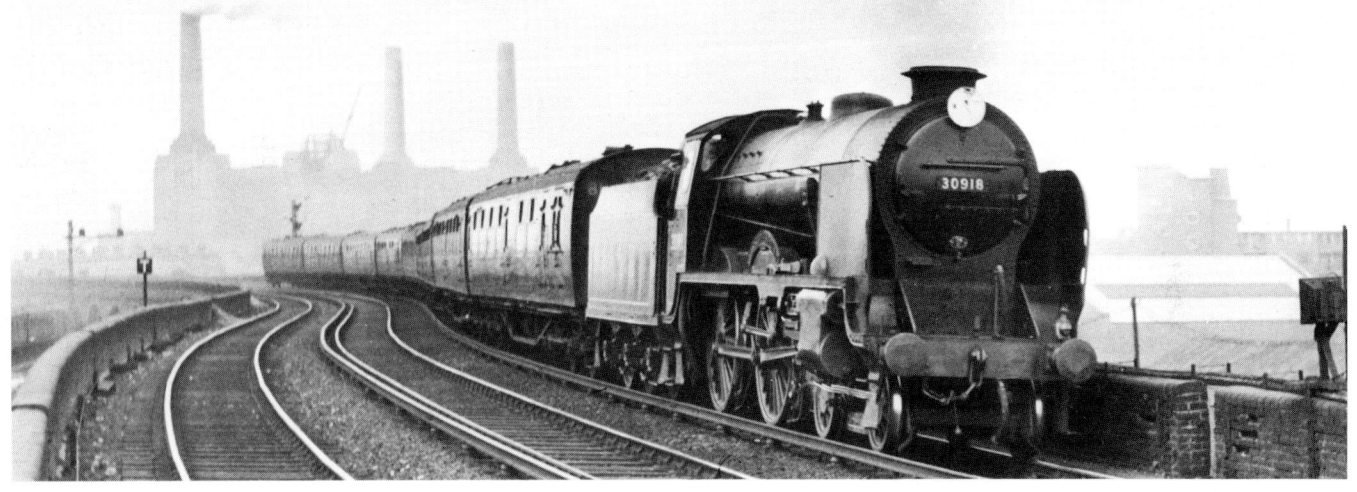

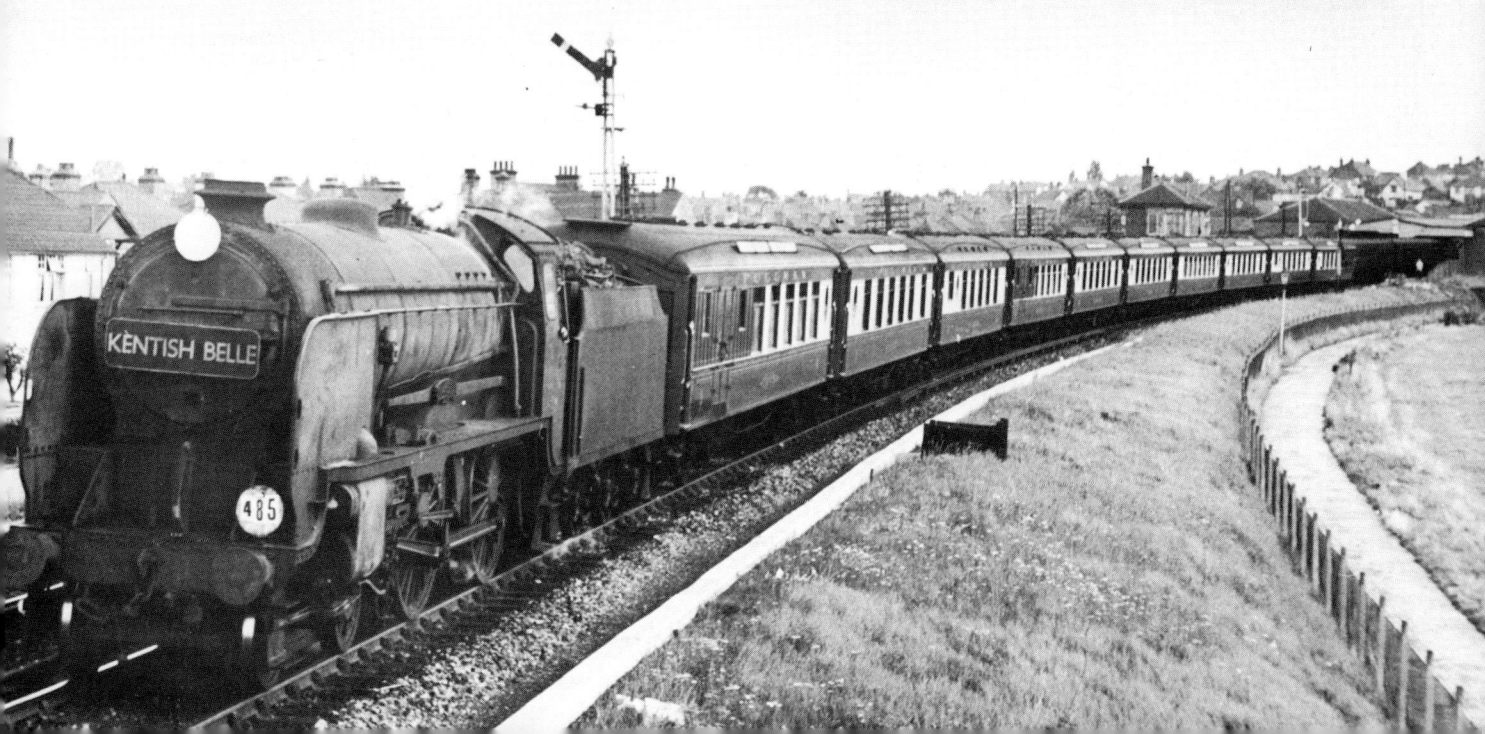

Left: No 30926 *Repton* sets out from Tunbridge Wells with an express for Hastings, 20 April 1957. *J. A. Coiley*

Above: No 30928 *Stowe* works hard at Knockholt with a Hastings train, 1950. *F. R. Hebron/Rail Archive Stephenson*

Below: Sevenoaks: a London Bridge–Folkestone train pauses behind No 912 *Downside*, c1947. *A. W. Croughton/Lens of Sutton*

Above: A down Kent Coast express east of Tonbridge on 16 February 1960 behind 'Schools' No 30938 *St Olave's*.
D. M. C. Hepburne-Scott/Rail Archive Stephenson

Left: The 'South American' Southampton Docks boat train at Waterloo on 4 February 1955, behind 'Lord Nelson' No 30856 *Lord St. Vincent*.   *N. Caplan*

Above right: No 30861 *Lord Anson* between Bournemouth West and Central stations with a Waterloo-bound express, 11 April 1955.
D. M. C. Hepburne-Scott/Rail Archive Stephenson

Right: Journey's end for No 30865 *Sir John Hawkins* as it brings an express from Waterloo past Weymouth shed, September 1957.
T. G. Hepburn/Rail Archive Stephenson

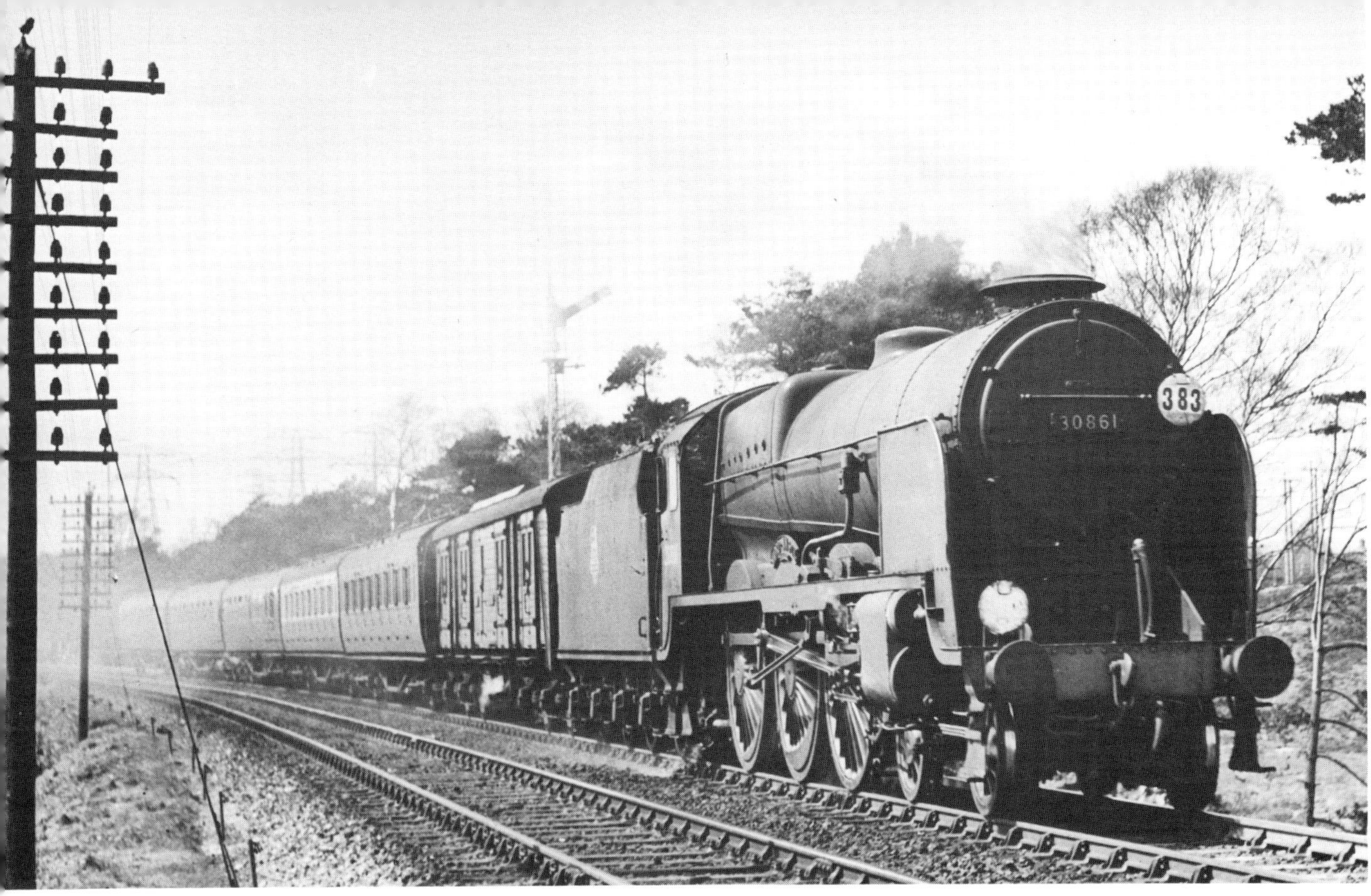
383
30861

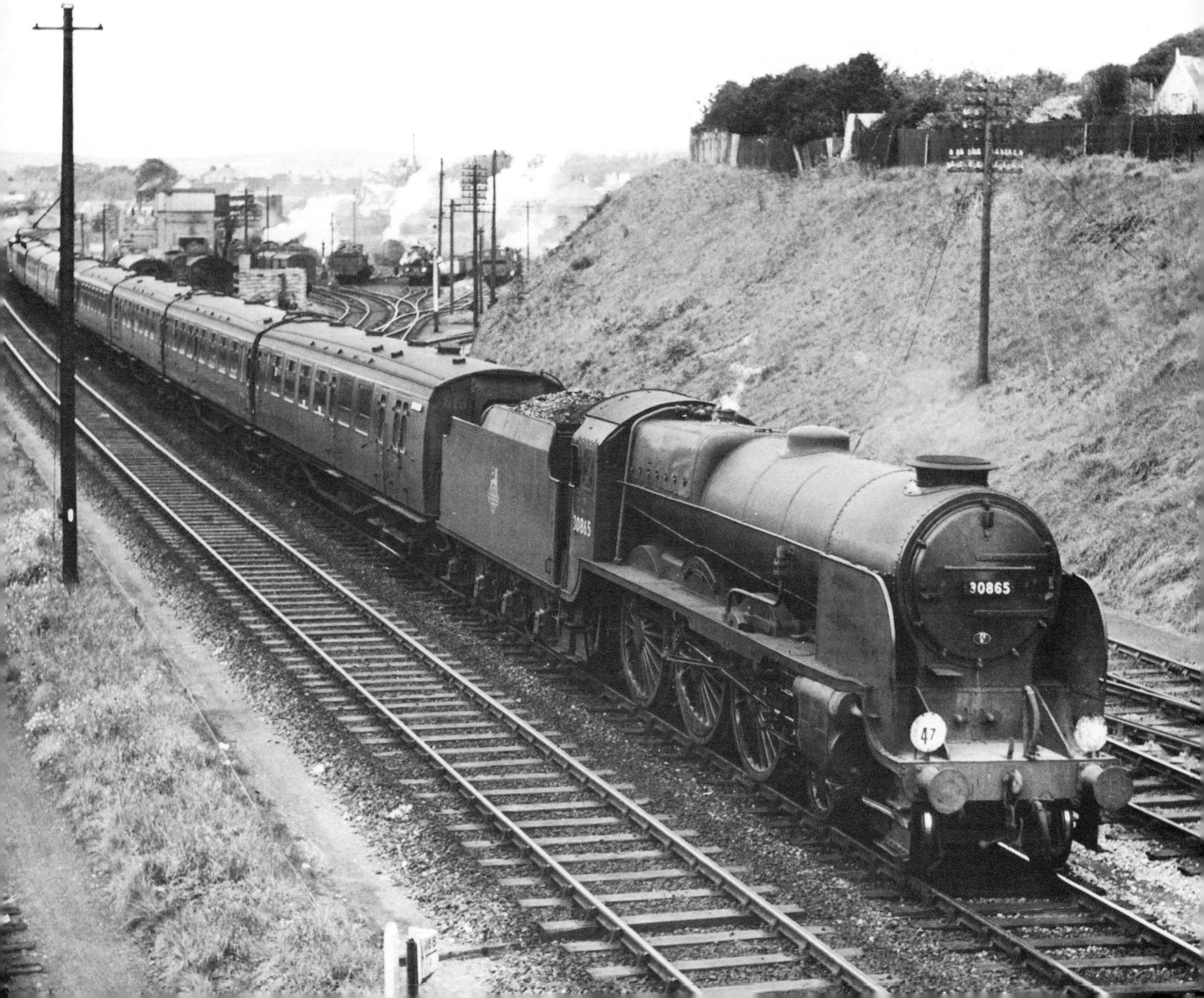
30865
47

14
In Preservation

In 1961, having conferred with a Consultative Panel made up of interested parties and locomotive historians, the British Transport Commission's Curator of Historical Relics, the late John Scholes, produced a list of steam locomotives that were scheduled for official preservation. That list was perhaps exceptional for what was not included, but it featured three Southern Railway express passenger locomotives, 'Arthur' No 777 *Sir Lamiel* (famed for its record run from Salisbury-Waterloo in 1936); No 850 *Lord Nelson* and 'Schools' No 925 *Cheltenham*. On withdrawal the three engines were stored. At one stage there was a suggestion that *King Arthur* himself would be kept for posterity instead, but in the event No 777 was retained. Subsequently, in the absence of space within the then Museum of British Transport at Clapham, all three led a peripatetic, if unproductive existence moving from one storage place to another. Fortunately, by 1982 resources of labour and time had made it possible for the three survivors to be restored to working order. The 'Arthur' and the 'Nelson' have been hard at work on special trains running on BR main lines and one aspect of this chapter is to relate the various interesting assessments that have been made of the two locomotives now in operation far from their former home territory. The 'Schools' has yet to be passed for working passenger trains. There are also two 'Schools' preserved by private owners.

First in the order of restoration is No 850. Its last workings were in 1962, and one of its final outings was on an enthusiast special from Paddington to Swindon Works that June. As it was a Sunday, the booked schedule was very easy, but a 13min late start provided an impetus for time recovery. With a 12-coach, 440ton gross train and in the hands of Western Region enginemen, it was good work to run the 31.00 miles out of Paddington to a signal check at Twyford in $32\frac{1}{4}$min, with speeds of 63-65mph sustained on almost level track. Perhaps this excursion was a hint that the 'Nelson' would henceforth work far from home in the hands of enginemen unused to it, but capable of showing that No 850 was a fine locomotive.

However, it was to be 1976 before *Lord Nelson* left Southern territory, after years of storage, for the prospect of restoration. It went first to the National Railway Museum, but agreement was reached that it should move to Steamtown, Carnforth for overhaul. For two years No 850 remained an unrestored, static object until funds and sponsorship could be made available for its rehabilitation. The boiler required an internal and external examination and complete retubing. This task was undertaken by the Babcock Power Company Ltd. The general mechanical parts restoration was carried out by Steamtown. As work began it was evident that various components were missing or wrongly

assembled and also that No 850 incorporated parts from about six sister engines. However, *Lord Nelson* proved to be fundamentally sound, although eventually 80 firebox stays had to be replaced.

In May 1980, No 850 was steamed for the first time in 18 years and the engine moved under its own power. On 23 May, it travelled in steam to take part in the Rocket 150 Cavalcade at Rainhill. Unfortunately, scale disturbed in the tender tank blocked the injectors and so No 850 missed the first day's Cavalcade in the three-day event, but duly appeared on 25/26 May. That problem with dislodged scale was to prove a nuisance on main line runs later in 1980, but at no time then or since has the locomotive been taken off a train, as the result of a failure.

Having returned to Carnforth, No 850 worked its first passenger train, as restored, on 1 July taking the 'Cumbrian Coast Express' from Sellafield to Carnforth. Twelve minutes were regained on schedule by LMS-trained Carnforth Driver Harry Bush and he was soon of the opinion that it was the best main line locomotive working from Steamtown. That was a vindication of the 'Nelson', for Steamtown Managing Director, George Hinchcliffe, had received letters and advice from Southern enginemen to the effect that in taking on No 850 he would have a 'lemon' on his hands. 'Foreign' enginemen would have difficulty in firing the engine, it was said, and disappointment was assured. That has been very far from the case. The 'Nelson' has cheerfully taken 500ton trains (for which it was designed to work) over the Settle & Carlisle line and it has earned itself an excellent reputation.

A few faults showed up when No 850 was back in harness. The engine had a tendency to lose the train brake vacuum suddenly, and the ejector has generally proved a little temperamental, and there have also been the problems of dislodged scale. The smokebox platework was partially renewed in early 1982. Coal consumption has been heavier than with the Gresley Pacifics working from Steamtown and an inspector has spoken of 'heavy shovelling' when working over the Settle & Carlisle. But despite published opinion to the effect that 'Nelsons' required careful firing in service, there have been no difficulties when working in the North of England. One fireman commented that 'we treat it like a "Royal Scot" and have never had any trouble'. Another Carnforth fireman, Alfie Butler, told the writer that it was a better locomotive than *Flying Scotsman* and a 'strong engine, particularly on the 1 in 100 of Dalton bank'.

A more remarkable example of *Lord Nelson's* capability came in June 1981. It stood in at short notice for the LMS 'Duchess' No 46229 on special trains running from Chester to Shrewsbury and Hereford and return. Despite never having seen a 'Nelson' before, the Shrewsbury crew made a record ascent of Gresford bank involving a minimum speed at the summit of 38mph with a 400ton train and, on the return trip northwards a week later, a Hereford crew reached Shrewsbury in 60min from Hereford for the 51.0 miles — a time that would have been regarded as excellent in steam days with the customary motive power. The broken climb of 14 miles between north of Ludlow and south of Church Stretton was achieved with a minimum speed of 53mph. Thanks are due to Mr S. A. Leyland through whose good offices details of these runs were received. No 850 continued northwards with a special over the ex-LNWR Manchester-Leeds route and made short work of the climb to Diggle. Elsewhere, it has impressed other BR crews, too, and a York inspector present on the footplate said that it had 'played' with an 11-coach train from York-Skipton in August 1982.

'Arthur' No 777 *Sir Lamiel* had little done to it since first preserved, despite being located at two different steam centres. In October 1976, agreement was reached between the National Railway Museum and the Humberside Locomotive Preservation Group for the engine to be restored to main line running condition at its premises in Hull. In June 1978 No 777 moved to Hull to be dismantled for overhaul. One immediate problem was the discovery of a frame fracture, a not uncommon ailment sustained by the class. An insert needed to be welded into the main frame and the large tubes required replacement. Much hard work was expended by the HLPG's small team in preparing the locomotive and delays in the delivery of tubes meant that it was February 1982 before the 'Arthur' was steamed for the first time in more than 20 years. After trial runs No 777 made its debut on a main line steam special on 27 March 1982. The BR motive power inspectors were unconvinced that the 'Arthur' was man enough to take a 400ton train unassisted over the Long Drag, from Settle Junction to Carlisle, and so for its first return run an LMS '5' was provided as pilot. The reputation of Maunsell locomotives for making light of hard work was soon established when a 13-coach train was taken from Leeds to Carnforth with ease.

In the summer of 1982, No 777 was extensively employed on main line special trains, based at Carnforth or York. The enginemen at York were full of praise for the 4-6-0: 'a strong locomotive', 'a Class 5-plus' were some of the comments made to the writer. Regarded as light on water, the only quibbles concerned a cab which seemed exposed as compared with the Gresley pattern and what was seen as an awkwardly operating regulator handle, moving from right to fully open. Poor coal had resulted in difficulty on one trip, the fireman involved pointing out that the closely spaced firebars made it a troublesome job when cleaning the fire. As with No 850, the virtues of the Maunsell/SR practice have outweighed minor irritations. No 777 is finished in 1920s/30s

sage green livery, and No 850 is in Bulleid malachite green, to the style applied from 1938/39.

The officially preserved 'Schools', No 925 *Cheltenham*, was moved to the National Railway Museum in 1977. It was prepared for inclusion in the Rainhill 150 Cavalcades in May 1980. However, pressure of time meant that it was restored to run light under its own power only, although it was turned out resplendent in the Southern Railway malachite green livery. On its return to York in the autumn of 1980 it ran in light steam with the preserved Midland Compound 4-4-0 No 1000, an interesting comparison in styles. Since then No 925 has been at York awaiting boiler repairs before it can take its place in working main line specials.

After withdrawal, No 928 *Stowe* was purchased by Lord Montagu of Beaulieu and moved to the National Motor Museum in February 1964, to be placed on static display with three Pullman cars. Some mechanical attention was given to the locomotive at Eastleigh Works in 1973 before transfer to the East Somerset Railway where, again, it was exhibited in non-working condition as there had never been any intention that it should be steamed. Arrangements were later made with Lord Montagu for the locomotive to be placed on loan with the Bluebell Railway and it arrived at Sheffield Park in July 1980. The 'Schools' was the recipient of an overhaul costing about £15,000 which included lifting the boiler from the frames, for examination and retubing, dismantling all working parts and repainting of locomotive and tender. Although it retained almost all its fittings, there had been an inevitable deterioration with disuse and the corrosion of platework with the result that the Bluebell Railway's engineers made a thorough and praiseworthy job of restoration. No 928 has been repainted in Maunsell era livery.

No 926 *Repton* was purchased by Steamtown Museum, USA and, after attention and repainting to SR livery at Eastleigh Works, was shipped to the United States in 1967. Subsequently, it spent at least a couple of seasons working passenger trains on the Cape Breton Steam Railway in Nova Scotia, Canada. Its present capabilities are unknown.

It is interesting that all the principal SR Maunsell types have survived to be preserved — except the 'H15' 4-6-0s — including more than one example of the 2-6-0 classes and no less than three 'S15' 4-6-0s. The general impression gained by those involved in the restoration and operation of these engines is that they are robust, well-constructed and, with those in steam, dependable and easily maintained. Locomotive preservation has caused some railway reputations to be reassessed, but in the case of the Southern Railway and its CME, R. E. L. Maunsell, the result has been to gain increased respect for the achievements of the smallest of the grouping companies, at times overshadowed by the 'big boys'.

Lord Nelson since restoration:

Right: In Bold Colliery sidings, ready for the Rainhill 150 Cavalcade, 26 May 1980. *Peter J. C. Skelton*

Below: After repainting, No 850 climbs towards Greenfield, on the LNW Manchester-Leeds line, heading the 'Yorkshire Pullman' of 20 June 1981; this run is referred to in the text. *Brian Dobbs*

Above: Homeward-bound, passing Dringhouses yard, York with an excursion for Carnforth, 16 August 1981. Driver B. L. Wharram, Fireman A. Hudson (York) are in charge. *John S. Whiteley*

Left: Riveting in progress at Steamtown, Carnforth on 15 May 1982, during renewal of the smokebox platework. *W. A. Sharman*

127

Left: After restoration and on its first trial trip at the head of a train: *Sir Lamiel* near Walton St Jn, Hull, bound for Bridlington on 23 March 1982.
John S. Whiteley

Below: *Lord Nelson* on a southbound 'Cumbrian Mountain Express' crosses Ais Gill Viaduct, 3 August 1982. *J. H. Cooper-Smith*

Right: *Sir Lamiel* on the favourably graded Leeds-York section, near Copmanthorpe with the outward 'Scarborough Spa Express' of 31 August 1982. *John Titlow*

Below: Heading the returning 'Scarborough Spa Express' of 2 September 1982, the last of that season, *Sir Lamiel* beyond Holgate Jn, York, bound for Leeds.
Brian Stephenson

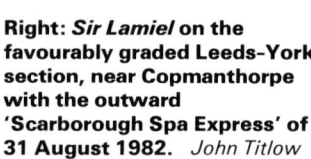

Above: 'Schools' No 925 *Cheltenham* at Bold Colliery, during Rainhill 150, on 24 May 1980. *Brian Stephenson*

Left: On its first public passenger train after restoration to working order by the Bluebell Railway, No 928 *Stowe* nears Horsted Keynes on 14 June 1981. *Brian Stephenson*

Below: No 926 *Repton* at Steamtown, USA. *Edgar T. Mead*

With the arrival of the Bulleid Pacifics, the 'Arthurs', 'Nelsons' and 'Schools' were increasingly diagrammed to secondary work, of the variety shown in the next few pages.

Above: Waiting at Seaton Junction for an approaching up express to precede, 'Arthur' No 30448 *Sir Tristram* heads an Exeter Central–Yeovil stopping train on 18 June 1949. SR malachite livery, BR identity. *S. C. Nash*

Below: No 30787 *Sir Menadeuke* at Battledown, west of Worting Junction with an Eastleigh-bound goods, 8 June 1954. *D. M. C. Hepburne-Scott/Rail Archive Stephenson*

Above left: Lemaître-fitted No 30737 *King Uther* on a down stopping train near Christchurch, 12 May 1954.
D. M. C. Hepburne-Scott/Rail Archive Stephenson

Left: 'Schools' No 30935 *Sevenoaks* approaches Three Oaks and Guestling Halt with the 5.38pm Hastings-Rye, 15 July 1956.
D. M. C. Hepburne-Scott/Rail Archive Stephenson

Below: No 30782 *Sir Brian* pulls away from Weymouth with a Bournemouth stopping train, September 1957.
T. G. Hepburn/Rail Archive Stephenson

Above right: No 30451 *Sir Lamorak* calls at Axminster with a down semi-fast, 27 June 1958. Urie tender in place of Drummond 'water-cart'. *John P. Wilson*

Right: 'Schools' No 30928 *Stowe* nearing Tonbridge with the 11.46am Charing Cross-Ashford train, 17 February 1960. Aws fitted. *D. M. C. Hepburne-Scott Rail Archive Stephenson*

Below: One of the thrice-yearly excursions from New Cross-Ramsgate via Oxted joins the Redhill-Tonbridge line by means of the Crowhurst spur, behind No 30924 *Haileybury* on 24 July 1960. *Derek Cross*

Left: A taxing job for a
'Schools' — the heavy
5.25pm London Bridge-
Reading South and Tunbridge
Wells with No 30916 *Whitgift*
topping Forest Hill bank on
9 August 1960. *John Scrace*

Below: No 30910 *Merchant
Taylors* in Clapham cutting
with a Waterloo-Basingstoke
train, 27 March 1961.
*D. M. C. Hepburne-Scott/Rail
Archive Stephenson*

Above: 'Schools' No 30905
***Tonbridge* near Steventon box**
with a Nine Elms–
Southampton goods,
18 September 1961. Running
with high-sided tender from
No 30932.
D. M. C. Hepburne-Scott/Rail
Archive Stephenson

Right: Fitted with aws gear,
No 30936 *Cranleigh* near
Eridge on a Tonbridge–
Brighton train, 24 June 1961.
D. M. C. Hepburne-Scott/Rail
Archive Stephenson

Below right: 'Arthur'
No 30796 *Sir Dodinas le*
***Savage* near Grateley with an**
up semi-fast train,
9 September 1961. Urie
tender in place of original
Ashford type.
D. M. C. Hepburne-Scott/Rail
Archive Stephenson

Above: No 30909 *St Paul's* leaves Earley with a Reading South-Redhill train, 16 September 1961.
D. M. C. Hepburne-Scott/Rail Archive Stephenson

Left: No 30451 *Sir Lamorak* near Oakley with a stopping train for Salisbury, 16 September 1961.
D. M. C. Hepburne-Scott/Rail Archive Stephenson

Below left: The only regular duty for a 'Nelson' on the West of England line in later years involved a return Waterloo-Salisbury semi-fast passenger working. No 30862 *Lord Collingwood* near Whitchurch on 13 January 1962.
D. M. C. Hepburne-Scott/Rail Archive Stephenson

Above: In its last summer of service, 'Schools' No 30936 *Cranleigh* **leaves Southampton Central with the 12noon summer Saturdays Waterloo–Lymington Pier, 25 August 1962.**
Michael J. Fox

Right: Shortly before withdrawal, 'Arthur' No 30765 *Sir Gareth* **pauses at Clapham Junction, 24 August 1962.**
Brian Stephenson

Below right: Similarly in its last days of service, 'Lord Nelson' No 30857 *Lord Howe*, **also at Clapham Junction.**
Brian Stephenson

Off the beaten track:

Above: 'Arthur' No 30789 *Sir Guy* with a 'B1' 4–6–0 in front at Nottingham Victoria on 30 July 1956, before returning to the SR with an excursion. *John. P. Wilson*

'Schools' No 30925 *Cheltenham* was used for a rail tour on 13 May 1962, the RCTS 'East Midlander':

Left: No 30925 returned south with the 12.30pm Nottingham Victoria-Marylebone service train on 16 May 1962, which it worked throughout. Seen at East Leake. *D. Holmes*

Below: It was used as pilot to LMS '2P' 4–4–0 No 40646, and the train is seen at Nottingham Victoria, bound for Darlington. *T. G. Hepburn/Rail Archive Stephenson*

Appendices 1 SR Route Availability

	'LN'	'N15'	'V'
Victoria (Eastern) to Ramsgate via Herne Hill and Chatham	√	√	√
Victoria (Eastern) to Dover — via Chatham and Faversham	√	√	√
via Tonbridge and Ashford			
Charing Cross and Cannon St to Chislehurst (prohibited, middle road and local lines, Charing Cross Bridge)	—	√	√
Tonbridge to Bopeep Jct	—	—	√
Swanley to Ashford	√	√	√
Ashford to Ore	—	—	√
Ashford to Minster Jct via Canterbury West	—	√	√
Folkestone Harbour branch	√	√	√
Dover to Ramsgate via Deal	√	√	√
Holborn Low Level and Holborn Viaduct to Herne Hill	—	—	—
North Kent East Jct to Charlton via Greenwich	—	—	√
Charlton to Maidstone West via Strood	√	√	√
Paddock Wood to Maidstone West	—	—	—
Victoria (Central) to East Croydon	√	√	√
London Bridge to Brighton via Redhill or Quarry	√	√	√
Three Bridges to Horsham	√	√	√
Keymer Jct to Eastbourne and Ore	√	√	√
Streatham South Jct to Arundel Jct via Dorking	—	—	—
Preston Park and Brighton to Havant	√	√	√
South Croydon to Hurst Green Jct and Tunbridge Wells Central	—	—	√

	'LN'	'N15'	'V'
Hurst Green Jct to East Grinstead	—	—	—
Tonbridge, Redhill and Guildford	√	√	√
Waterloo and Reading	√	√	√
Guildford and Reading via Blackwater or Frimley and Ascot	60	60	60
Waterloo to Weymouth, and Exeter St Davids	√	√	√
Waterloo to Portsmouth Harbour via Woking or Cobham	√	√	√
Exeter to Okehampton	—	40	—
Okehampton to Plymouth	—	—	—
Brookwood to Winchester via Alton	√	√	√
Eastleigh to Portsmouth via Botley	√	√	√
St Denys to Fareham (20mph over Hamble Viaduct)	—	—	√
Basingstoke to Reading	√	√	√
Enborne Jct (Newbury) to Shawford Jct	—	—	—
Southampton to Salisbury via Nursling or Eastleigh	√	√	√
Romsey to Andover (from Kimbridge Jct)	—	—	—
Brockenhurst to Lymington Pier	—	—	—
Brockenhurst to West Moors	—	—	—
West Moors to Hamworthy Jct	√	√	√
Salisbury to West Moors (from Alderbury Jct)	—	—	√
Templecombe to Broadstone	—	50	50
Coleford Jct to Ilfracombe	—	—	—

√=permitted; 40=speed limit 40mph; —=barred

Note: Route permission was given by the Civil Engineer on the basis of daily running. On some prohibited routes, occasional trips were permitted in emergency or for special trains.

Below: 'Arthur' No E767 *Sir Valence* steams through Bromley South station with the 11.00am Victoria-Dover Marine boat train, 1927. *F. R. Hebron/Rail Archive Stephenson*

140

2
SR Tender Locomotives (circa 1938/39)

20,000lb tractive effort and over		Total
'Nelsons'	4-6-0	16
'Arthurs'	4-6-0	74
H15	4-6-0	26
S15	4-6-0	45
T14*	4-6-0	10
N15X†	4-6-0	7
N, N1	2-6-0	86
U, UI	2-6-0	71
K	2-6-0	17
Q	0-6-0	20
700	0-6-0	30
H‡	4-4-2	11
'Schools'	4-4-0	40
D15	4-4-0	10

18,000lb tractive effort and over		Total
C	0-6-0	108
C2, C2X	0-6-0	48
C3	0-6-0	8
E, E1	4-4-0	26
L, L1	4-4-0	37
S11	4-4-0	10
K10, L11	4-4-0	80
B4, B4X	4-4-0	13

Under 18,000lb tractive effort		Total
O1	0-6-0	54
0395	0-6-0	18
B1, F1	4-4-0	41
D, D1	4-4-0	51
L12	4-4-0	20
T9	4-4-0	66
T6	4-4-0	1
X6, T3	4-4-0	6
X2	4-4-0	1
B4	4-4-0	7
A12	0-4-2	13

*'Paddleboats'; †'Remembrances'; ‡Atlantics

Above right: No E791 *Sir Uwaine* has just taken over a cross-country express for Bournemouth, at Oxford, c1926. *Lens of Sutton*

Right: A Ramsgate 'Schools', No 30913 *Christ's Hospital*, just ex-works from Eastleigh, accelerates away from Hinton Admiral with a stopping train to Southampton on 21 May 1954.
D. M. C. Hepburne-Scott/Rail Archive Stephenson

3
Locomotive Summaries

'KING ARTHUR' CLASS 4-6-0s
Urie LSWR 'N15' class

SR No	Name	Date built	Date withdrawn	Shed allocation 2/51	Shed allocation 3/53	Final Shed	Notes
736	Excalibur	8/18	11/56	Bournemouth	Bournemouth	Bournemouth	1
737	King Uther	10/18	6/56	Bournemouth	Bournemouth	Bournemouth	1
738	King Pellinore	12/18	3/58	Bournemouth	Bournemouth	Basingstoke	
739	King Leodegrance	2/19	5/57	Bournemouth	Bournemouth	Bournemouth	
740	Merlin	3/19	12/55	Bournemouth	Bournemouth	Bournemouth	
741	Joyous Gard	5/19	2/56	Bournemouth	Bournemouth	Bournemouth	1
742	Camelot	6/19	2/57	Bournemouth	Bournemouth	Bournemouth	
743	Lyonnesse	7/19	10/55	Bournemouth	Bournemouth	Bournemouth	
744	Maid of Astolat	9/19	1/56	Basingstoke	Nine Elms	Basingstoke	
745	Tintagel	11/19	2/56	Basingstoke	Basingstoke	Basingstoke	
746	Pendragon	6/22	10/55	Eastleigh	Eastleigh	Eastleigh	
747	Elaine	7/22	10/56	Eastleigh	Eastleigh	Eastleigh	
748	Vivien	8/22	9/57	Eastleigh	Eastleigh	Basingstoke	
749	Iseult	9/22	6/57	Eastleigh	Eastleigh	Basingstoke	
750	Morgan le Fay	10/22	7/57	Eastleigh	Nine Elms	Basingstoke	
751	Etarre	11/22	6/57	Eastleigh	Nine Elms	Basingstoke	
752	Linette	12/22	12/55	Eastleigh	Nine Elms	Eastleigh	1
753	Melisande	1/23	3/57	Eastleigh	Basingstoke	Eastleigh	
754	The Green Knight	2/23	1/53	Eastleigh	—	Eastleigh	2
755	The Red Knight	3/23	5/57	Eastleigh	Nine Elms	Nine Elms	1

Maunsell SR 'N15' class

SR No	Name	Date built	Date withdrawn	Shed allocation 2/51	Shed allocation 3/53	Final Shed	Notes
448	Sir Tristram	5/25	8/60	Salisbury	Salisbury	Salisbury	
449	Sir Torre	6/25	12/59	Salisbury	Salisbury	Salisbury	
450	Sir Kay	6/25	9/60	Salisbury	Salisbury	Salisbury	
451	Sir Lamorak	6/25	6/62	Salisbury	Salisbury	Salisbury	
452	Sir Melliagrance	7/25	8/59	Salisbury	Salisbury	Salisbury	
453	King Arthur	2/25	7/61	Salisbury	Salisbury	Salisbury	
454	Queen Guinevere	3/25	11/58	Salisbury	Salisbury	Salisbury	
455	Sir Launcelot	3/25	4/59	Salisbury	Nine Elms	Basingstoke	
456	Sir Galahad	4/25	5/60	Salisbury	Nine Elms	Basingstoke	
457	Sir Bedivere	4/25	5/61	Salisbury	Nine Elms	Nine Elms	
763	Sir Bors de Ganis	5/25	10/60	Stewarts Lane	Stewarts Lane	Eastleigh	
764	Sir Gawain	5/25	7/61	Stewarts Lane	Stewarts Lane	Bournemouth	
765	Sir Gareth	5/25	9/62	Stewarts Lane	Stewarts Lane	Basingstoke	
766	Sir Geraint	5/25	12/58	Stewarts Lane	Stewarts Lane	Stewarts Lane	
767	Sir Valence	6/25	6/59	Dover	Stewarts Lane	Eastleigh	
768	Sir Balin	6/25	10/61	Dover	Stewarts Lane	Eastleigh	
769	Sir Balan	6/25	2/60	Dover	Stewarts Lane	Eastleigh	
770	Sir Prianius	6/25	11/62	Dover	Stewarts Lane	Basingstoke	3
771	Sir Sagramore	6/25	3/61	Dover	Stewarts Lane	Salisbury	
772	Sir Percivale	6/25	9/61	Dover	Stewarts Lane	Bournemouth	
773	Sir Lavaine	6/25	2/62	Dover	Stewarts Lane	Eastleigh	
774	Sir Gaheris	6/25	1/60	Dover	Stewarts Lane	Nine Elms	
775	Sir Agravaine	6/25	2/60	Dover	Dover	Feltham	
776	Sir Galagars	6/25	1/59	Dover	Dover	Dover	
777	Sir Lamiel	6/25	10/61	Nine Elms	Dover	Basingstoke	4
778	Sir Pelleas	6/25	5/59	Nine Elms	Dover	Nine Elms	
779	Sir Colgrevance	7/25	7/59	Nine Elms	Dover	Nine Elms	
780	Sir Persant	7/25	7/59	Eastleigh	Nine Elms	Bournemouth	
781	Sir Aglovale	7/25	5/62	Eastleigh	Nine Elms	Bournemouth	
782	Sir Brian	7/25	9/62	Eastleigh	Bournemouth	Bournemouth	
783	Sir Gillemere	8/25	2/61	Eastleigh	Bournemouth	Salisbury	
784	Sir Nerovens	8/25	10/59	Eastleigh	Eastleigh	Eastleigh	

SR No	Name	Date built	Date withdrawn	Shed allocation 2/51	Shed allocation 3/53	Final Shed	Notes
785	*Sir Mador de la Porte*	8/25	10/59	Eastleigh	Eastleigh	Eastleigh	
786	*Sir Lionel*	8/25	8/59	Eastleigh	Eastleigh	Eastleigh	
787	*Sir Menadeuke*	9/25	2/59	Eastleigh	Eastleigh	Eastleigh	
788	*Sir Urre of the Mount*	9/25	2/62	Eastleigh	Eastleigh	Eastleigh	
789	*Sir Guy*	9/25	12/59	Eastleigh	Eastleigh	Eastleigh	
790	*Sir Villiars*	9/25	10/61	Eastleigh	Eastleigh	Eastleigh	
791	*Sir Uwaine*	9/25	5/60	Nine Elms	Stewarts Lane	Eastleigh	
792	*Sir Hervis de Revel*	10/25	2/59	Nine Elms	Stewarts Lane	Eastleigh	1
793	*Sir Ontzlake*	3/26	8/62	Stewarts Lane	Stewarts Lane	Basingstoke	
794	*Sir Ector de Maris*	3/26	8/60	Stewarts Lane	Stewarts Lane	Basingstoke	
795	*Sir Dinadan*	4/26	7/62	Stewarts Lane	Stewarts Lane	Basingstoke	
796	*Sir Dodinas le Savage*	5/26	2/62	Stewarts Lane	Dover	Salisbury	
797	*Sir Blamor de Ganis*	6/26	6/59	Bricklayers Arms	Dover	Dover	
798	*Sir Hectimere*	6/26	6/62	Bricklayers Arms	Dover	Salisbury	
799	*Sir Ironside*	7/26	2/61	Bricklayers Arms	Bricklayers Arms	Salisbury	
800	*Sir Meleaus de Lile*	9/26	8/61	Ashford	Bricklayers Arms	Eastleigh	
801	*Sir Meliot de Logres*	10/26	4/59	Ashford	Bricklayers Arms	Eastleigh	
802	*Sir Durnore*	10/26	7/61	Ashford	Ashford	Eastleigh	
803	*Sir Harry le Fise Lake*	11/26	8/61	Ashford	Ashford	Eastleigh	
804	*Sir Cador of Cornwall*	12/26	2/62	Ashford	Ashford	Eastleigh	
805	*Sir Constantine*	1/27	11/59	Ashford	Ashford	Eastleigh	
806	*Sir Galleron*	1/27	4/61	Hither Green	Hither Green	Eastleigh	

Notes

Building details: 448-57, 736-55 and 793-806 built at Eastleigh, 763-792 built by the North British Locomotive Co —
Hyde Park Works Nos 23209-23228 and 23279-23288
Renumbered by BR as 30736-55, 30448-57 and 30763-806
1) *Fitted by Bulleid with multiple-jet blastpipe and large-diameter chimney, later removed from 792.*
2) *First King Arthur to be withdrawn.*
3) *Last King Arthur to be withdrawn.*
4) *Preserved as part of the National Collection. Restored to main line running condition by the Humberside Locomotive*
   Preservation Group, 1982.

'LORD NELSON' CLASS 4-6-0s

SR No	Name	Date built	Date withdrawn	Shed allocation 2/51	Shed allocation 10/58	Final shed	Notes
850	*Lord Nelson*	8/26	8/62	Eastleigh	Eastleigh	Eastleigh	1
851	*Sir Francis Drake*	5/28	12/61	Eastleigh	Eastleigh	Eastleigh	
852	*Sir Walter Raleigh*	7/28	2/62	Eastleigh	Eastleigh	Eastleigh	
853	*Sir Richard Grenville*	9/28	3/62	Eastleigh	Eastleigh	Eastleigh	
854	*Howard of Effingham*	10/28	9/61	Eastleigh	Eastleigh	Eastleigh	
855	*Robert Blake*	10/28	9/61	Eastleigh	Eastleigh	Eastleigh	
856	*Lord St. Vincent*	11/28	9/62	Eastleigh	Eastleigh	Eastleigh	
857	*Lord Howe*	12/28	9/62	Eastleigh	Eastleigh	Eastleigh	
858	*Lord Duncan*	1/29	8/61	Nine Elms	Eastleigh	Eastleigh	
859	*Lord Hood*	3/29	12/61	Nine Elms	Eastleigh	Eastleigh	
860	*Lord Hawke*	4/29	8/62	Nine Elms	Bournemouth	Eastleigh	
861	*Lord Anson*	9/29	10/62	Bournemouth	Eastleigh	Eastleigh	
862	*Lord Collingwood*	10/29	10/62	Bournemouth	Eastleigh	Eastleigh	
863	*Lord Rodney*	10/29	2/62	Bournemouth	Eastleigh	Eastleigh	
864	*Sir Martin Frobisher*	11/29	1/62	Bournemouth	Bournemouth	Eastleigh	
865	*Sir John Hawkins*	11/29	5/61	Bournemouth	Bournemouth	Eastleigh	

Notes

Renumbered by BR as 30850-65
1) *Officially preserved as part of the National Collection. Restored to working order in 1980, it is currently at*
   Steamtown, Carnforth.

'SCHOOLS' CLASS 4-4-0s

SR No	Name	Date built	Date withdrawn	Shed allocation 2/51	Shed allocation 10/58	Final shed	Notes
900	*Eton*	3/30	2/62	St Leonards	Brighton	Brighton	1
901	*Winchester*	3/30	12/62	St Leonards	Brighton	Brighton	1
902	*Wellington*	4/30	12/62	St Leonards	Nine Elms	Nine Elms	
903	*Charterhouse*	4/30	12/62	St Leonards	Nine Elms	Nine Elms	
904	*Lancing*	5/30	7/61	St Leonards	Basingstoke	Basingstoke	
905	*Tonbridge*	5/30	12/61	St Leonards	Basingstoke	Basingstoke	2
906	*Sherborne*	6/30	12/62	St Leonards	Nine Elms	Brighton	
907	*Dulwich*	7/30	9/61	St Leonards	Nine Elms	Brighton	1
908	*Westminster*	7/30	9/61	St Leonards	Stewarts Lane	Basingstoke	

SR No	Name	Date built	Date withdrawn	Shed allocation 2/51	Shed allocation 10/58	Final Shed	Notes
909	St Paul's	7/30	2/62	St Leonards	Stewarts Lane	Guildford	1
910	Merchant Taylors	12/32	11/61	St Leonards	Ramsgate	Nine Elms	
911	Dover	12/32	12/62	Ramsgate	Ramsgate	Brighton	
912	Downside	12/32	11/62	Ramsgate	Ramsgate	Nine Elms	3
913	Christ's Hospital	12/32	1/62	Ramsgate	Ramsgate	Nine Elms	1
914	Eastbourne	12/32	7/61	Ramsgate	Ramsgate	Redhill	1
915	Brighton	5/33	12/62	Ramsgate	Stewarts Lane	Brighton	1
916	Whitgift	5/33	12/62	Ramsgate	Ramsgate	Brighton	
917	Ardingly	5/33	11/62	Ramsgate	Ramsgate	Brighton	1
918	Hurstpierpoint	6/33	10/61	Ramsgate	Ramsgate	Nine Elms	1
919	Harrow	6/33	1/61	Bricklayers Arms	Ramsgate	Brighton	1
920	Rugby	10/33	11/61	Bricklayers Arms	Ramsgate	Brighton	1
921	Shrewsbury	10/33	12/62	Bricklayers Arms	Ramsgate	Nine Elms	1
922	Marlborough	11/33	11/61	Dover	Ramsgate	Brighton	
923	Bradfield	12/33	12/62	Dover	Bricklayers Arms	Brighton	4
924	Haileybury	12/33	1/62	Dover	Bricklayers Arms	Redhill	1
925	Cheltenham	4/34	12/62	Dover	Bricklayers Arms	Basingstoke	5
926	Repton	5/34	12/62	Dover	Bricklayers Arms	Basingstoke	6
927	Clifton	6/34	1/62	Dover	Bricklayers Arms	Nine Elms	
928	Stowe	6/34	11/62	Bricklayers Arms	Bricklayers Arms	Brighton	7
929	Malvern	7/34	12/62	Bricklayers Arms	Bricklayers Arms	Brighton	1
930	Radley	12/34	12/62	Bricklayers Arms	Bricklayers Arms	Brighton	1
931	King's Wimbledon	12/34	9/61	Bricklayers Arms	Bricklayers Arms	Nine Elms	1
932	Blundell's	2/35	1/61	Bricklayers Arms	Bricklayers Arms	Ashford	8
933	King's Canterbury	2/35	11/61	Bricklayers Arms	Bricklayers Arms	Nine Elms	1
934	St Lawrence	3/35	12/62	Bricklayers Arms	Bricklayers Arms	Basingstoke	1
935	Sevenoaks	5/35	12/62	St Leonards	Bricklayers Arms	Nine Elms	
936	Cranleigh	6/35	12/62	Bricklayers Arms	Bricklayers Arms	Nine Elms	
937	Epsom	6/35	12/62	Bricklayers Arms	Stewarts Lane	Nine Elms	1
938	St Olave's	7/35	7/61	Bricklayers Arms	Stewarts Lane	Nine Elms	1
939	Leatherhead	7/35	6/61	Bricklayers Arms	Stewarts Lane	Nine Elms	1

Notes

Renumbered by BR as 30900-39
All locomotives built at Eastleigh
1) *Fitted with Lemaître multiple jet blastpipe and wide chimney by Bulleid from 1938.*
2) *Coupled latterly with high-sided tender off No 30932.*
3) *Coupled latterly with bogie tender from Lord Nelson class.*
4) *Named* Uppingham *at first.*
5) *Preserved as part of the National Collection. Restored to running order by National Railway Museum, 1980.*
6) *Restored to SR livery and shipped to Steamtown, USA.*
7) *Preserved at the Montagu Motor Museum after withdrawal and restored to SR livery, repainted in 1973 at Eastleigh before going to the East Somerset Railway at Cranmore. Subsequently transferred to Bluebell Railway and restored to running order in 1981.*
8) *Fitted with a high-sided tender, later transferred to No 30905.*

Bibliography

Berridge, P. S. A.; *The Girder Bridge*; Robert Maxwell, 1969.

Bradley, D. A.; *Locomotives of the London & South Western Railway (Parts 1/2)*; Railway Correspondence and Travel Society 1965, 1967.

Cocks, C. S.; *History of Southern Railway Locomotives to 1938*; Institute of Locomotive Engineers proceedings, Vol xxxviii, 1948.

Darwin, B.; *War on the Line*; Southern Railway Co, 1946.

Dendy-Marshall, C. F.; *The History of the Southern Railway*; Reprinted Ian Allan, 1982.

Holcroft, H.; *Locomotive Adventure*; Ian Allan.

Kidner, R. W.; *The Southern Railway*; Oakwood Press, 1958.

Moody, G. T.; *Southern Electric 1909-1968*; Ian Allan, 1978.

Nock, O. S.; *Southern Steam*; David & Charles, 1966.

Nock, O. S.; *British Steam Locomotives at Work*; George Allen and Unwin, 1967.

E. S. Cox, W. A. Tuplin, John Powell, P. G. Johnson; *Royal Scots of the LMS*; Ian Allan, 1970.

Saklatvala, B.; *Arthur; Roman Britain's Last Champion*; David & Charles, 1967.

White, H. P.; *A Regional History of the Railways of Great Britain* Vol II; Reprinted David & Charles, 1982.